INCORPORATIONS

INCORPORATIONS

Race, Nation, and the Body Politics of Capital

Eva Cherniavsky

University of Minnesota Press
Minneapolis
London

Chapter 1 was originally published as "Subaltern Studies in a U.S. Frame," *boundary 2* 23, no. 2 (1996): 86–110; copyright Duke University Press; reprinted with permission from Duke University Press. Chapter 3 was originally published as "Tribalism, Globalism, and Eskimo Television in Leslie Marmon Silko's *Almanac of the Dead*," *Angelaki: Journal of the Theoretical Humanities* 6, no. 1 (2001): 111–26; reprinted with permission of Taylor and Francis, http://www.tandf.co.uk/journals. Chapter 6 originally appeared as "Karmic Realignment: Transnationalism and Trauma in *The Simpsons*," *Cultural Critique* 41 (1999): 139–57.

Published by the University of Minnesota Press
111 Third Avenue South, Suite 290
Minneapolis, MN 55401-2520
http://www.upress.umn.edu

Library of Congress Cataloging-in-Publication Data

Cherniavsky, Eva, 1960–
Incorporations : race, nation, and the body politics of capital / Eva Cherniavsky.
p. cm.
Includes bibliographical references and index.
ISBN-13: 978-0-8166-4604-3 (hc : alk. paper)
ISBN-10: 0-8166-4604-X (hc : alk. paper)
ISBN-13: 978-0-8166-4605-0 (pb : alk. paper)
ISBN-10: 0-8166-4605-8 (pb : alk. paper)
1. Race. I. Title.
HT1521.C445 2006
305.8—dc22 2006003497

Printed in the United States of America on acid-free paper

12 11 10 09 08 07 06 10 9 8 7 6 5 4 3 2 1

For Tom and Ivan

Contents

Acknowledgments

This book has been longer in the making than it is wise to admit, yet through its varied incarnations has been enabled, engaged, and supported by a steadfast cohort of friends, students, colleagues, and co-agitators. My debt to these interlocutors is not one I can repay, but it is a pleasure to acknowledge what I owe. Pat Brantlinger, Diana Fuss, Judith Kegan Gardiner, Barb Klinger, Susan Jeffords, Alberto Moreiras, and Joseph Heathcott have provided feedback on ideas and on drafts, recommended the project, or afforded me valuable opportunities for further critical exchange. Students in my seminars on gender, race, and nation and on mediating whiteness, as well as the members of my dissertation writing group, have enabled me to sound and refine many of the ideas developed in this work, and I am especially grateful to Tyrone Simpson, Hamilton Carroll, Yuan Shu, and Brian Carr for their conversation and tenacious interest. My editor, Richard Morrison, grasped the import of this project so quickly and accurately that I scarcely needed to make a pitch; he has seen the manuscript through to publication with skill and tact. Jim Naremore generously shared with me his encyclopedic knowledge of film noir and drafts of his own work-in-progress, and encouraged my preoccupations with whiteness and noir at a point where I was far from secure in my approach. Don Pease's interrogation of my investments and procedures in this book has provoked my appreciation (always), my resistance (on occasion), and raised the bar for what I mean when I think of intellectual generosity. Joan Hawkins and Purnima Bose provided expert commentary on particular chapters, grrrl talk, and abiding friendship. Jan Radway was an ideal reader, who engaged the work with care and sensitivity and offered invaluable suggestions for revision at a key moment. Robyn Wiegman knew what this book was about before I had brought myself to see it, has read every line (and many lines more than once), and compelled me to know and to say why this project matters. Her conversation has animated the book, and her friendship sustained its writer. I reserve my deepest thanks for my partner, Tom Foster, who has inhabited the work with me. He has been my keenest and most committed reader, as well as my best refuge when writing turned to compulsion—and no doubt this book is better for his knowing when to switch on the TV. Our son, Ivan, was born just as the contours of this project were becoming clear to me. He spins his own stories now but is patient with his parents' less inventive narrations. I dedicate this book to Tom and Ivan with love and gratitude.

Audiences at the Kinsey Institute, the University of Louisville, the Summer Institute on the Futures of American Studies, the Contemporary Art Museum of St. Louis, and Dartmouth University have engaged with various parts of this work and helped me sharpen my arguments. An Indiana University Summer Faculty Fellowship funded my research in its early phase and a College Arts and Humanities Institute grant supported the final revisions. Jasmine Trice accomplished the video captures under deadline with resourceful efficiency and good cheer.

Introduction

The Body Politics of Capital

This book is concerned with raced bodies—with how bodies were and are produced (quantified and qualified, institutionally and customarily) under the aegis of "race." *Incorporations: Race, Nation, and the Body Politics of Capital* has emerged, in its present form, from a series of apparently discontinuous starts: my ruminations on the intraterritorial dynamics of U.S. colonialism, the contemporary disarticulations of nation and state, the cinematic mediation of whiteness, whiteness studies, and the politics of identification. My writing on these matters was a guilty pleasure, a distraction from a projected book manuscript on racial fetishism whose aims and design continued to elude me. *Incorporations* sprang already half-grown, an unlovely adolescent, from the recognition that these discrete inquiries converged on a common animus. The sidelines and tangents of my research bore out what the (putative) center could not hold: my dissatisfactions with the critical study of *racial imaginaries*, which increasingly seemed to foreclose on pressing questions about the longevity of racial distinctions in what is now widely regarded as the dawn of a "postracial" epoch and the terms of our critical intervention in their reproduction. In writing this other book to a finish, it has not been my aim to efface its scattered origins, still less to rear the adolescent to maturity. This book's project is explicitly deformative: to think not so much against as simply apart from a critical tendency to refer matters of race to questions of identity and difference. Consequently, *Incorporations* maintains a positive investment in its own contingent form. I make no claim for the necessity—the transparency—of my beginnings, and my endings are not arrivals. My aim has been to consider what is elided in the fixation on race as difference and what it could mean to suspend this noisy analytic engine.

"The very use of the term 'race,'" remarks Ruth Frankenberg, "raises the idea of difference, for 'race' is above all a marker of difference, an axis of differentiation. What kind of difference race is and what difference race makes in real terms are the questions that are contested in competing modes of thinking through race" (138). Frankenberg delineates this approach with a graceful economy of prose, an economy made possible, in turn, by the nearly axiomatic status of the assumptions on which this approach rests. I want to suggest how the inquiry into the "difference race makes" is at least partially foreclosed by the language of "idea," "axis," and (above all) "marker" or, in other words, by an utterly unremarkable discourse of racial antiessentialism, which for that very reason need no longer account for its terms. The postcolonial intellectual tradition, grounded in such figures as W. E. B. Du Bois and Frantz Fanon, that relocates race to the cultural imaginary—to the arena of contingent self-other relations and the practices of exclusion, projection, and internalization that support them—has crucially delegitimated the discourse of recalcitrant racial essences across the terrain of Western knowledge production, from the humanities to the human sciences. Its triumph is recorded in the now-hegemonic status of the "culturalist" viewpoint, in a reclamation of racial common sense that by the turn of the twenty-first century has tainted the belief in innate racial qualities with the stigma of a racism that only a relative minority of the new world order's elite will avow. But this triumph has been at once too uneven and too complete. On one side of the ledger, we witness racial essentialism's perennial reappearance, as nativisms, ethnonationalisms, and state policies of containment or removal crafted for the management of unassimilable—and invariably racialized—populations. On the other, we witness the lure of identificatory free play:

from the suburban mall to the "alternative" arts scene, opportunities proliferate for assuming and exchanging racial identities, vested in consumable/disposable commodities, styles, and images. Confronted with the proofs of a durable essentialism, we reach for more or less nuanced versions of this cultural dialectics. Race is "a marker of difference," a relation between bodies and embodied subjects that therefore inheres, as a proper or authentic attribute, in none. There is no raced body prior to or apart from this relation between subjects—and now as ever, the stakes in the relation are the subordination or emancipation of the differentiated term. Confronted with capital's proliferation and leveling of racial differences, we insist on the asymmetries of racial identities and their irreducible historical density. So we argue with Frankenberg that race is *only* difference even as we argue that difference *matters*.

There is, of course, nothing contradictory in asserting that race is both inessential and material, but to the extent that we simply oscillate between one and the other claim, we generate little insight into why any particular category of difference acquires or retains its material weight. In general, the study of race as difference, and of difference as a "mark," defers the project of a genealogical analysis, in other words, as it permits us to know "according to what rules has a particular statement been made [or a particular difference has been asserted], and consequently according to what rules could other similar statements be made," but largely fails to address "how is it that one particular statement [or difference] appeared rather than another?" (Foucault 27). By studying race as a differentiating mark, we learn how this particular difference plays, rather than why this category of difference is the one in play at any given moment. This critical limitation is signally expressed in the belief that race has now outlived itself—the brainchild of a (discredited) racial "science," crosshatched with the (defunct) administrative categories of colonial justice. Like sightings of Elvis, this claim is everywhere: across the spectrum of mass-mediated common sense and academic scholarship, of right-wing punditry and Left critique, race figures as a residue—a lingering effect of a metropolitan modernity already superseded in our post–civil rights and (or) postmodern moment. Yet the reluctance to account for the continuing social and political effectiveness of race, except as some kind of protracted aftershock, serves paradoxically to make of race a fixed and indelible predicate, because bound to its own internal logic.

Despite her insistence on the status of race as "difference," Frankenberg's conceptualizing of racially differentiated embodiment finds a limit in the reference to racial "marker[s]." To situate race as a bodily inscription is to posit that race makes a difference to the figuration of the body, exclusively, not to the fundamental condition of embodiment itself. From this vantage, in other words, race appears as the cultural differentiation of essentially similar organic human forms—although for many, of course, their racial inscription serves precisely to elide this human likeness. Nonetheless, the culturalist analytic is oddly democratic, insofar as it assigns a discrete organic form to bodies across racial lines. On the one hand, to read race as a *bodily* mark is to recognize that bodies are formed dialectically (in a relation to alterity) and consequently that our sense of bodily self-containment, our incorporated state, is not our own, intrinsic property. On the other hand, to read race as a bodily *mark* is to assume the body's priority with respect to its markings and thus to recuperate incorporation as a generalized, existential norm.

The collapse of difference into similarity at the level of corporeal form is at least potentially resolved when we shift from a model of racial inscription to one of racial performativity, and the more sophisticated critique of subjective and bodily interiority that it supports. The premise of performative identity is that no body precedes its cultural determinations or offers an already constituted surface for inscription. Instead, this analysis seeks to account for the cultural production of bodies and bodily surfaces—how bodies take shape, in the first place, through activating and deactivating specific bodily zones, affects, and receptivities. The investigation of performative race therefore holds open the possibility that not all bodies may adhere to the same compositional logic of organic (good) form.[1] In the context of this investigation we might ask, though few have done so, whether incorporated embodiment is normative for all racial subjects or, conversely, whether the integrity of the body is equally imaginary across racial lines.

Incorporations elaborates an understanding of "race" as an apparatus (a set of institutionalized practices) for the (re)production—the (dis)assembly—of human bodies, rather than an apparatus for their inscription. In this reading, race signals the radically uneven capacity of bodies to serve as the shell (the organic container) of the subjects they embody. Even if one wishes to insist that our sense of the body as a bounded domain is only the perception of our "real" biological condition as discrete organism, there is certainly nothing given or immediate in the way that boundary is observed, maintained, patrolled, investigated, and violated. There is no a priori element in the way that boundary matters, in other words—and the admittedly episodic and nonlinear story I wish to tell about racial embodiment begins with the novel ways in which bodily bounds come to matter at the broad historical juncture where traditional society yields to modernity. I am calling "incorporation" or "incorporated embodiment" a specific idea of the body as the proper (interior) place of the subject, and my claim is that incorporation emerges as the privileged form of embodiment for a modern social and economic order predicated on mobility: the geographic mobility of the labor force relative to centralized manufacturing zones, for example, or the abstract mobility of "free" economic agents to enter into and to terminate contractual relations. From this perspective, then, incorporated embodiment represents an *articulation of bodily form for the subject at risk of dispersal.*

This historical conjugation of mobile personhood with interiorized embodiment is strikingly evident in the institution of wage labor, which negotiates the wage earner's alienation in the marketplace precisely by establishing a proper/proprietary relation to an embodied selfhood. As C. B. Macpherson has shown, in his brilliant exposition of the foundational assumptions in Hobbes, Locke, and other seventeenth-century political economists, wage labor, as well as the social contract theory that it exemplifies, rests on the notion of a "possessive individualism" that detaches individuals from all traditional supports and obligations by binding them to the interior (inalienable) core of themselves:

> Thus: since the freedom, and therefore the humanity, of the individual depend on his freedom to enter into self-interested relations with other individuals, and since his ability to enter into such relations depends on his having exclusive control of (rights in) his own person and capacities, and since proprietorship is the generalized form of such exclusive control, the individual is essentially the proprietor of his own person and capacities. (263–64)

The framing of self-determination as self-ownership, of rights as property rights, informs the delineation of freedom as the freedom to dispose of one's capacities on the open market. Social relations are made and dissolved through the rational calculation of self-proprietors or, in Macpherson's words, "human society consists of a series of market relations" (264). However, the individual's freedom to alienate his property in himself is crucially limited by the requirement that he not cede title to his personhood in its totality, since to do so would be precisely to renounce the basis of this defining independence from the wills of others. Therefore Macpherson stresses, "The individual cannot alienate *the whole of his property in his own person*"; he cannot relinquish the condition of discrete and autonomous personhood, in other words, even though self-interest demands that he sell to best advantage the creative abilities through which (one might assume) his personhood is realized (264, my emphasis).

But what is the inalienable portion of human personhood in which its integrity is vested—that which guarantees the person against the centrifugal force of commercialized social relations? This essence acquires a name in the elaborations of nonpersonhood that accompanied (and heralded) the institutionalization and normalization of possessive individualism, and nowhere is this essence more commonly invoked than in the abolitionist discourse that reckoned, so as to denounce, the dispossession of the New World slave. Ultimately, as David Brion Davis has argued, abolitionist discourse flourished in the ideological service of industrial production (which accounts for abolitionism's relatively later emergence in the United States), since the indictment of unfree labor doubled as an explicit or implicit defense of wage earning, represented by contrast as an equitable transaction between capitalist and laborer. In perhaps the most commonplace gloss on the distinction between self-proprietors and slaves, abolitionists decried slavery as the expropriation of the captive subject "body and soul"—a formulation especially telling in its linkage of the human body to the term that normally opposes and displaces it within the major epistemological and religious traditions of the West, that is, in the linkage of the perishable body to the eternal soul against which corporeal existence is habitually reckoned base and transitory. In the routine rhetorical twinning of these terms by which the slave's dispossession is measured, a twinning central to the opposition of chattels to free men, one begins to distinguish the terms on which the body acquires its value as inalienable property for the unsubjected (consenting) subject of bourgeois social discipline: not as quantity of physical matter, still less as the repository of sensual pleasures, but as the support, as the organic form, or figure, of identity (soul). For liberal political theory, in other words, the relation of the individual to self pivots on the body's status—not because the body would be valued for itself but because the coherence and continuity of a definitionally mobile and alienated personhood comes to rest on the integrative power of the person's embodied condition. The body that rises to the status of inalienable property is an interiorizing figure of the human subject within a capitalist formation characterized by invasive market relations, by the compulsory objectification and circulation of the subject's proper abilities—of physical and intellectual labor. From this perspective, the body is protected from exchange so that the "free" person's other attributes are opened to it.

If this is so, then it is not sufficient to think plantation slavery as inscribing bodies with a servile condition, although no doubt the obsession with the legible servility of the captive body's surfaces was pervasive, encompassing enlightened men of science no less than slavery's most vulgar apologists. But the very primeness of the slave body's surfaces for inscription, for the breathtaking superfluity of bizarre and contradictory renderings that Hortense Spillers so aptly terms "pornotroping," is an index to the crisis in—the suspension of—incorporated embodiment for the slave. The captive body is all surfaces; it is the scene of the evacuation of the captive person, rendered wholly soluble in capital. Rather than incorporate the mobile subject of contractual social relations, then, this body tropes the conditions of the chattel slave's dispersal as so many atomized, exchangeable quantities. In the context of plantation slavery, I am proposing that race marks the status of the body that is not one—an inorganic body, fully opened to capital.

From this perspective, the institution of slavery in the United States represents a limit case for the European colonizers' partial and uneven assimilation of the colonized: emerging from the Middle Passage, quite possibly the most radical dislocation of human subjects that modernity has produced, the African undergoes a compulsory *extroversion,* marked by the incapacity to designate anything as properly his or her own. Slavery constitutes an absolutely modern, because absolutely deracinated, labor force, without the most minimal protections or consolations of interiority. But to situate chattel slavery at the limit of colonial practice is, conversely, to imply that colonialism more generally refuses the benefits of incorporated embodiment to subjugated peoples. Colonialism in nearly all its permutations involves expanding metropolitan capital into zones of precapitalist production—only to claim down the line that the "backwardness" of indigenous productive modes and social relations requires withholding modernity's social benefits (democracy, rule of law) from the colonized. Arguably, then, a defining feature of colonialism in general is its absorption of colonized populations into heterogeneous regimes, marked at once by the time-space relations of the metropolitan culture (increased spatial mobility, spurred by centralized systems of agricultural production and resource extraction, and by the creation/expansion of administrative centers) and the "feudal" relations of production along the periphery (indentured/conscripted rather than "free"/wage labor).

Elaborating on Antonio Gramsci, particularly his writing on the relation of Italy's agricultural south to its industrialized north, Stuart Hall observes how "different modes of production can be *combined* within the same formation," citing migrant labor, colonial enclaves, and peasant economies in developing nations among other examples of such combinations (24–25). Hall's examples pertain to "backward" or "underdeveloped" zones (or populations) internal to the nation-state, but this model of "combined" formations usefully specifies, as well, the organization of "classic" (extraterritorial) colonial domination, which is similarly shaped by the conjunction and collision of different modes of production within an overarching administrative apparatus. Considered in this light, the crucial distinction between the paradigmatically colonial context and the various "combined" formations Hall describes is that the colony's extranational location makes it relatively easier to rationalize the uneven allocation of rights and protections across racial lines (the colonized are subjects, not citizens), at least in comparison with an intranational colonialism, where the raced population of the so-called backward sector is positioned within the nation's political boundaries. In any case, the crucial point is that the feudalism or underdevelopment of the (neo)colony is nurtured by *the colonizing power* no less than the traditional elite, insofar as colonial law generally refuses the colonized both property in the self and the bodily protections it requires and confers. From this perspective, the heterogeneity of the "combined formation" signals not the incompleteness of the colonial project, the still-unfinished business of assimilating the periphery, but rather the irreducible discontinuity between metropolis and (neo)colony, which capital not only tolerates but requires. The attenuated personhood or nonpersonhood of the colonized is not the consequence of their belated emergence into modernity but a distinctly modern construction.

Critical for Hall's discussion is the remarkably consistent link between the differential incorporation of the "backward" sector and racist manifestations. "Theoretically, what needs to be noticed is the persistent way in which these specific, differentiated forms of 'incorporation' have been consistently associated with the appearance of racist, ethnically segmentary, and other similar social features," he observes (24–25). If the proposition is also reversible, as I am suggesting—if "the appearance of racist . . . social features" is "consistently associated" with the event of differential incorporation—then race presents itself, like class, as expressing the social relations of production. As class articulates the mode of production to the social order within advanced/industrialized contexts, so does race within "combined formations." By no means do I suggest, however, that we consider race and class to be homologous: one reason, of course, is that race intersects and (re)mediates rather than substitutes for existing relations of caste and class within the different modes of production that are "combined" (but not superseded) in the formations Hall describes. Equally important, I am arguing that the industrial wageworker and the (raced) laborer in combined systems of (neo)colonial production are wrongly conceived as mirror images of each other (on either side of an inter- or intranational division of labor), inasmuch as race vitiates or suspends the proprietary structure of embodiment on which the social relations of industrial capital, including the civic apparatus of liberal democracy, come to rest.

Certainly, the condition of the differentially incorporated laborer is always the potential, menacing fate of the industrial wageworker—a proximity registered, for instance, in the polemical reframing of wage labor as "wage slavery." Yet they represent fundamentally asymmetrical modes of existence within the civic institutions of modernity, an asymmetry marked in the relative force (juridical, ideological) of the claim to interiority, to a register of personhood (an embodied self) that *does not circulate.* If chattel slavery effects the most thorough extroversion of personhood, renders the entire (non)person of the slave susceptible to commodification; if outside the infamous forts of the West African coast or the auction blocks of the antebellum South the colonized body is rarely bought and sold *outright* (much less with the explicit legal sanction of the state); still, the raced subject, in general, I argue, is characterized by a missing or attenuated hold on interior personhood—by an openness to capital(ization) without the conventional protections (legal, social, political) of embodied individuals.[2] My counterintuitive claim is that the raced subjects lack essence, except in the quite particular and paradoxical sense that they are cast as essentially lacking, and that raced bodies notably fail to bind and envelop this (missing) core—which explains why "essentialist" colonial tropologies belabor the indistinctness of black and brown flesh, the impossibility of differentiating among members of a subject race (e.g., one can scarcely tell the natives apart), who reduce to serial racial type. From this vantage, we may speculate that the figure of the masses, of overabundant (proliferating) and indistinct bodies, always carries a racial charge—while, conversely, the massification of a white, working class in the metropolis (at moments of strike or riot) enacts as crisis a state of embodiment, of depthless and dispersed corporeality, that is normative for raced subjects in the colonies and the "backward" sectors of the nation.[3]

This understanding of race and of racial essentialism, to which the chapters of my book are variously committed, offers an enabling perspective on the persistence of race in a postmodern context, marked by the (arguable) disappearance of organic bodies in favor of proliferating corporeal signs—codes and images that may be dis- and reassembled at will. In Paul Gilroy's words, the second half of the twentieth century has seen a "move away from the biopolitics of 'race' and toward its nano-politics," a move characterized, in his estimation, by the increasing, if unevenly acknowledged, irrelevance of rac(ial)ist thinking (19).

> Whether the distinguishing marks, organs, and features were discovered on the external surface of the body or were thought to dwell somewhere inside it where the hidden properties of racially differentiated blood, bone, and sinew were imagined to regulate social and cultural manifestations, the modern idea of race favored a specific representational scale and operated within the strictest perceptual limits. Our situation is demonstrably different. The call of racial being has been weakened by another technological and communicative revolution, by the idea that the body is nothing more than an incidental moment in the transmission of code and information, by its openness to the new imaging technologies, and by the loss of mortality as a horizon against which life is to be lived. . . . *Screens*

> *rather than lenses now mediate the pursuit of bodily truths.* This is a potent sign that "race" should be approached as an afterimage—a lingering effect of looking too casually into the damaging glare emanating from colonial conflicts at home and abroad. (36–37, my emphasis)

Thus, for Gilroy, the loss of a certain organic density—the transition from peering technologies (that look in on the body) to screening technologies (that turn the body inside out, a quantity of information manipulated on a computer screen)—in a word, the depthlessness of contemporary human bodies, renders racial consciousness "an anachronistic, even a vestigial phenomenon" (37). Compelling in its utopian reach, in its vision of genetic mapping as a (potentially) *post*-racial science, Gilroy's argument for the residual nature of race mirrors a wider consensus within the cultures and institutions of the multicultural metropolis that race has outlived the conditions from which it arose; that the now-*visible* irrationality of racial knowledge—as exemplified, for instance, in the discredited protocols of comparative anatomy—makes racial categories increasingly irrelevant to embodied existence in the twenty-first century. I am arguing instead that the raced body (the "bodily truth" of race), while born of the lens, was destined for the screen; that race vexes interiority and arises from the conditions of empire and diaspora where the claims to interiority are most vexed; that comparative anatomy is not the ground of colonial hierarchy but its alibi, marked by the contradictory insistence on the inherence of qualities that evacuate personhood among the "lower" races, that open these black and brown and yellow bodies to the a(na)tomizing calculus of capital—which is why comparative anatomy can yield no surprises, why the inner function of the colonized races so invariably affirms the absence of social competence already heralded on the slick and hardened surface of the orientalist and primitivist stereotype.[4] Far from requiring organic bodies, then, race manifests in the zones where the interiority of embodied subjectivity and of national bodies unfolds, and announces the limits of organicism in the face of capital's expansionist drives.

This angle of approach to the study of race and nation carries pointed implications for the critical investigation of "whiteness," especially as this venture is now (re)assigned to the discrete terrain of (something called) "whiteness studies." Around the mid-1980s, the call for a critical engagement with whiteness as a racial formation came from African American and ethnic studies scholars resistant to the persistent alignment of race matters with nonwhite populations, as though whiteness, in Hazel Carby's words, was "without color" and therefore "not implicated in a society structured in dominance by race" (194). "Are only the so-called colored to be the subjects of a specialized discourse of difference?" she goes on to ask. "And most important, do existing power relations remain intact and unchallenged by this discourse?" Carby's urgent call has been answered unevenly, at best—not least because so much of the critical work on whiteness shares (with Frankenberg) an emphasis on racial "markers" and narrowly equates the privilege of whiteness with the pretension to colorlessness (unmarking). Thus, for instance, a good deal of the recent scholarship counters the (supposed) invisibility or universality of whiteness by (re)positioning white subjects within the bounded specificity of white bodies. In so doing, however, we miss the way in which it is precisely the boundedness of white embodiment vis-à-vis capital that confers on white personhood an interior core—a property in the self that appears to precede every social mediation and thus upholds the colonizer's sense that the world is only a function of his seeing it, and he himself its unmarked and original point of reference.[5] From this perspective, the critical work of de-universalizing whiteness risks merely reconstituting the white subject and/in its protected relation to capital, as I argue more fully in later chapters. Likewise, a burgeoning scholarship on the dialectics of white identity, which seeks to foreground its dependence on racial alterity, often misses the extent to which privilege might be vested precisely in the dialectical form of the relationship—in other words, in a capacity to incorporate (appropriate) difference that consolidates rather than prostrates white personhood.[6]

The first section of this book seeks to elucidate and elaborate the triangulated relation of race, nationalism, and colonial domination. My focus in this section's three chapters is on "incorporation" as normative for national bodies (individual and collective) and, more specifically, on the relation between incorporation, hegemony, and subalternity. Chapter 1, "Subaltern Studies in a U.S. Frame," dwells on the importance of thinking the United States as a nation split internally between an assimilative nationalism and modes of capital expansion that entail the specifically colonial administration of targeted populations within the nation's own borders. In her influential introduction to *Cultures of United States Imperialism* (1993), Amy Kaplan observes both the belated attention of postcolonial studies to the United States and the belated attention to postcolonial scholarship within the field(s) of American studies. Yet the *Cultures* collection and the variety of critical efforts it served to focus tend to treat extra-territorial domination as paradigmatic of colonialism as such, so that the discussion of U.S. imperialist and colonial ventures is keyed to 1898 and after (the Philippines, Cuba). This treatment may reflect, in turn, the uneven career of "internal colonization," a concept frequently reproached with obfuscating more than it illuminates, eroding the meaning of "colonialism" to the point where it loses critical and historical specificity and becomes a too-generalized synonym for "domination" as such.[7] Chapter 1 argues that this loss of specificity follows, quite the contrary, from eliding the matter of intraterritorial colonialism—the problem, in Hall's words, of the " 'colonial' enclave within the development of metropolitan capitalist regimes" (24–25)—and suggests, as well, how the work of the Subaltern Studies Group furthers the critical engagement with differential incorporation and its effects. Subaltern studies provides both a name for those subsumed by a political power to which they are not assimilated (the subaltern) and, more significant, a critical practice for tracing the imprint and effects of racial subalterns on hegemonic U.S. culture and the (re)production of elite identities. As such, subaltern studies is invaluable to the project of a "postnational" American studies, as it seeks to disengage from the inevitably normative impulse of nationalist historiography.

Chapter 2, "After Bourgeois Nationalism," pursues the question of incorporation and its limits in a contemporary context, marked, as I contend, by the gradual withdrawal of the state from the assimilative project of the nation. The increasingly evident divestment of the state (as administrative power) from reproducing an organic imagined community (a nation) correlates with the growing obsolescence of self-possessed individualism, as either a desirable or a sustainable norm for transnational capital. More exactly, chapter 2 explores how raced embodiment, which emerges historically from colonial expansion and combined formation, is increasingly generalized under a new state ethos of "flexible" labor. Along the way, this chapter elaborates more fully the relation of nationalism, citizenship, and embodiment to the social reproduction of labor as commodity. A crucial point is that the dismantling of organic corporeality and the opening of bodies-in-general to the invasive force of capital does not imply the leveling of racial hierarchy (as though all subjects were flexible in the same manner), only that capital no longer maintains an interest in reproducing self-proprietors. This chapter's final section moves to consider possibilities for countering new disciplines of "flexible" labor and resisting the state's role in creating such tractable subjects, without simply reverting, however, to the discourse of incorporation (to the defense of borders and the promulgation of nationalist and proprietary claims).

Chapter 3, "Eskimo Television and the Critique of Whiteness (Studies)," extends these reflections through a reading of tribalism and fourth world militancy as conceptualized in Leslie Marmon Silko's novel *Almanac of the Dead,* which doubles as the "almanac" of its title: a book of days that links "tradition," repetition, and unofficial knowledge to calendrical time, production, and futurity. If the almanac as a historical genre has centrally to do with articulating the premodern to the modern, the novel specifically refuses (and derides) the association of the tribal with anterior time. In *Almanac,* the confrontation of modernity with tribalism is the confrontation of expansionist capital (incorporation through abstraction) with a mode of collective existence (and a world-historical vision) that does not rely on an incorporative strategy—and so rejects the value of nationalism and of identitarian claims to resistance. The practice of Silko's tribal subalterns opens onto a critique of identity as a(nother) form of capitalist property relations, and chapter 3 seeks to develop the implications of this critique for a "whiteness studies" that has proven centrally invested in the (re)construction of white identities.

The book's second section, the final three chapters, addresses visual culture and the racing of screen bodies. The scholarship on race and cinema, in particular, has primarily engaged with race as a topical concern, related to the content of images and of narrative genres. Chapter 4, "Hollywood's Hot Voodoo," draws attention to the racial grammar of Hollywood cinema—the rules that govern the composition of screen bodies—as it emerges from the context of the colonial administration of race, particularly in the United States. If "race" is the very condition of depthless embodiment (the body that is all surfaces), then it follows that screen bodies bear more than an incidental, or thematic, relation to race matters. Following on the work of Laura Mulvey and other feminist film critics, who have shown how the ordering of masculine and feminine bodies within narrative cinema adheres to a patriarchal discipline, chapter 4 considers how Hollywood's classic style is implicated in colonial rule.

One important innovation of cinema, rarely remarked, is its transmutation of white bodies into commodities—more particularly, into an anticipation of what Mitsuhiro Yoshimoto terms the "commodity-image," an ideal because absolutely ephemeral object.[8] The movie star as mass-mediated icon, whose glamour and allure are crucially staked on the "dazzle" of whiteness (in Gilroy's phrase), thrives in the context of its own impossibility: the most lustrous white skin cannot properly signify whiteness—cannot signify the white subject's property in the self—when it circulates as a detached and exchangeable image. Chapters 4 and 5 trace the industry's (uneven) management of this contradiction in and by a visual grammar that conjugates white corporeality with glow. Richard Dyer's valuable discussion of classic lighting methods in *White* usefully documents the dominance of this compositional principle in Hollywood film, although in his reading the star's glowing body simply extends the idealization of white skin (as trope of purity and spirituality) already evident throughout the past millennium of Christian iconology in the visual arts. Starting from the different premise that the methods for illuminating white skin reflect the function and organization of the cinematic medium (rather than a generalized Christian tropology), chapter 4 explores how the film star's glow (re)mediates her implication in the commodity form. Dissolving at its edges in an aura of white light, the stellar body refuses resolution: it remains visually indiscrete, but for that very reason elusive and inappropriable. As her bodily glow diffuses through the object world—through the world of American commodities that comprise the setting for so much of Hollywood's product—the star transforms from an object of visual consumption into a figure of consumer pleasures.

My use of feminine pronouns and possessives gestures toward the interplay of race and gender in the composition of the filmic image. White women's juridical and social self-possession is, of course, historically belated and decidedly tenuous when measured against the legal and conventional protections extended to white men—a point that brings us back within the compass of Mulvey's analysis and her insistence that femininity is visually given over to the masculine spectator. At the same time, however, white women's claim to a protected interiority receives the widest cultural sanction, insofar as white women are required to embody interiority *for others*—to serve as the bearers of a familial and a national domestic. For this reason, the emergence of the white female body as commodity-image proves especially vexing for the narrative (re)production of white racial prerogatives, even though white women themselves are only the partial and uneven beneficiaries of individual and national incorporation. The exchangeable body of the white female star thus becomes the site of the exacerbated grammatical *and* narrative maneuver that I trace in chapter 5, "White Women in the Age of Their Mechanical Reproduction." This chapter attends to film noir as it registers a crisis of domestic interiority, wrought precisely by the traffic across national boundaries in the sexualized body-image of the white female star. The genre's narrative fixation on financial and sexual intrigues that spill into border zones, third world locations, and racial/ethnic enclaves allegorizes the global reach of Hollywood film and particularly the dissemination of white female sexuality to nonwhite markets in Latin America, Asia, and Africa.

As my initial chapters on incorporation traced the implications for proprietary selfhood of the shift from industrial capitalism to flexible accumulation, so the section on visual culture weighs the implication of this shift in the organization of production for screen bodies. Chapter 6, "Fast Capitalism and Consumer Ordeals," suggests how the maneuvers of classic cinema yield to more explicitly cynical (re)mediations of the white body's relation to the commodity form, particularly when the production of iconic whiteness shifts from the United States to zones of low-wage labor (*The Simpsons* is made in South Korea). The chapter centers on this canny series' representation of white, middle-class consumption—which for classic cinema is at once the particular prerogative of its narratives' white protagonists *and* the medium's universalizing hail of the comprador classes along the colonial/decolonizing periphery. In *The Simpsons,* however, consumerism transforms from the sign of racial privilege into a measure of the white person's damaging intimacy with commodity culture, a transformation hyperbolized in this animated series, where the priority of subjects over objects dissolves (animation levels the distinction between human and other forms, as well as the distance between foreground and background). Here property in the self becomes the ability to accumulate properties that fill the place of the missing subject—a subject reduced to the effects of the appetites that capital prescribes for him (and in contrast to Hollywood cinema, the paradigmatic consumer in this series is male). In the world of *The*

Simpsons, commodities lay siege to the white consumer, invading and disfiguring this body. The series thus registers the disintegration of white embodiment through an overproximity to commodity culture supported, precisely, by white people's relative economic advantage—what George Lipsitz has termed the "possessive investment in whiteness."

Throughout this book, my emphasis falls on how race (and the institutions that govern its reproduction) effects embodiment (rather than simply marks the body)—on how it regulates the assembly and disassembly of the organic human form in modernity. My texts and contexts remain necessarily fluid and reversible as I move from chapter to chapter: the result of this movement is a series of possible trajectories through matters of race, nation, capital, colonialism, and their visual mediation, rather than anything on the order of a map. If race appears where interiority fails, as I argue in these pages, then the study of race also precludes most forms of mapping—of marking territory—in any case. By the same token, the study of race and (as) the politics of embodiment is critical to the articulation of any post-nationalism worth its name.

Chapter 1

Subaltern Studies in a U.S. Frame

What had she lost or gained, and why?
And what else might be done?
—*Octavia Butler,* Dawn

Theorizing colonial history for a postcolonial critical practice, Ranajit Guha observes: "*Bourgeois culture hits its historical limit in colonialism.* None of its noble achievements—Liberalism, Democracy, Liberty, Rule of Law, etc.—can survive the inexorable urge of capital to expand and reproduce itself by means of the politics of extra-territorial, colonial dominance" ("Dominance" 277). My project in this chapter is to consider how we might critically trace this historical limit in the context of specific forms of colonial domination that place in crisis the delineation of inside and outside implicit in Guha's notion of "*extra*-territorial" expansion.[1] To map the vectors of colonial power in the United States is to turn the spaces of Guha's postcolonial historiography inside out. Indeed, U.S. history is marked by a convergence of nationalism and colonialism, so that independence transfers power from imperialist interests abroad to imperialist interests on American soil—from white men to white men. We can discern the contours of the new nation's territorial ambitions, as well as its specifically colonial administration of annexed populations within its own expanding borders, in the following features of early national life, very broadly sketched: (1) the genocide of indigenous peoples and the displacement of surviving populations to increasingly marginalized spaces (reservations) within the territorial United States; (2) the (re)coding of an indigenous, or mestizo, labor force as a foreign (Mexican) element; (3) the expansion of capital by importing the African as a captive labor force; and (4) the expansion of capital by importing a Chinese labor force defined as irreducibly foreign (not subject to naturalization).[2] If we take as axiomatic of colonial rule in general Guha's claim that British rule in India represented "dominance without hegemony"—in other words, that the colonized were consistently "coerced" rather than "persuaded"—then the United States arguably achieves hegemony through exercising a colonial dominance that systematically displaces both indigenous peoples and nonwhite labor from the social and symbolic territory of the consensual Euro-American state.

In one sense, at least, in the case of the United States, capital appears effectively to exceed its own historical limit and assimilate the extraterritorial to its logic. Significant classes of people whose land and (or) labor is expropriated under this colonial rule, classes that comprise, for Guha and subaltern studies, the category of "the people" as such, are at various junctures of U.S. history forcibly externalized with respect to what is constituted as the space of an "American" national politics and culture ("Dominance" 44).[3] In this internalization of extraterritorial spaces and extroversion of colonized peoples, we encounter the figure of an achieved colonial rule, which is also, I will suggest, the figure of bourgeois culture delimited not at its periphery but at its center. If postcolonial critical practice emerges in, and in response to, the failures of decolonization (to the impossibility of simply unraveling colonial power, of "substituting," in Gayatri Chakravorty Spivak's words, "the lost figure of the colonized"), a postcolonial approach to U.S. history and culture would speak to the contradictions of a naturalized/nationalized colonial domination ("Can the Subaltern Speak?" 295). The U.S. colonial context unravels the spatial metaphorics of Guha's claim, insofar as any demand that colonial power be returned to its "own" (national) borders has been rendered unintelligible. However, the instability in the U.S. frame of the mirror couple interiority/exteriority invites rather than precludes what Spivak characterizes as the deconstructive historiographical method of subaltern studies, with its emphasis on colonialism as the historical disarticulation of rational bourgeois culture.

More specifically, this chapter contends that theorizing the "intraterritorial" dimension of colonial dominance in the U.S. context is critical to understanding the reproduction of racial embodiment. If colonization entails a people's simultaneous subjection to the power of a nation-state and exclusion from its polity—entails incorporation without assimilation—as Guha intimates, it would be difficult to overlook that the various features of an intraterritorial U.S. colonialism, which I began by enumerating, *invariably* pertain to racialized populations. Unless we assume (with the colonial apologists) that indigenous peoples and mestizos, Africans and Asians, were selected for differential treatment by virtue of race (that bodily difference motivated practices of domination), then we need to ask instead how the colonial administration of subject peoples has constituted raced bodies in the United States. This chapter therefore seeks to maintain a persistently doubled focus on the specifically colonial character of racial domination in the United States and on the specifically racial determination of bodies under the conditions of colonial rule. I am interested in race as a bodily articulation of Guha's "historical limit" and so, by implication, as the scandal of bourgeois nationalism in the United States.

Post-American Narratives?

As Edward W. Said observes, the "discourse insisting on American specialness, altruism, and opportunity" has been "so influential... that 'imperialism' as a word or ideology has turned up only rarely and recently in accounts of United States culture, politics, history" (8). Nonetheless, with the emergence of postcolonial literatures and theory as a legitimated disciplinary category within American academic institutions, the discourse of American exceptionalism that has reigned in the field of American studies virtually since its institutional inception has suddenly and startlingly begun to yield to the recognition of U.S. participation in the world-making histories of imperialism and colonial domination.[4] Indeed, "recently," and despite their long historical invisibility, the New Americanist criticism (so called) has come abruptly and emphatically to acknowledge imperialist practices, and their realization in systems of colonial administration, as structuring dimensions of U.S. history. Yet I would argue that this swift, overdue, and welcome transformation in the landscape of American studies is taking place in the absence of sustained critical inquiry into the specifically North American configurations of imperialism and colonialism, so that these terms find their ways into an Americanist critical practice in notably un- or undertheorized forms. I want to raise some cautions about the consequent leveling of distinctions between capitalist and colonial domination in the important and influential arena of New Americanist work while suggesting how a subaltern studies approach might benefit this collective critical project.[5]

On the one hand, New Americanist criticism typically articulates questions of imperialism within a problematic of extraterritoriality, even as the limits of this spatialization are acknowledged. As John Carlos Rowe concedes, "By 'extraterritorial,' I mean 'outside the North American continent,' and I realize that the term is itself something of a contradiction, since the territory of the North American continent was from the very outset of European exploration and settlement an 'extraterritorial' region of European colonization. But this great paradox of United States history remains as difficult to communicate today as it must have been in Melville's nineteenth century" (256). Although Rowe's essay aims nonetheless to discern in Melville's writing some degree of critical engagement with the paradoxes of American territorial domination, much of the recent New Americanist work on U.S. imperialism continues to emphasize the lines of this paradoxical history's imaginary resolution.[6] If Manifest Destiny is now routinely cited as an imperialist ideology, Americanists, for the most part, remain enamored of its efficacy, its apparently seamless consolidation—borrowing Wai-Chee Dimock's terms—of empire under the sign of liberty. Thus, for instance, the point of Dimock's own study is to implicate American individualism in a cultural logic of imperialism. While usefully insisting on the territorialization of individuality and discursive authority, however, Dimock has little to say about the logic of U.S. imperialism as such, as a form of both extra- and intraterritorial domination that points, if only by occlusion, to the heterogeneity of the continental nation.

On the other hand, allusions to the intranational dynamics of U.S. colonialism are commonplace in the register of a New Americanist "body" criticism, which is focused on the relation of embodied subjectivity to the abstractions of citizenship and national identity. More or less explicitly postmodern in its assumptions and emphases, this type of New Americanist study considers the body as surface rather than organism or essence, as the overdetermined topography of a corporeal existence that only appears to precede its historical determinations. In this compelling critical frame, it is not only the case that bodies are figurable as territories, subject to foreign invasion and administration; more to the point, the postmodern treatment of the body as a surface/site in effect functions to privilege a metaphorics of colonization, as *the* figuration of the body's relation to capital and bourgeois nationalist formation. Insofar as any marked body is made susceptible to its decoding as colonized body, however, the historical differences both between disparate modalities of colonial domination and between specifically colonial and other appropriations of "the body" are evacuated. For example, Rowe puts his claim about Melville's *Typee,* and its recognition of the continuities between colonialism and slavery, this way: "This scene [in which a Polynesian woman admires a white sailor's tattoos] enacts at once the westerner's expectation of the Polynesian woman's licentiousness and *her* recognition that she shares this sailor's 'marked' body. In the 'India ink' of his tattooed body, he shares with this woman and the New-World slave the 'mark' that is variously figured by the colonizer as race, class and gender" (275). In this formulation, all forms of domination exercised by the white masculine bourgeois subject are made commensurate; the white masculine laborer and the indigenous woman of color are said to share the mark "variously" but also, it appears, interchangeably "figured . . . as race, class and gender." Rowe's gesture toward a flat-out equivalence of bodily marks is perhaps atypical, yet finds subtler echoes in the treatment of embodied identities throughout New Americanist criticism. In a generally compelling elaboration of the ways that commodity culture beckons to disqualified social subjects, for instance, Lauren Berlant posits the appropriation by a colonizing power of both black and white women's bodies: "In *Imitation of Life,* when women make pancakes, picnics and movies, *the colonized female body* is not abstract, but hyper-embodied, an obstacle and not a vehicle to public pleasure and power" ("National Brands" 114, my emphasis). While Berlant, unlike Rowe, goes on to distinguish forcefully between the forms of white and black women's colonization, her analysis nonetheless supplies no particular historical or theoretical rationale for thinking of Bea Pullman's (or Claudette Colbert's or Lana Turner's) white bourgeois female body as "colonized." Or rather, colonialism becomes synonymous here with territorialization and commodification. To pose the question in Guha's terms, we might ask in what sense white bourgeois femininity, whether abstract or embodied, is traversed by the "historical limit" of bourgeois culture in the United States?

How Americanists theorize, or fail to theorize, imperialism and colonialism in a U.S. frame has an important bearing on how this disciplinary category might be "post-ed."[7] Mapping such a post-Americanist critical discourse in his introduction to *National Identities and Post-Americanist Narratives,* Donald Pease aligns "postnational narratives" with those subjects debarred from full participation in the abstract universality of national identity:

> Instead of accepting this assumption as the basis for their social identities, the socially disenfranchised figures within emancipatory political movements understand that the universality of the national identity depends on their externality for its integrity. In the wake of this recognition, these movement figures offered themselves up not for integration within the national narrative but, by way of what I am calling postnational narratives, actively contested its social arrangements. (3)

And again:

> Whereas the national narrative resulted in the assimilation of difference to the self-sameness of ruling assumptions, whose universality was predicated upon their inapplicability for peoples construed as of "another Nature," the postnational narratives dismantle this opposition. The agents of this dismantling were the national subject peoples, figures of race, class, and gender, who had been previously interpellated within the hegemonic category of disqualified social agency. (4)

Much like Rowe's, Pease's formulation largely brackets the distinction between particularized/externalized subjects by aligning variously "othered" people with one and the same "externality." While a critically valuable notion of "disqualified social agency" here displaces Rowe's amorphous concept of the "shared bodily mark," still, in this way of situating particularized subject peoples, it is their very particularity we risk eliding—how the various emancipatory movements of the past quarter century, and the "figures of race, class, and gender" who belong to them, might be quite differently mapped in relation to national identity and assimilationist ideologies of citizenship. As a result, a metaphorics of binary space (inside/outside) seems incongruously to survive the post-ing of national narratives; the concept of bounded national territory is *not* assigned to the logic of an always phantasmic interiority, at least to the extent that both inside and outside continue to figure as discrete and coherent sites. In a stunning and suggestive move, what Pease alters, or rather inverts, is the nationalist hierarchy, so that the nonintegrationist outside now becomes the repository of a (post-)American alterity. And yet the critical and political force of this gesture is compromised, insofar as it preserves the territorializing logic of the nation: finally, it seems uncertain how or why to associate "these movement figures"/"figures of race, class, and gender" with "*post*national narratives," insofar as *post-* implies an at least doubled position both "inside" and "outside" a national order. Pease is sensitive to the contradiction and, in a curious turn, instead aligns the hybridized position of a (more recognizably) "*post*national" subject with the New Americanists, the (generally leftist) interdisciplinary and (in this anthology predominantly white) cultural critics: "[The essays in this collection] configure individually and collectively *post*national narratives as the surfaces on which New Americanists have constructed their identities. The term *post*national indicates New Americanists' multiple interpellations: their different identifications with the disciplinary apparatuses in the new American Studies, as well as with social movements comprised of the 'disenfranchised groups' already cited" (4). Having constructed the "figures of race, class, and gender" as an ideally recalcitrant "outside," then, Pease (re)assigns marginality to the cultural critics, whose negotiations of cultural interspace, between disciplinary structure and emancipatory movement, thereby claim center stage in the production of "postnational narratives." In one sense, this argument provocatively moves to imagine a place for white intellectuals in unthinking the terms of their privileges within the nation-state. At the same time, such a configuration of the "post-American" field tends to preserve and perpetuate the privilege of these historically universalized subjects to be everywhere and nowhere, to travel freely between center and margin, indeed to reinscribe the boundary in the very exercise of their free passage.

Siting Colonialism

Implicit in Rowe's allusion to "the colonization of workers, women and people of color" (277), or in Berlant's reference to "the colonized female body," is an assumption that colonialism is coextensive with the cultural logic of capitalism, so that colonialism reduces to a form (the privileged form) of capitalist incorporation, and, conversely, the commodification of bodies and labor in general become figurative colonizations. While both Rowe's and Berlant's formulations gesture suggestively toward an analysis of colonial power relations at the center, this analysis of U.S. colonialism is all-too-seamlessly assimilated to an analysis of social, political, and economic domination within metropolitan bourgeois culture. Implicitly defined as the extension of capitalist relations of production (to extraterritorial locations), colonialism readily becomes the figure for the multiple forms of capitalism's progress. As Partha Chatterjee remarks, however, with reference to the formation of the colonial and the modern state, if "the colonial state is simply another specific form in which the modern state has generalized itself across the globe," then "the specifically colonial form of the emergence of the institutions of the modern state would be of only incidental, or at best episodic, interest" (14). By analogy, where colonialism designates simply another specific form in which capital has mobilized subjects and citizens of the United States, then the specifically colonial forms of subject peoples' economic and political subordination would be of only incidental or episodic interests to the study of U.S. nationalism. Yet, for Chatterjee, as well as for Guha, colonialism crucially figures both a historical *expansion* of capital and the historical *limit* to its totalizing self-reproduction. Subaltern studies thus sites colonialism where a mode of production, a social formation, and (or) a temporal-spatial order we might variously apprehend (to different emphases) as advanced or industrial capitalism, bourgeois culture (Guha), or modernity (Chatterjee) fail to assimilate the new elements they incorporate.

Rather than one particular form of capitalist expansion (among others), that is, colonialism represents *an expansion of capital that falls at least partially outside the logic of capitalist production.* As Guha repeatedly emphasizes, the "extraterritorial" expansion of British capital operates on the subcontinent through indigenous precapitalist modes of production, so that colonial Indian society is "largely semi-feudal" ("Dominance" 277). It is from this vantage that Guha observes, in the conclusion of this passage, "Colonialism stands thus not merely for the historical progeny, *ãtmaja,* of industrial and finance capital, but also for its historic Other." In specifying this doubled relation of colonialism to industrial and finance capital, subaltern studies provides a critical model of colonialism with applications for a postcolonial historiography of the center; more particularly, it suggests a strategy for mapping colonial domination across the heterogeneous cultural space of metropolitan formations. By insisting on the import of differential productive modes within the scene of capitalist expansion in the colonies, subaltern studies implicitly engages the colonial dimensions of metropolitan life in Europe and North America in those contexts and locations where labor is extracted outside the terms of a capitalist wage-labor economy. For instance, through the lens of subaltern studies, we can expand our grasp of the (intraterritorial) colonialism that Aijaz Ahmad has begun to describe in his account of U.S. slavery and national formation:

> Bourgeois hegemony [in the United States] was established before the full consolidation of the classes of industrial capitalism and under a leadership ideologically as advanced as in revolutionary France but drawn, in its class composition, substantially from the plantation economy of slaveowners, with the predominantly commercial and petty capitals of New England occupying a subordinate position. The contradictory consequence was that the American revolution was, simultaneously, in some fundamental ways even more advanced than the French, while it retained some aspects so retrograde that its full elaboration spanned virtually a whole century and was completed only in 1864 with the destruction of the plantation economy and the assimilation of the slave population first into sharecropping and then increasingly into wage-labour circuits. (50)

Although the disparity in this instance is not between an indigenous and an imported mode of production, since commercial capital and chattel slavery are equally foreign to the preinvasion Americas, nonetheless capitalist development in the antebellum United States is crucially heterogeneous to its proper productive modes.[8] By extension, a critique of capitalist class relations cannot adequately acknowledge and engage the situation of a captive, racialized labor force.

For Ahmad, the insistence on the historical heterogeneity of metropolitan capitalist formation dovetails with a critique of "Three Worlds" theory, particularly as it plays out in Fredric Jameson's elaboration of a "third world literature" as an aesthetic and analytic category. At issue for Ahmad is a disjunction between Jameson's characterization of first and second world orders "in terms of their production systems (capitalism and socialism, respectively)" and of the third world "purely in terms of an 'experience' of externally inserted phenomena." This classification of global order imposes a distinction "between those who make history and those who are mere objects of it," Ahmad contends, even as it crucially fails to account for the place of the third world in international relations of production: "If only the First World is capitalist and the Second World socialist, how does one understand the Third World? Is it pre-capitalist? Transitional? Transitional between what and what?" (99–100). In Ahmad's revisionist mapping, a model of transglobal contradiction and discontinuity in capitalist formation displaces the binary opposition of advanced (first world) and backward (third world) capitalism:

> But one could start with a radically different premise, namely the proposition that we live not in three worlds but in one; that this world includes the experience of colonialism and imperialism on both sides of Jameson's global divide (the "experience" of imperialism is a central fact of all aspects of life inside the U.S. from ideological formation to the utilisation of social surplus in military-industrial complexes); that societies in formations of backward capitalism are as much constituted by the division of classes as are societies in the advanced capitalist countries; that socialism is not restricted to something called the second world but is simply the name of a resistance that saturates the globe today, as does capitalism itself. (103)

Contesting the consolidation of the first world under the sign of advanced capitalism and the disarticulation of the third world under the sign of its historical violations, Ahmad usefully expands the terrain of postcolonial analysis to the first world and implicitly underwrites an attendant critical shift from the liberal-multiculturalist emphasis on global diversity to what Homi K. Bhabha distinguishes as the "conceptualizing of *inter*national culture, based . . . on the inscription and articulation of culture's *hybridity*" (38, my emphasis).[9]

Like Ahmad, albeit to different purpose, Stuart Hall insists, as well, on the presence and effects of heterogeneous productive modes within advanced capitalist arenas. At issue for Hall is the way differences of race and ethnicity mark the social organization of production across a variety of (neo)colonial formations at the center:

> Moreover, his [Gramsci's] analysis does also point to the way different modes of production can be *combined* within the same social

> formation leading not only to regional specificity and unevenness, but to differential modes of incorporating so-called "backward" sectors within the social regime of capital (e.g. Southern Italy within the Italian formation; the "Mediterranean" South within the more advanced "northern" sectors of industrial Europe; the peasant economies of the hinterland in Asian and Latin American societies on the path to dependent capitalist development; "colonial" enclaves within the development of metropolitan capitalist regimes; historically, slave societies as an integral part of primitive capitalist development of metropolitan powers; "migrant" labor forces within domestic labor markets; "Bantustans" within so-called sophisticated capitalist economies, etc.). Theoretically, what needs to be noticed is the persistent way in which *these* specific, differentiated forms of "incorporation" have consistently been associated with the appearance of racist, ethnically segmentary and other similar social features. (24–25)

If class articulates the social relations of production within the zones of industrial capitalist development, then we may speculate, following Hall's implication, that race or ethnicity marks the social relations of production in "differentially incorporated" sectors. Chatterjee similarly links the social and political mobilization of race to the circumstances of differential incorporation in his account of Indian colonial history. The developing insistence on race is aligned with the project of social consolidation and administrative rationalization, he argues, so that race appears to "emphasize the specifically colonial character of British dominance in India" at precisely the point where "the logic of a modern regime of power" pushes colonial officials toward "the normalization of the objects of its rule" (19). Thus, for Chatterjee, as for Hall, "the appearance of racist . . . social features" is the sign of an assimilation that suspends the reproduction of the same. As Chatterjee's analysis suggests, the racialized body registers the irreducible contradiction of capital's social regime, which cannot assimilate the colonized if it is to dominate them; at the same time, the racialized body veils this contradiction by assuming it as the "fact" of its own visible difference.

Siting the Center

In claiming the usefulness of subaltern studies for analyzing differential metropolitan formations in general, and the United States in particular, I am compelled by Gayatri Spivak's account of this historiographical method, even as, paradoxically, my effort to elaborate a subaltern studies approach to U.S. racial formations places me at odds with Spivak's own assessment of metropolitan and postcolonial race relations and their incommensurate histories. Crucially, for Spivak, subaltern studies speaks to a colonial context historically absolutely differentiated from class relations at the center:

> The position implicit in the work of the "Subaltern Studies" group of historians is that, since the colonies were not the theater of the development of industrial-capitalist class differentiation, if postcolonial intellectuals keep themselves strictly to the discourse of class analysis and class-struggle, they might produce a *Mischmasch der Kentnisse.* The peculiar historical development of colonial society, however, does not exclude the critique of class-analysis as a normative imposition of an instrument of reading. Insofar as such a critique represents a group with a name, it is the subaltern. ("Who Claims Alterity?" 273)

Furthermore, insofar as postcoloniality is not simply a rupture but also a repetition of the "colonial episteme," postcolonial experience is asymmetrical to the experience of race or ethnicity in a metropolitan context: "The stories (or histories) of the postcolonial world are not necessarily the same as the stories coming from 'internal colonization,' the way the metropolitan countries discriminate against disenfranchised groups in their midst" (274). Implicit in this construction of global "theaters" is the inapplicability of subaltern studies to the analysis of metropolitan formations. As Spivak suggests elsewhere, racial differentiation at the center is imbricated in industrial class differentiation, creating a continuity between the operations of racial and class domination that promptly unravels when we shift to a colonial frame of reference:

> Can the subaltern speak? What must the elite do to watch out for the continuing construction of the subaltern? The question of "woman" seems most problematic in this context. Clearly, if you are poor, black and female you get it in three ways. If, however, this formulation is moved from the first-world context into the postcolonial (which is not identical with the third-world) context, the description "black" or "of color" loses persuasive significance. The necessary stratification of colonial subject-constitution in the first phase of capitalist imperialism makes "color" useless as an emancipatory signifier. Confronted by the ferocious standardizing benevolence of most U.S. and Western European human-scientific radicalism (recognition by assimilation), the progressive though heterogeneous

> withdrawal of consumerism in the comprador periphery, and the exclusion of the margins or even the center-periphery articulation . . . the analogue of class-consciousness rather than race-consciousness in this area seems historically, disciplinarily and practically forbidden by Right and Left alike. It is not just a question of *double* displacement, as it is not simply the problem of finding a psychoanalytic allegory that can accommodate the third world woman with the first. ("Can the Subaltern Speak?" 294–95)

In this analysis, it becomes symptomatic of the historical divide between the first world and the postcolonial contexts that the economic disadvantage of "the poor, black and female" subject in the United States can be meaningfully addressed in the frame of antiracist discourse. The stratification of colonial subject-constitution, however, disjoins race and class in ways that render a Euro-American race-consciousness meaningless and expose the normative agenda in the models of class-consciousness predicated on an industrial capitalist formation. It would be difficult to quarrel with Spivak's remarks on the historical disparity between advanced capitalist and colonial formations that renders first world critical models unequal to the analysis of postcoloniality, whether by the transposition or the multiplication of terms. Here, however, Spivak also effects a homogenizing of first world space that both Hall's and Ahmad's observations usefully function to query. If it is true that race-consciousness in the United States opens a critical perspective on class relations (e.g., on the status of a growing urban subproletariat overwhelmingly composed of African Americans and other peoples of color), the reverse has not been the case. That is, a critique of industrial capitalist class differentiation does not account for the operation of race in the United States either "historically, disciplinarily [or] practically," underscoring Ahmad's observation that the most ideologically advanced formations may comprise the most retrograde and heterogeneous elements. In this context, I would suggest that the value of subaltern studies to a reading of race, nationalism, and postnationalisms in the United States lies precisely in forbidding the erosion of the distinction between colonialism and industrial capitalism in critical formulations such as Rowe's or Berlant's. It is not by siting colonialism at the center that we elide "the peculiar historical development" of the periphery, in other words, but rather by failing to do so *carefully:* at any rate, the alternative to the theorization of differential incorporation and its bearing on race within advanced capitalist formations has not been an enhanced sense of world history that would respect the profound asymmetries between metropolitan and colonial societies but just the contrary, an inclination to equate the territorializing operations of capitalism as such with the operations of colonialism.

Yet even as Spivak insists that the colonial situation has no metropolitan analogue (set off between diacritical marks, "internal colonization" is also implicitly set aside as a model lacking critical and historical coherence), her reading "against the grain" of subaltern studies suggests precisely how we might trace the figure and effects of the colonial subaltern in a U.S. frame. In Spivak's reading, the ostensibly positivist project of subaltern studies—restoring the colonial subaltern as the subject of history—stands as a "strategic use of positivist essentialism" (*In Other Worlds* 205). The affirmation of the "sovereignty," "consistency," and "logic" of "rebel consciousness" in subaltern studies, Spivak argues, represents a politically invested break with a deconstructive critical practice that at the same time tacitly enables these historians' treatments of sovereign subjectivity as "subject-effect" (Guha, cited in *In Other Worlds* 207). Citing Guha's analysis of the "counter-insurgent" text as her exemplary instance of subaltern studies methodology, Spivak weighs Guha's claim that the colonial administration's extensive record on peasant insurgencies represents not simply the "will" of the authors but also that of the insurgents. The elite will-to-suppress is necessarily contingent on the subaltern will-to-rebel, and thus the colonial archives are marked by the deliberative subaltern consciousness that is, *as such,* unsignifiable in this discursive regime. Spivak concludes:

> Thus do the texts of counter-insurgency locate a "will" as the sovereign cause when it is no more than *an effect of the subaltern subject-effect,* itself produced by the particular conjunctures called forth by the crises meticulously described in the various *Subaltern Studies*. . . . Reading the work of Subaltern Studies against the grain, I would suggest that elements in their text would warrant a reading of the project to retrieve the subaltern consciousness as the attempt to undo a massive historical metalepsis and "situate" the effect of the subject as subaltern. (204–5, my emphasis)

Thus in Spivak's reading of Guha, the latter's work contributes to a post-structuralist critical practice its missing historical register, supplementing the antihumanist critique of subjectivity (human consciousness as effect rather than cause) with the critique of imperialism (human consciousness as effect of inhumane power and of those less-than-human subjects called forth by imperial institutions and practices). While Spivak assigns subaltern studies to a specific cultural and historical domain—to what she ostensibly wishes to distinguish from the metropolitan as the properly colonial context—the figure of the colonial subaltern in Spivak's formulation is not proper to any domain, in the sense that it is she who cuts the border:

> The arena of the subaltern's persistent emergence into hegemony must always and by definition remain heterogeneous to the efforts of the disciplinary historian. The historian must persist in *his* efforts in this awareness, that the subaltern is necessarily the absolute limit of the place where history is narrativized into logic. (207)

The subaltern is heterogeneous to history, insofar as history is necessarily inscribed within a specific economy of cultural (re)production. I would argue that, understood in this way, as marking the absolute limit of hegemonic culture, the subaltern and its effects might be traced in a variety of colonial configurations across global divides and that the value of such a project lies in the potential of subaltern studies to enable a different siting of the center. To "situate the effect of the subject as subaltern" in any particular historical situation would be to trace the limits of national sovereignty and of elite agency.

From this vantage, we might reconsider the figure of "the poor, black and female subject" in the United States, whom Spivak cites as the locus of an exemplary discontinuity between the logic of postcoloniality and of racial "discrimina[tion]" in metropolitan countries. If, as Guha observes, "subalternity is materialized in the structure of property" ("Prose of Counter-Insurgency" 45), then the juridical determination of black men and women *as* alienable property situated these captive subjects as subaltern within a national social formation that "combined" (to borrow Hall's term) capitalist development and chattel slavery. Stripped of the ownership in his or her own labor that informs the subject of industrial capitalism—rendered heterogeneous to the principle of possessive individualism that operates bourgeois representation—the black subaltern thus sites the historical limit of hegemonic culture in the metropolitan United States.[10]

A subaltern studies approach to black female subjectivity here rejoins Hortense Spillers's groundbreaking analysis of black female reproduction under, and in the wake of, slavery. In a brilliant revision of a history intelligible to the terms of nationalist narrative only as a pathological aberration (e.g., the Moynihan report), Spillers reflects on the female slave's marginality to the logic of capitalist production (a body transmuted directly into capital) and of patriarchal reproduction alike. The astonishing capacity of the captive black woman to *re*produce capital requires that she transmit her own "condition" to her offspring rather than mediating the transmission of the father's name. As such, Spillers argues, the black woman designates the site, or position, in an "American grammar" where a patriarchal syntax, or genealogy, is disrupted; the captive mother's "condition" ambiguously indexes the condition of her existence under slavery and her condition as the proscribed subject of a *paralogical* history: "But what is the 'condition' of the mother? Is it the 'condition' of enslavement the writer means, or does he mean the 'mark' and 'knowledge' of the mother upon the child, that here translates into the culturally forbidden and impure?" (79).

If we (re)read Spillers's claim through the lens of Spivak's "reading against the grain," then the doubled "condition" of the black female subaltern bespeaks the "conditional," or contingent, status of *elite* subjectivity in the United States. First, in the sense that U.S. national culture coheres only on condition of muting the subject Spillers here invokes, a subject marked by her knowledge of "the culturally *forbidden* and *impure*." In other words, the consensual Euro-American state forms itself in the act of countering the potential insurgency of the black female subject, who undergoes either assimilation to hegemonic identity or the most radical objectification as racial/sexual other. From this vantage, however, white masculine/patriarchal agency is less a cause than an effect of black female subalternity. Second, in the sense that the black female subaltern's proscribed knowledge is the knowledge of a national impropriety. The black mother marks her progeny with the knowledge of capitalism's systemic contradictions (the plantation economy at the center of U.S. capitalist development) and of U.S. culture's systematic violation under slavery of its founding prohibition on miscegenation.[11] The juridical disavowal of miscegenation, through the erasure of white paternity, displaces onto the racialized "black" body the "mark" and "knowledge" of a *national* "condition."

In the final section of this chapter, I turn to the first volume in Octavia Butler's science fiction trilogy *Xenogenesis*, titled *Dawn*, which I read as a postcolonial novel written in, and for, a U.S. context. I do not intend for this "turn" to function as a departure (a turn away) from theoretical and historiographical concerns, as if these had been sufficiently belabored and with contexts now elucidated we could return to the matter of textual analysis. Indeed, I turn to *Dawn* not as a literary instance of an already delineated American post-coloniality but as a critical model in its own right—as a text that implicitly elaborates Spillers's work in the direction of what we might call, following Pease, a "post-Americanist" historiography. In the defamiliarized landscape of the science fiction text, Butler offers a polemical vision of U.S. slavery as an explicitly colonial practice, even as the novel moves forward to imagine the conditions for the emergence of both the colonizer and the colonized as postnational subjects. While in Pease's account the boundary-crossing (white) academic harnesses the alterity of the dispossessed, Butler's novel mobilizes the paralogical history of the black female subaltern to trace her "mark" and "knowledge" on the bodies and the persons of *white* men and women.

The Dawn of History

Butler's novel about the forced genetic adulteration of the human species grafts a reproductive scenario profoundly reminiscent of slavery in the United States onto the imagined encounter between a decimated humanity and an alien race of interplanetary "traders." The human survivors of nuclear war have been captured and removed from the global fallout zone by the Oankali, a species of Medusa-like beings, with smooth, gray flesh covered in tentacles that double as sensory organs and lethal stingers. Since the tentacles replace eyes and ears, the Oankali have nothing by way of a face; and although they are bipedal, with a vaguely human body contour, their joints effect a radically nonhuman articulation of body parts. To their human prisoners, the Oankali body is horrifying, abject, a phantasm of alienness. Although, like the human body, the Oankali body is sexed, Oankali sexual organization is triadic. Reproduction requires a male, a female, and a neuter partner, with the male and female both assuming what counts, at least in a phallic economy of human gender, as passive positions in the sexual act. In other words, Oankali sex involves the penetration of both the male and the female by the neuter Oankali, called ooloi, who acquire in adolescence a specialized set of organs for this purpose. The ooloi and, to a lesser extent, male and female Oankali are biologically equipped to perceive and control DNA directly, so that Oankali reproduction represents a form of genetic engineering, a willed manipulation of genetic materials. *Dawn* opens as the Oankali are preparing to revive their human captives, most of whom have been held in suspended animation, and return them to earth, which has been made newly habitable thanks to the painstaking ooloi reconstruction of terrestrial ecosystems at the cellular level. The price of this renewal is something the Oankali term a "trade," which Lilith, the African American survivor whose initiation into Oankali life is the subject of *Dawn,* defines as "crossbreeding... no matter what you call it" (42).[12]

An African American in a colonized population slated for controlled "crossbreeding," Lilith's "condition" in the text invokes the "condition" of her captive ancestors—the systematic dispossession of the African American subject and "theft of the body" itself (Spillers 67). Furthermore, as a woman whose reproductive function is enhanced, and disciplined, through biotechnological intervention, Lilith's "condition" also obliquely evokes that of a late-twentieth-century white female elite, who form the consumer base of a burgeoning industry in artificial insemination, in vitro fertilization, and other reproductive services. As Valerie Hartouni has argued, contemporary reproductive biotechnologies must be understood in terms of their specifically nationalist appeal to a class of professional women, whose exercise of reproductive choice has imperiled the proper allocation of national resources: "Both [the] text and subtext [of fertility research] are straightforward," she points out. "White women want babies but cannot have them, and black and other 'minority' women, coded as 'breeders' within American society (and welfare dependents with Reagan's America), are having babies 'they' cannot take care of and 'we' do not want" (46). Interestingly, by aligning elite reproductive practices with the female subaltern's body, Butler effects a strategic refiguration of the fertility clinic (and its ethos of voluntarism) as captive breeding zone. Thus, Lilith wonders, as she begins to fathom the Oankali's agenda, "Was that what she was headed for? Forced artificial insemination. Surrogate motherhood? Fertility drugs and forced 'donation' of eggs? Implantation of unrelated fertilized eggs. Removal of children from mothers at birth... ? Humans had done these things to captive breeders—all for a higher good, of course" (62). Lilith remembers an array of contemporary reproductive practices with a difference—not as an extension of women's reproductive options but as a biotechnological arsenal serving the always partial interests that define the general good. Her defamiliarizing recollections serve to draw a crucial distinction between consumer choice and reproductive freedom. Indeed, if under the conditions of slavery black women reproduce property, in the contemporary fertility clinic, white women's reproduction is made (over) into a corporate property—reproduction as patented technological procedure. The transformation into capital of the black female body under slavery and of white women's reproductive activity under the terms of today's research remain wholly incommensurate historical phenomena, yet by running them together in this way, Lilith's ruminations insist that reproduction is never unmediated by the forces of production. From this perspective, the interest of the female subaltern would lie not (or not only) in her accession to an elite femininity's privilege of naturalized reproduction (her emergence into a hegemonic experience of motherhood) but in a critical reassessment of the limits of that privilege, made visible precisely when the reproduction of whiteness cannot be separated from the reproduction of blackness.

Two other features of Lilith's condition among the Oankali, and more generally of the way the novel maps human-Oankali relations, are worth discussion. First, Lilith and the colonized humans are mute subjects within the dominant Oankali culture. Insofar as the Oankali privilege the language of the human body, its genetic codes and capabilities, it matters relatively little what languages (human or Oankali) the colonized will speak or even what linguistic (inter)spaces they may limn. Given the Oankali installation of the genetic as a universal, or transspecies, biocultural discourse, it falls to the colonizer to articulate the meaning of the captive subject: "Your body said one thing. Your words said another," Lilith's ooloi Nikanj informs her human lover Joseph, when he resists the ooloi's sexual advances (200). Later, Nikanj assures Lilith, dismayed to find that she is pregnant with a mixed-species, human-Oankali child, that "nothing about you but your words reject this child" (262). As Lilith herself concedes, "It's like a language that they have a special gift for. They know our bodies better than we do" (178). Put another way, as that which speaks (in) us, the Oankali occupy the place Jacques Lacan identifies with the symbolic order itself, the place where the "I" of the speaking subject is engendered as an effect of this alienation in the social/other.[13] From this perspective, the condition for the colonized humans' speech can only be their emergence into Oankali hegemony.

Second, the human discourse of resistance to Oankali domination grounds the subject's humanity in an organic corporeality, that is, in an ideology of the body as proper(ty). Thus, from the perspective of the captive humans, "human" history *can* be narrativized beyond apocalypse, beyond genocide and devastation on a planetary scale, but not beyond the adulteration of human genetic material. As Lilith puts it, "Some will think the human species deserves at least a *clean* death" (261, my emphasis). But this predication of human history on the preservation of an original, and thus authentic, human identity is shown to uphold a specifically masculine (and historically white masculine) privilege; the rallying cry of the disaffected human males is the profanation of their manhood, being "taken like a woman" in the Oankali sexual act (216). Against this threat of feminization, "human" identity is asserted through possessive heterosexual mating. When one of the human women refuses male companionship, two of the human males proceed to rape her, in an act represented by their supporters as merely exacting her allegiance to humanity: "It's her duty to get together with someone. There aren't that many of us left. . . . We pair off! One man, one woman. Nobody has the right to hold out. It just causes trouble" (187). Ironically, then, it is not the Oankali but the humans whom Lilith must remind that "nobody here is property. Nobody here has the right to the use of anybody else's body" (188).

Lilith's injunction against rape, phrased as an injunction against holding human property, invokes the historical circumstances of slavery and inscribes a critique of organic corporeality from the vantage of a subaltern subjectivity absolutely liminal to this discursive logic. Here, the novel requires us to contemplate the (re)production of "human" identity in, and through, the figure of the human/commodity that marks its historical borders, that is, in and through the history of a body without boundaries, a body rendered absolutely and impossibly improper insofar as it becomes (another's) property. However, her historically vexed relation to the privilege of organic embodiment becomes Lilith's critical privilege in the novel, which permits her to decipher, as the attraction of Oankali culture, its displacement, or post-ing, of human (re)production. If to the residual human population the genetic alteration of the human body would mark the end of human history, for Lilith's Oankali interlocutor, it is the logic of human history that, like radioactive fallout, threatens the perpetuation of the species:

> "There must be ruins," she [Lilith] said softly.
> "There were. We've destroyed many of them."
> She seized his arm without thinking. "You destroyed them? There were things left and you destroyed them?"
> "You'll begin again. We'll put you in areas that are clean of radioactivity and history. You will become something other than you were."
> "And you think destroying what was left of our cultures will make us better?"
> 'No. Only different." (35)

While Lilith mourns the obliteration of the blasted ruins, the Oankali understand her cathecting of the past, of ruined, or original, things, as a lethal form of historical identification.[14] The Oankali predicate a continued history *for* humans on the end of human history, on the genetic mutation, or becoming other, of humanity. As one of Lilith's captors explains, the "essence" of Oankali identity lies in the "drive" to displace itself, so that this identity is visibly constituted in its alienation, or division:

> "We are Oankali." . . .
> "What does it mean in your language?"
> "Several things. Traders, for one." . . .
> "What do you trade?"
> "Ourselves."
> "You mean . . . each other? Slaves?"
> "No. We've never done that."
> "What, then?" . . .
> "We trade the essence of ourselves. Our genetic material for yours. . . . We're not hierarchical, you see. . . . But we are powerfully acquisitive. We acquire new life—seek it, investigate it, manipulate it, sort it, use it. We carry the drive to do this in a minuscule cell within a cell, a tiny organelle within every cell of our bodies. . . . One of the meanings of Oankali is gene trader. Another is that organelle—the essence of ourselves. (23, 41–42)

If the Oankali are thus genetically coded for capitalism, Oankali social formation admits neither the reproduction of property in slavery nor genetic engineering as a corporate property. Rather, the Oankali practice reproduction as a form of corporate/corporeal impropriety, in which they perpetuate "their" identity and agency by displacing themselves across the historical and territorial limits of Oankali culture. Thus the Oankali's essentialist rhetoric and their ostensibly organicist sensibilities (it is, after all, human biology whose language they fathom, rather than humans themselves) here sustain neither a universalist conception of Oankali culture nor even a sense of its original integrity. The point about Oankali colonialism is that the colonizers understand their expansionist "drive" as an abdication of sovereignty and the embodied Oankali subject is marked by the knowledge of his/her/its radically contingent relation to the (bio)cultural reproduction of non-Oankali. As Lilith discovers, what she perceives as "the Oankali" are, in fact, complexly hybridized beings, who display the genetic imprint of their millennia of "trade." In this frame, I would argue that the Oankali is the Euro-American subject refigured as an effect of its planetary *dis*locations. Butler's "post-Americanist" narrative thus situates the promise of the postnational subject in a rearticulation of whiteness as an embodiment fully conditional on what can never be proper to it. The novel suggests how the affiliation of white subjects with marginal or subaltern cultures that Pease defines as central to the post-ing of American national identity depends not simply on their mobile sympathies but on a critical racialization of whiteness.

In a discussion of "'transnational' reproduction," Mary Layoun queries, "Is there reproduction that allows another order of things? That allows for the agencies of female desire and sexuality and of reproduction? For the reconsideration of boundaries of the 'nation' and of what they contain and exclude?" (72). From one perspective, in the defamiliarized (post)national landscape of *Dawn,* there is no other kind; Oankali reproduction is a function of national, historical, and biocultural boundary crossings. Lilith's sexual and reproductive agency, however, as yet finds its articulation only in her recognition of its loss. When Nikanj informs Lilith, at the novel's end, that she is pregnant, with a girl he has "mixed" to be her "she-companion," she protests: "It won't be a daughter. . . . It will be a thing—not human." She stared down at her own body in horror. "It's inside me, and it isn't human!" (262).

Invaded by cultural forces that turn her inside out, Lilith can only articulate what the child is *not*—not human, not her own. But we might imagine that Lilith nevertheless finds her voice in this anguished (ac)knowledge(ment) of the child's nonidentity and her own, and that, in her articulation of a permanently vexed interiority, she marks the postnational space where she may eventually know to inscribe a different name.

Chapter 2

After Bourgeois Nationalism

One important new feature of global cultural politics ... is that nation and state are at each other's throats, and the hyphen that links them is now less an icon of conjuncture than an index of disjuncture.
—*Arjun Appadurai,* Modernity at Large

Who knows what we humans have that others might be willing to take in trade for a livable space on a world not our own?
—*Octavia Butler, afterword to* Bloodchild and Other Stories

These days, discussions of the nation-state in the era of globalization often invoke one side or another of a supposed debate on its continuing relevance to the study of capital's social and cultural regimes. One side argues that the operations of mobile capital, and in particular the accelerated transfers of labor, commodities, and information across national borders, bring about the erosion of the nation-state, a position routinely attributed to Arjun Appadurai and to Masao Miyoshi; the other contends that the nation-state continues to exert a significant disciplinary function on the lives of its citizens and of noncitizens within its borders, a position often linked to scholars such as Roger Rouse and Bonnie Honig. The debate results primarily from a reductive citational practice, in which certain lines of argument are severed from a more complex analytic frame. Thus, for instance, Appadurai may propose new "macrometaphors" for the study of "fractal" cultural shapes, as "configurations of people, place, and heritage lose all semblance of isomorphism" (47, 46), yet he also finds a future for patriotism in "the spread of *national* forms that are largely divorced from territorial states" (169). Similarly, Rouse may stress the continuing complicity of capital and state, yet he, too, avers that "the relationship between the state as emblem of the nation, the population that resides within its borders, and the corporations that do business there is more disjunctive than at any time in . . . [U.S.] history" (368). For each of these commentators, then, the point is not to decide whether the nation-state has a future but to excavate from among the layers of residual, dominant, and emergent organization the futures it may hold; to investigate, that is, the increasingly disjunctive relation between the nation (as imagined community) and the state (as administrative apparatus)—a disjuncture that does not portend the simple dissolution of either term.

Notwithstanding the nationalist responses to migration and immigration on which Honig, for instance, builds her reading of nationalism's resurgence; indeed, notwithstanding the eruption of ethnonationalisms worldwide, I want to suggest, following Appadurai's lead, that what we may be witnessing today is the separation of nationalism's incorporative functions from the operations of the state. This is not to say that nationalism vanishes altogether as strategic ideological referent from state-sponsored discourse, but that the *normative* or assimilative project of the modern nation seems increasingly marginal to the exercise of state power on subject populations. If, as Miyoshi remarks, "the state did, and still does, perform certain functions for which there is as of now no substitute agency," what he goes on to characterize as the state's ailing condition seems rather to reflect a failure, or more precisely a lapse, of its integrative, national component.

> The state as a political authority seems biased and compromised. It is not the nation as an integrated whole but certain classes, the privileged in it, that receive a major portion of benefits from the state performing these tasks. The state fails to satisfy most of its sectors and leaves most of its citizenry resentful. (92–93)

Is the uncoupling of the historical union between integrative nationalism and state formation most usefully understood as a failure in the operations of the modern state? What changes has the divorce—or, at any rate, the estrangement—of nation and state begun to work on those who have prospered by their marriage, as on those for whom the domestic arrangements of the nation-state have always seemed "biased" in someone else's favor? In brief, I want to ask what is lost and what is gained when the state fails to satisfy—fails, that is, to interpellate its citizenry as national subjects. What are the implications of a postnational state for the disposition of embodied subjects under its administration? To what extent does the state's retreat from nationalism mark a transformation in the social (re)production of embodied subjects within the broader context of transnational capitalism and the rise of an informational economy?

Dominance without Hegemony? The Politics of Dissatisfaction

Should we or, more to the point, can we afford to regret the collapse of the state's at least apparently mediatory function, its now-all-too-visibly servile relation to a ruling class? The power of Miyoshi's observation rests in his canny linkage of the disintegrating nation-state to the matter of satisfaction—to the practice of hegemony, in other words. After all, the disaffection of a disappointed citizenry signals a crisis in the hegemonic exercise of state power and not by any means an attenuation of state power as such. Just the reverse. Assuming, to borrow Michael Warner's language, that the citizenry no longer consents to its own coercion, then we revert to the prospect of a purely coercive state (111). Thus the state's ostensible failure to subject its citizens in the double sense of that term—to subject them to its power and to authorize them as "freely" consenting subjects—would reduce the state to an apparatus of subjection in the merely singular sense, to an exclusively repressive function. From this vantage, Miyoshi's disappointment appears all too fitting, since the state's reorientation to serving an elite stratum (rather than to reproducing an "integrated whole") would sound the death knell of the modern state's progressive impulses toward universal suffrage, however vexed.

Thus the state's contemporary "failure" returns us to the contradiction of the modern nation-state, dedicated at once to the welfare of its people (to the health of the social organism) and to the preservation of private property (to the advancement of the propertied class). Yet paradoxically, it is the modern state's lack of autonomy, its elision with the interests of the dominant class, that inaugurates its progressive, mediatory function, as Antonio Gramsci so acutely discerns:

> The revolution which the bourgeois class has brought into the conception of law, and hence into the function of the State, consists especially in the will to conform (hence ethicity of the law and of the State). The previous ruling classes were essentially conservative in the sense that they did not tend to construct an organic passage from other classes into their own, i.e. to enlarge their class sphere "technically" and ideologically; their conception was that of a closed caste. The bourgeois class poses itself as an organicism in continuous movement, capable of absorbing the entire society, assimilating it to its own cultural and economic level. The entire function of the State has been transformed; the State has become an "educator," etc. (260)

If the modern state satisfies, it is only because it teaches satisfaction, diffusing bourgeois productive and reproductive—work and sexual—disciplines among the broadest segment of the popular masses. As Gramsci goes on to remark, the bourgeois "will to conform[ity]" falls necessarily short of its mark, to the extent that it continues to rely on the law and on the state. "A class claiming to be capable of assimilating the whole of society, and which was at the same time really able to express such a process," he observes, "would perfect this conception of the State and of law, so as to conceive the end of the State and of law—rendered useless since they will have exhausted their function and been absorbed by civil society" (260). Thus the limits of the state's pedagogical success are signaled in the continued existence of the state itself—and indeed, in the state's absorption, or colonization, of civil society, so that, in Gramsci's words again, "by 'State' should be understood not only the apparatus of government, but also the 'private' apparatus of 'hegemony' or civil society" (261).

But what becomes of hegemony with the eclipse of the bourgeoisie and its revolutionary organicism? In a wonderfully prophetic, if elliptical passage of the *Prison Notebooks* (the opening sentence, at any rate, reads as a notation or sketch of an idea to be written out later), Gramsci envisions how the unraveling of the bourgeois class may entail not (in conventionally Marxist terms) the state's dissolution through the ascendance to power of a genuinely universal proletariat but rather a return of sorts to a premodern state formation, characterized by the external imposition of force, rather than the inculcation of internalized disciplines.

> How this [assimilative] process comes to a halt, and the conception of the state as pure force is returned to, etc. The bourgeois class is "saturated"; it not only does not expand—it starts to disintegrate; it not only does not assimilate new elements, it loses part of itself (or at least its losses are enormously more numerous than its assimilations). (260)

It is neither new nor controversial, I suspect, to remark that the middle class's dominance in America is over (or, at any rate, fading quickly). But Gramsci implies a startling corollary: that the middle class's disintegration signals an end to hegemonic power and the state's regression to a regime of force. Gramsci thus primes us to see how a decline in the fortunes of the bourgeoisie wrought by the complex transformation in production (often tagged as the shift from an industrial to a postindustrial society) may also entail a collapse of bourgeois nationalism's *ethos*—and the state's reversion to the exercise of a dominance without hegemony that, in Ranajit Guha's brilliant analysis, represents not only the practice of the premodern state but also the condition of colonial rule, where the subordination of the colonized does not coincide with their interpellation as the citizen-subjects of national capital.[1]

Certainly, if we look to the United States, there is no lack of evidence that the decline of the middle class has wrought a crisis in the exercise of hegemonic power as such, so that the condition of dominance without hegemony once peculiar to the colonial periphery is now becoming *generalized* within the metropole. There are U.S. policies of welfare "reform," for example, designed to force the unemployed into service work at below-subsistence wages and thereby actively support the expansion of a prostrated (sub)proletariat absolutely marginal to the traditional institutions of civic discipline (schools, benevolent associations, nuclear family) and to the arena of consumption through which civic entitlement is increasingly secured.[2] In the current drive to dismantle welfare, we witness the state as it participates in the forced development of a class external to the public and the private apparatus of its hegemony. There is also the state's swiftly expanding use of incarceration as a tactic for the management-by-force of certain target populations, most notably poor people of color, and especially African American men. Equally telling, the construction and administration of prisons is now routinely outsourced to private corporations, for whom the prison population represents not only access to lucrative government contracts but a potentially enormous reservoir of unpaid labor. Within the context of the prison as "growth industry," the reformist ethos that underwrites the modern penal system, at least in theory, gives way to the increasingly transparent internment-for-profit of disqualified citizens for whom no alternate destiny (no redemptive discipline) is any longer envisioned.

If we shift our gaze from the ever-expanding margins to the center, from the subaltern to the agent of state power, hegemony's future seems just as uncertain. Does it make sense any longer to speak of a ruling *bloc*—or do we speak, more aptly, of a ruling *caste,* whose restricted ranks are visible not only in the increasing concentration of wealth among an increasingly minute fraction of the global population but also in the transfer of a tiny roster of personnel between key corporate and state postings (e.g., from Enron, Halliburton, and Chevron to the White House)? This continual redeployment of the same personnel not only highlights the indifference of the ruling elite to public perception—to how any of this looks—but would also seem to suggest that the ranks of the power brokers are relatively thin.[3] At the same time, faith in the continuity of hegemonic power seeks proof in the ongoing performance of electoral politics and in the requirement (which follows historically, at any rate) that the ruling class successfully hail the lower classes (or, in more contemporary terms, that it hail the mass public). Yet the signs that elections have increasingly less bearing on the disposition of state power are everywhere: the 2000 presidential election, and the seemingly inconceivable way in which the negation of the popular vote by a state-appointed body failed to register as scandal, is only the most obvious. The conditions of possibility for this simultaneously hypervisible and undisclosed usurpation of power, moreover, inhere in the broader erosion of a hegemonic state signaled by the near-total collapse of the two-party system and the ever-plummeting voter turnout. As the organizers of the grassroots, Internet-based MoveOn.org political action committee noted in a postelection e-mail to contributors, less than 20 percent of the electorate voted in the November 2002 elections. While one hears from the Right and the Left alike that the electorate's indifference has caused the decline of electoral politics, a less moralizing and more persuasive claim is that voters have quite astutely recognized how popular consent becomes an ever more marginal consideration to the exercise of state power.

At issue, then, in the state's contemporary practices is not only the disregard for something approximating the welfare of "the people" (a regard that has always been partial and uneven at best, overwritten by the imperatives of property) but also a dwindling concern with the crafting of a perceived public interest that the state can claim to secure. The dubious fate of hegemony as a form of power is legible both in the exacerbated promotion of elite interests and (what does not necessarily follow) in the increasingly overt display of the state's mercenary dedication to those interests. In the manner of Poe's thieving minister, who conceals the purloined letter in plain view, the state makes barely an effort to disguise its bias and thus claims in transparency protection from the critical force of disclosure. Disclosure or, more exactly, the idea that disclosure matters, that it has weight and consequence, supports (and finds support in) the architecture of rule by consent: insofar as the state is supervised by an anonymous public, citizens can conceive of their subordination to its power as a voluntary measure, as a free acquiescence in a power that defines and constrains that freedom. Viewed in this way, the political scandal performs a crucially hegemonic function; it takes down a particular set of agents and agencies, in order to enact the legitimacy of state power as such. Thus the shift to a regime of state where abuses lie on the surface—impossible to penetrate and demystify because *already exposed*—indexes a historical juncture where bourgeois hegemony's intricate two-step falters, and the spectacle of power's dispersal (in the public; in every individual, consenting subject) is replaced by the spectacle of its concentration.

Yet despite the proliferating contexts of state domination without hegemony, it would be too simple to claim that the state has renounced its pedagogical function altogether. Rather, I think, the task is to reconstruct the ethical project of the state in the absence of an assimilative, or universalist, agenda on the part of the ruling class. To posit an end to the bourgeoisie's hegemonic governance is to suggest that the value of bourgeois disciplines is eroding under the conditions of late capitalism, as the system of industrial production underwritten by proprietary selfhood, free labor, and the work ethic yields to a postindustrial order, in which the ongoing utility of such normative constructions is by no means self-evident. The sections that follow limn the tenets of a postindustrial discipline and the features of the citizen-subjects it calls forth. In so doing, I aim to elucidate new directions in state pedagogies after bourgeois nationalism.

The Ethics of (Post)industrialism?

The demise of the bourgeois class as "an organicism in continuous movement" coincides with a significant transformation in labor as a form of social relation. Historically, we must reckon with the contradiction that the bourgeoisie's organicist ethos accommodates a commodification of labor that thoroughly atomizes workers: how to reconcile the decomposition of embodied subjects within alienated labor (the hyperutilization of specific corporeal and mental functions; the irrelevance and atrophy of others) with the organicism of bourgeois sociality? The work of the Canadian political scientist C. B. Macpherson usefully illuminates this contradiction, and I want to linger for a moment on his revisionist reading of social contract theory, to think both the hegemonic construction of wage (or "free") labor and what comes to displace it in the late capitalist era. Reading (perhaps) somewhat aslant of Macpherson's own investments, I take his "theory of possessive individualism" as a compelling account of how the organic social body is articulated to the fragmented bodies of its individual members through an idea of property. By "theory of possessive individualism," he means "the social assumptions . . . common to the main seventeenth-century political theories from Hobbes to Locke," particularly as they are "relevant to the problems of later liberal-democratic society," and he frames this theory as a series of foundational propositions (263). His critical preoccupations are with the matter of logical priority—what follows from what in establishing the necessity of a modern market society. While the first two propositions concern a definition of freedom as independence from the will of others, so that all legitimate social relations must be voluntary and serve the interests of both parties, the third and fourth function to delineate the worker's relation to the labor market:

(i) What makes a man human is freedom from dependence on the wills of others.

(ii) Freedom from dependence on others means freedom from any relations with others except those relations which the individual enters voluntarily with a view to his own interest.

(iii) The individual is essentially the proprietor of his own person and capacities, for which he owes nothing to society.
(iv) Although the individual cannot alienate the whole of his property in his own person, he may alienate his capacity to labour.
(v) Human society consists of a series of market relations.
(vi) Since freedom from the wills of others is what makes a man human, each individual's freedom can rightfully be limited only by such obligations and rules as are necessary to secure the same freedom for others.
(vii) Political society is a human contrivance for the protection of the individual's property in his person and goods, and (therefore) for the maintenance of orderly relations between individuals regarded as proprietors of themselves. (263–64)

In this way of rendering the social contract, it is evident that the assumption of self-ownership outlined in the third proposition is meaningless apart from the conditions of a "possessive market society" cited in the fourth proposition. As Macpherson points out, the fifth proposition, "human society consists of a series of market relations," may also be understood as the ground from which all the prior propositions proceed, in reverse sequence (264). Stressing how possessive individualism starts from this premise at which it claims to arrive, Macpherson implicates the juridical production of property in the body as a legitimation strategy for the systematic expropriation of bodily labor under capitalism: by installing absolute title to one's body as the (supposed) condition of its abstraction and fragmentation in the labor market, in other words, the bourgeois state instructs its citizen-subjects to cathect an atomizing social process as a universally protected self-interest.

The significant reorientation in the international division of labor signaled by the increasing movement of production to third world sites, as well as the rise of a service economy within the former industrial centers of the first world, constitutes a significant reorganization in the "market relations" comprising "human society." If the contemporary forms of (post)industrial production still depend on the expenditure of human beings' physical and mental energies, we might anticipate that the restructuring of market relations over the past several decades must occasion, in turn, a transformation in the social (re)production of labor as commodity. Most glaringly, perhaps, the migration of manufacturing to industrially "underdeveloped" zones of high unemployment and cheap, nonunionized labor assails the presumption of "free" labor that finds its fair and proper value on the open market. The radically uneven integration of a global economic order, in other words, renders increasingly palpable the contingency of labor's value within a highly irrational system—for example, a system that prostrates labor even as it seeks to maximize consumption. Thus the always precarious idea of labor as a rational transaction between capitalist and worker—a level exchange of the body's capacities for wages—gives way to the practice but, above all, perhaps, to the ever-present prospect of what Manuel Castells has termed "absolute exploitation." Addressing Latin America's integration into the global economy, he glosses "absolute exploitation" as one of two antithetical models that currently govern the "development" of third world regions:

> One closer to Pinochet's Chile, based on absolute exploitation of population and devastation of the environment to support cut-throat competition in external markets; or a different one, closer to that of democratic Chile in the 1990s, linking up external competitiveness, social well-being, and expansion of the internal market, on the basis of redistribution of wealth and stepped-up technological/managerial modernization. (132)

Here the very alternation between the "absolute exploitation of population" and its (redemptive) reconstitution as an "internal market" would seem to erode the claim that (anything we might plausibly call) the wage earner's own interests finds expression in the relation of labor to capital. Particularly devastating to the terms of bourgeois hegemony—to the sense of wages as appropriate (if not always sufficient) compensation; to the belief that "what the market will bear" reflects the plural, the mutual interests of a society's members—is the articulation of "absolute exploitation" with progress or advancement in a global economy where, to cite Castells again, "*structural irrelevance*... is more threatening than dependency" (135).

At the same time, the notable expansion of a service economy in the former industrial zones of the (over)developed first world erodes the premises of wage labor in another way. Michael Hardt and Antonio Negri have argued that

> whereas the process of modernization was indicated by a migration of labor from agriculture and mining (the primary sector) to industry (the secondary), the process of postmodernization or informatization

> has been demonstrated through the migration from industry to service jobs (the tertiary), a shift that has taken place in the dominant capitalist countries, and particularly in the United States, since the 1970s. . . . [Service] jobs are for the most part highly mobile and involve flexible skills. More important, they are characterized in general by the central role played by knowledge, information, affect, and communication. (285)

In line with well-known accounts such as Robert Reich's on the new centrality of "symbolic-analytical services," Hardt and Negri thus rehearse and amplify the claim of labor's increasing "immaterial[ity]" within the postindustrial economies of the first world. As opposed to productive labor, they contend, the labor of the service provider finds no objective expression; "immaterial labor" consists not, or at any rate not primarily, in the production of durable goods but rather in establishing, sustaining, and elaborating circuits of interactivity. By implication, the contemporary value of a uniform labor force, composed of individuated and formally equivalent monads, would seem dubious at best; the ideal worker is precisely unbound and adaptable, the product of social disciplines that cultivate a heightened capacity for interface. "Today we increasingly think like computers," Hardt and Negri note, "while communication technologies and their model of interaction are becoming more and more central to laboring activities. One novel aspect of the computer is that it can continually modify its own operation through its use" (291).

In addition to the domain of analytic and symbolic tasks (both creative and routine) and to the production and manipulation of affect ("labor in the bodily mode"), Hardt and Negri align the category of "immaterial labor" with modes of industrial production that have been fundamentally transformed through technologies permitting a "continual interactivity or rapid communication between production and consumption" (290). Their analysis thus highlights the communications feedback loop on which just-in-time production relies, but also a computerization of production that increasingly distances workers from the objects of their labor (292). "The labor of computerized tailoring and the labor of computerized weaving may involve exactly the same concrete practices—that is, manipulation of symbols and information," they note. While tools have "always abstracted labor power from the object of labor to a certain degree," computerization intensifies this abstraction, insofar as the computer becomes the "universal" or "central tool, through which all activities might pass"

(292). It is this third aspect of "immaterial labor" within the context of industrial production that brings "backward," third world economies into the frame of Hardt and Negri's analysis. Their observation that many underdeveloped economies did not complete the phase of industrialization before emerging into aspects of an "informational economy" proves central in establishing the global scope and relevance of this "postmodern" shift from industry to service. "The geographical differences in the global economy are not signs of the co-presence of different stages of development," they argue; instead, "the hybrid, composite economy" *is* the newest face of capital "that varies not in kind but in degree across the globe" (288–89).

But Hardt and Negri's analysis—relatively congruent with the prevailing accounts of postindustrialism to this point—takes a more polemical turn with the claim that the abstraction of labor through computerization coincides with a revolution in the character of labor, which no longer depends on capital to cultivate its social, or cooperative, aspect. In computerized production, as in the symbolic-analytic and affective forms of "immaterial" labor, Hardt and Negri aver

> *cooperation is completely immanent to the laboring activity itself.* This fact calls into question the old notion (common to classical and Marxian political economics) by which labor power is conceived as variable capital, that is, a force that is activated and made coherent only by capital, because the cooperative powers of labor power (particularly immaterial labor power) afford labor the possibility of valorizing itself. Brains and bodies still need others to produce value, but the others they need are not necessarily provided by capital and its capacities to orchestrate production. Today productivity, wealth, and the creation of social surpluses take the form of cooperative interactivity through linguistic, communicational, and affective networks. In the expression of its own creative energies, immaterial labor thus seems to provide the potential for a kind of spontaneous and elementary communism. (294)

Taken together, the point of Hardt and Negri's somewhat oracular pronouncements would seem to be that the networking technology of the computer (as both a medium and a model for cooperative relations) wrests from capital the exclusive power to transform individual into social labor. Computerization means the insertion of laborers into rhizomatic networks that operate necessarily in excess of capital's designs, so that the capacity for collective creativity is no longer the upshot of careful management (through the employment of large numbers of workers by a single employer; through the synchronization and aggregation of labor processes, etc.), but rather the precondition of "immaterial labor" that is neither prescripted nor exhausted in advance by the particular ways in which capital may seek to mobilize this energy.[4] For the industrial laborers Marx describes, "their union into one single productive body, the establishment of a connexion between their individual functions, *are matters foreign and external to them,* are not their own act, but the act of the capital that keeps and brings them together" (331); but for the "immaterial" laborers of Hardt and Negri's *Empire,* the capacity for productive interface inheres in—which is to say, defines—the "laboring activity itself." "Immaterial labor" is therefore not, or no longer, alienated from its social or collective aspect.

Anticipating by several years Hardt and Negri's assertion that the shift to an informational economy has had a transformative impact on labor, Castells reads the altered conditions of industrial production quite differently, specifically refuting claims of the service sector's exponential growth and countering, as well, the idea that computer technology possesses an agency, or efficacy, independent of the ends to which it was implemented. Noting that the category of "services" has functioned within employment statistics as a catchall rubric for a wide range of disparate occupations, "historically originated from various social structures and productive systems," Castells interrogates the coherence of "service" as a tertiary sector, composed of all that is not "agriculture, mining, construction, utilities, or manufacturing."

> Attempts at defining services by some intrinsic characteristics, such as their "intangibility" as opposed to the "materiality" of goods, have been definitively voided of meaning by the evolution of the informational economy. Computer software, video production, microelectronics design, biotechnology-based agriculture, and so on, and many other critical processes characteristic of advanced economies, merge inextricably their information content with the material support of the product, making it impossible to distinguish the boundaries between "goods" and "services." (205)

In a precise inversion of Hardt and Negri's argument that the thing manufactured is remote from the practices of computerized production (since labor and management alike, they contend, are manipulating information, rather than shaping matter), Castells stresses that "information processing is most productive when it is *embedded in material production or in the handling of goods,* instead of being disjointed in a stepped-up technological division of labor" (211, my emphasis). From this vantage, as Castells asserts, it becomes necessary to differentiate between distinct categories of "service" (e.g., producer services, social services, personal services), rather than assign any and every articulation of an informatics with the work process to a discrete "sector" of wholly abstracted (nonmaterial) production.

Equally important, Castells decisively counters the claim that technology determines the conditions and quality of labor. While not explicit in Hardt and Negri's line of reasoning, their account everywhere implies the causal chain: the rise of a computer-based, informational economy results in the varied forms of wholly abstracted, immaterial, and yet (what also seems to follow from the circumstances of service sector production) unalienated labor. Castells takes issue with just this kind of causality when he confronts the familiar argument that computer technologies have polarized labor by prompting the growth of high-prestige symbolic analysis jobs, on the one hand, and of low-skill (repetitive), poorly paid activities, on the other. Citing studies that track the quite varied effects of technological advancement in different national contexts, Castells observes that technology eliminates jobs (and thus drives people to low-end, part-time, or temporary employment) only when it is specifically implemented to that end. "Studies conducted on the interaction between technological change and capitalist restructuring during the 1980s also showed that more often than not, technologies were introduced, first of all, to save labor, to subdue unions, and to trim costs, rather than to improve quality and enhance productivity by means other than downsizing" (Castells 249). In other words, it is not technology that results in the reduction of full-time, salaried positions and the increase in "flexible" labor but rather the reorganization of the workplace in response to the changing imperatives of capital that motivates technological innovation in the first place. Similarly, one might argue that the activity of labor in an informational economy acquires its "immediately" cooperative character only insofar as the network technology has been structured to yield this effect. For one thing, it is by no means clear that all forms of interface are social in nature. A data entry or a food service worker may be linked to a network, but the experience of that link as something "live," as a cooperative relation to other subjects in the network, remains contingent on the workplace's structure and the corporation's ethos, as well as on circumstances relating to the worker's subject formation both in and beyond the workplace (such as affiliation with coworkers through labor organizations and community groups).[5] Even in contexts where we might want to concede the necessarily social quality of the labor—for instance, symbolic analysis at the professionalized levels, or affective services—we should wonder whether the sense of participation in an intrinsically integrated activity links workers to each other, or to capital. In Marx's analysis, it is precisely the laborer's alienation from a cooperative labor process that appears external to him, imagined and overseen by capital, which generates, in turn, a friction, or resistance. "As the number of co-operating labourers increases," Marx observes, "so too does their resistance to the domination of capital, and with it, the necessity for capital to overcome this resistance by counter-pressure" (331). The alienated worker retains an awareness of mediation: the worker's relation to the collective, producing body is neither transparent nor voluntary. From this perspective, to orchestrate a cooperative labor process no longer experienced as an external imposition by the workers yet still fully affirmative of capitalist ends (still producing value for the capitalist) constitutes a notable achievement *for capital*—an advance in its organizational abilities. Insofar as an informational economy allows forms of affiliation not completely dependent on the aims of capital, we should remember that this semiautonomy is effected at capital's behest—and that it serves to eliminate resistance by collapsing any distance between capital's and labor's designs at least as much as it opens possibilities for workers' reclamation of their own collective creativity. Far from a "spontaneous and elementary communism," then, new organizations of cooperative labor are no less (potentially) repressive than (potentially) liberatory.

Drawing on Castells's important correctives to the commonplace account of postindustrialism, as well as on the more persuasive elements of Hardt and Negri's at times strangely utopian interpretation, we might view labor in the contemporary moment as "disposable" in both possible senses of this word: disposable because any notion of wage earning as an exchange between self-interested parties (the quid pro quo of labor for wages) has become simply untenable in a world where the laborer's interest is so visibly—so spectacularly—beside the point. When capital fashions its labor force from among the prostrated populations of the globe, to demand a living wage is to confront the prospect that somewhere, someone will work for less.

If the requirement to reproduce labor constituted, in Marx's analysis, a kind of minimal constraint on capital (an incitement to subsistence-level wages), it no longer seems clear that mobile capital has any stake at all in the reproduction of labor, of which there is, henceforth, a perpetual surfeit. In this sense, the laborer becomes so much detritus. Disposable, too, because the social organization of labor within an informational economy transforms labor from a detachable bodily product into a function of the laborer's bodily and intellectual disposition. If we accept as persuasive Castells's rejection of a technologically driven shift to "immaterial labor," Hardt and Negri are equally persuasive in their emphasis on workers' adaptability, the need to meet (and to create) demand not through uniform processes of acceleration and coordination but through variable forms of participation in multiple and always evolving interfaces. Indeed, this part of their analysis tallies well with Castells's own insights into the decentralization of labor, though significantly he cites this development as a turn away from socialized production toward increasingly individualized work. "We are witnessing the reversal of the historical trend of salarization of work and socialization of production that was the dominant feature of the industrial era," Castells writes. "New information technologies allow at the same time for the decentralization of work tasks and for their coordination in an interactive network of communication in real time, be it between continents or in the same building" (265). Castells thereby distinguishes two distinct processes (individualization *and* networking of work) where Hardt and Negri see only one (labor's "immediate" integration in a network). Either way, the increasing irrelevance, indeed incoherence, of wage labor traditionally conceived—the worker as self-alienating self-proprietor—is palpable. The capacity for labor appears less and less as a part of himself or herself that the worker separates from his or her person and exchanges for compensation.

Instead, as Castells insinuates, "customized markets" mean customized workers, whose bodily, intellectual, and psychic contours are continually reevaluated and redesigned to suit a particular work assignment or adapt to a particular interface. Labor becomes inseparable from the disposition of the entire embodied person, and, to that extent, it seems doubtful that the capacity for (what I am calling) disposable labor will ever be glossed as the birthright of the autonomous subject—as an attribute of discrete and interiorized personhood. In one sense, the fading of proprietary selfhood and the full immersion of embodied persons in capital—so that we can hardly distinguish any longer between "customization" and self-realization—suggests that *the condition of raced embodiment within (neo)colonial formations is now the general condition of bodies under transnational capital;* in other words, no embodied persons maintain any longer a proper relation to capital. From this perspective, it would seem, there is a certain case to be made, in the contemporary moment at least, for the elision of colonialism with capitalism that I disputed in chapter 1. Yet it is crucial to distinguish between the dismantling of the organic self-proprietor and the leveling of racial hierarchies, which would suggest that capital disposes of all bodies in the same way, or at any rate that the variable disposition of laboring bodies proceeds without respect to the (merely residual) categories of racial differentiation. To the contrary, the present disposition of labor depends absolutely on the legacies of "uneven development" to continue and to accelerate the differential incorporation of "backward" sectors into a globalized economy. The labor of which capital disposes in the first sense of the term—prostrates and discards—is overwhelmingly composed (in the first world as in the third) of people of color, whose susceptibility to forms of "absolute exploitation" is as much the consequence of colonial world-making as it is the hallmark of a new world order.

If the state's withdrawal from the assimilative project of the bourgeois class would seem to herald the diminished usefulness of bourgeois social disciplines to capital, as I suggested earlier, conversely, in contemplating the shift from alienated to disposable labor, one might well anticipate the demise of the bourgeoisie's universalist ethos. Alienated labor registers a fundamentally hegemonic transaction: lose the greater part of oneself in return for the attribution of a self (an interiorized being) that can agree to the loss. The historical reality that large segments of the industrial labor force have perennially withheld agreement marks the limits of bourgeois hegemony but does not alter the hegemonic ambition legible in this form of labor relation. But there is no benefit to cultivating a uniform individuality when capital thrives precisely on the difference in living standards between different regions and on the flexibility of workers who can meet not only the demand for specific things but above all the demand for convergence, for the meeting itself. Disposable labor obviates the need to manage and console for the laborer's diminished existence by dismantling the figure of the individual self-proprietor—the person who precedes (stands apart from or outside) capitalist social relations and who withholds some part of himself or herself (an inalienable core) from the exchange.[6] Rather, in the shift to an informational economy, capital cultivates a relation of continuity between self-production and production—between the self-fashioning of the worker as embodied person and the creation of (surplus) value. The calculus—the gamble—is that consent is irrelevant in the absence of distance, of another (anterior or subterranean) scene for the realization of social subjects.[7] Here again, it seems useful to recall Castells about the larger threat of "structural irrelevance": we might speculate that capital need no longer assimilate subjects when participation in its circuits of production and exchange are synonymous with survival—in a world where to be inaccessible, or unattractive, to capital is to lack futurity, to await one's own extinction. It is on these terms, I would suggest, that one should think the affinity of corporate media for disseminating images of mass human suffering; the mute figures of the sick and starving and displaced are cast not as the victims of capital but as the luckless nonparticipants, the left-behind—with the mark of death upon them.

Octavia Butler's Postindustrial Allegory

In Octavia Butler's short story "Bloodchild," I read an allegory of disposable labor, which investigates some of the possibilities and risks that attend it. When I began laying out the design of this book, I did not anticipate the return to Butler's science fiction in this chapter, but I was drawn back in the writing, and my circuit responds to Butler's own absorption in the study of disincorporations. Her fiction lingers on the unprotected and assailed interiority, bodily and psychic, of the colonized but displaces it into a postcontemporary moment, after the unthinkable, the apocalypse, when the world is not, or no longer, "our own." Like *Dawn,* "Bloodchild" explores the futures of human subjects for whom the alternatives are "irrelevance" or "dependency," slow extinction or compulsory remaking by an overproximate, no-longer-simply-alien power. "Bloodchild" suggests how the decline of an assimilationist ethos does not signal the end of an ethical, or hegemonic, dimension to the exercise of state power as such, only the thoroughgoing reconfiguration of the relations between coercion and consent.

Despite the resonance of Butler's science fiction with this chapter's concerns, it may seem surprising that I turn at this juncture to a literary text—to *any* work of literary fiction—rather than to ethnography or other varieties of social science data in order to think through some implications of disposable labor and the state's role in creating and maintaining such disposable subjects.[8] In claiming a critical usefulness for Butler's allegory (alongside these more consecrated forms of sociological evidence), I draw on Walter Benjamin's canny reflections, in particular what I take as his emphasis on allegory's dialectical reassertion of transformative prospects—possibilities for intervention—in a reified world order. Admittedly, Benjamin's reflections on allegory are set in the wider context of his writing on German tragic drama. Yet despite the national and epochal distance between baroque *Trauerspiel* and Butler's SF, Benjamin's account of allegory in its broad strokes illuminates Butler's fiction, even as "Bloodchild" suggests the contemporary salience of allegorical writing. Critical to Benjamin's analysis are both the propensity of allegory to "the frenzy of destruction, in which all earthly things collapse" and the melancholy contemplation with which the allegorist fixes this loss (*The Origin of German Tragic Drama* 232). Allegory's investment is in the spectacle of lifeless, ruined things—an emblem of human transience, the ruin itself is eternal, immutable—but this denuded, unyielding landscape throws us back, in Benjamin's reading, on the historical time of the melancholy gaze. It is precisely the fixation of allegory on ultimate things—on history's end—that unfixes the vision, sweeps away "the final phantasmagoria of the objective," insofar as the very fixation refers us to the activity of the pensive subject, rather than the inert and lifeless objects of his contemplation (232). For Benjamin, allegories disinter the transformative temporality of history from the very scene of its ruination, an organizing gesture in which "Bloodchild" also participates. Yet, crucially, in "Bloodchild" the reinstallation of history's human subjects does not entail their reappropriation of the world as a thing of their own making. Rather, their historical agency must be reclaimed in and for a world order that relentlessly, efficiently disposes of them.

Like *Dawn,* "Bloodchild" posits a hypothetical mode of material exchange, what Butler calls "trade," to investigate the forms of both intimate (familial) and economic relation such a trade would require and enable. As in the *Xenogenesis* trilogy for which she is perhaps best known, Butler here envisions a trade between a remnant of humanity that has barely survived genocidal warfare on earth and an alien species, which derives value from humans in ways the humans themselves find intensely disquieting. Yet in "Bloodchild," as in the trilogy, the social and economic relations that emerge in the contact zone between species decode as an unprecedented and inhuman arrangement primarily from the viewpoint of the human males, who hold to the notion of their autonomous and inviolable interiority—to the racial and gendered privilege, that is, of property in the self. In part, the novelty of interspecies trade lies in the way that a feminized posture of psychic and corporeal receptivity becomes the new standard of human commercial functionality, to the detriment of industrial capitalism's gender and sexual disciplines. In this way, "Bloodchild" plays out the near-future scenario Nick Dyer-Witheford envisions, when he notes that originally the term "'proletarian' designated someone who has no function but to reproduce himself." While "in Marxist usage, this has conventionally been understood as a person who has nothing to sell but his or her labor power," Dyer-Witheford posits that soon the term may also apply "to someone whose only economic assets are gestational capacity and genetic heritage" (107). The version of interspecies trade in "Bloodchild" thus limns the features of the postindustrial service economy and of a state-sponsored ethics that dismantles rather than hails the organic social subject.

"Bloodchild" is set among a contingent of human refugees who have found sanctuary on an alien planet dominated by a species of large, intelligent worm, the Tlic. The humans' arrival (some generations before the narrative present) finds the Tlic in desperate straits, as this species depends on "hosts" for incubating its ova, and the animals best adapted to this end have ceased to accommodate the eggs. "The animals we once used began killing most of our eggs after implantation long before your ancestors arrived," a Tlic recalls, with the result that the Tlic population, reduced to the use of hosts chosen from among the planet's lower forms of life, has grown increasingly weak and infirm (25). As the narrative unfolds, we come to understand the reason for the original hosts' belligerence, as the newly hatched grubs are indiscriminately voracious and proceed to eat their way out of the host body, if not promptly removed by a vigilant Tlic parent. Thus the price of a "livable space" turns out to be human consent to the implantation of Tlic eggs inside human bodies—and particularly inside human males, since the females are usually exempted in order to bear the next generation of human hosts. "Bloodchild" is a coming-of-age narrative, in which a human adolescent male, Gan, must reckon with his impending role as a disposable body in the economy of human-Tlic exchange.

Several aspects of this scenario are worth remarking. First, human accession to the terms of this exchange proves at least as necessary to the welfare of the humans themselves as it is to the welfare of the Tlic. Because the consumption of sterile Tlic eggs has a narcotic and pacifying effect on human users, the Tlic might easily compel the humans to a wholly involuntary participation in the Tlic reproductive cycle. "Back when the Tlic saw us as not much more than convenient, big, warm-blooded animals," one human recalls, "they would pen several of us together, men and women, and feed us only eggs," thereby assuring the perpetuation of the human species and a continuous supply of host bodies (9). Had the practice persisted, the speaker notes, Terrans would swiftly have become "little more than big, convenient animals" (10). Hence the righteous ring of one Tlic's recollection that her species came to see humans "as people . . . when they still tried to kill us as worms" (25). For the humans, the alternative to trade is not self-sufficiency but subjection—either the absolute prostration of their personhood at the hands of a coercive state or their emergence into Tlic hegemony.

Second, participation in this service economy is explicitly rendered as a form of parasitism—but parasitism in "Bloodchild" transforms from a critical trope (e.g., the vampire capitalist) into a social norm. Indeed, the Tlic state seems no more than usually embarrassed to inculcate parasitism as benevolent social mission. Successfully cultivating the humans' consent to their corporeal infestation, the Tlic state suggestively bears out Gramsci's observation that the project of the ethical state, of conforming the masses to the apparatus of production, leads to the evolution "even of physically new types of humanity" (242). At the same time—and this is the critical aspect of the narrative I wish to flag—the humans' assumption of their disposable embodiment does not entail their satisfaction, as we begin to see when Gan confronts a hatching gone wrong.

> Pale worms oozed to visibility in Lomas's flesh. I closed my eyes. It was worse than finding something dead, rotting, and filled with tiny animal grubs. . . . I had been told all my life that this was a good and necessary thing Tlic and Terran did together—a kind of birth. I had believed it until now. (16–17)

The problem is less that the material reality of the process swamps the ideology of Tlic-Terran cooperation, I would suggest, than that the very circumstances of the trade suspend any simple distinction between coercion and voluntarism. In the aftermath to this crisis of faith that constitutes the narrative denouement, Gan comes at once to realize that (unlike the parasitized animal he thinks he sees in Lomas) he may choose whether to trade on his gestational capacity, but that (unlike the subject of bourgeois hegemony) his choice is not—and indeed no longer appears to be—free. A choice cannot be styled free unless the will to choose appears intrinsic or original to the one who chooses—but it is the very priority and privilege of interiority that the ethics of parasitism displaces. Put another way, Gan (situated in my reading as a paradigmatic subject of Tlic hegemony) cannot both embrace as "good and necessary" the image of Lomas's crawling flesh and imagine that he does so from a position of prior, uncontaminated autonomy. As it promotes conformity to service, then, the Tlic state strives to incarnate not the interiorized subject of bourgeois disciplines but a model of disposable personhood vested in the capacity for interface. Thus the voice of Tlic state pedagogy, a "government official" named T'Gatoi to whom Gan's services have been promised, does not refute Gan's protestation that "you use us." Rather, her reply collapses the distance between using and cultivating human personhood. "We do," she answers. "We wait long years for you and teach you and join our families to yours. You know you aren't animals to us" (24). The problem for human agency embedded in T'Gatoi's reply is not that Gan lacks choice, or even that his choice remains irrelevant, but rather that he can choose only from within the discipline of a humanity already defined as usable—or disposable—by the state. Although by narrative's end Gan has overcome his disaffection to the extent of agreeing to his own implantation, he remains unreconciled to state power and state ends—dissatisfied, ironically, not because the state has grown too alien, has failed or rebuffed him, but because it looms too near, because he cannot project himself outside or apart from its effects.[9]

Under these conditions, the state has nothing to gain by effacing its role in the productive disposition of Tlic and Terran subjects. So, for example, the relations of the bourgeois family to the bourgeois state (where the state claims only to uphold the sanctity of family as a private zone of affective self-cultivation) are superseded by an arrangement in which family and state are overtly coextensive. Yet tellingly, the highly visible hand of the state in the constitution of Tlic-Terran families does not preempt mobilizing the family as an instrument of state pedagogy, although familial affect no longer functions to elide the compulsory nature of subjects' participation in its (re)productive operations (or, in other words, compulsion need not be cathected as choice). T'Gatoi's hegemonic vision thus demands that she preserve the family as a relay in the economy of Tlic-Terran commerce, but does not require that the family (or, indeed, any other sphere of Tlic or Terran life) appear to stand outside or apart from the imperative to generate surplus value. As Gan observes:

> T'Gatoi was hounded on the outside. Only she and her political faction stood between us and the hordes who didn't understand why there was a Preserve—why any Terran could not be *courted, paid, drafted, in some way made available to them.* Or they did understand, but in their desperation, they did not care. She parceled us out to the desperate and sold us to the rich and powerful for their political support. Thus we were necessities, status symbols, and an independent people. She oversaw the joining of families, thus putting an end to the final remnants of the earlier system of breaking up Terran families to suit impatient Tlic. (5, my emphasis)

While T'Gatoi rejects (what we might call, borrowing from Castells's account of the two Chiles) the "absolute exploitation" of humans in favor of more broadly distributed possibilities for "social well-being," she does not dispute or contest the crucial conflation of terms: courtship (cultivation of affective ties), payment (wage labor), and drafting (state-supported conscription), as she, too, apportions humans, sells them, *and* joins families. Despite the simple exchange vaguely intimated in the concept of "trade," humans in "Bloodchild" are better understood as the variable capital that enables the creation of a surplus: laboring to reproduce themselves, the humans produce a value greater than what they themselves embody—in this case, they (re)produce Tlic. Here, however, their constitution as variable capital depends on running together the registers of love and sacrifice (family), compensation (wages), and compulsion (submission to the state)—a restructuring of social spheres that provides the condition and context for the making of "available" subjects.

Plainly indicated by the selection of names, but otherwise unremarked, Gan's Chinese ethnicity positions him in an ambiguous relation to the seeming novelty of his formation as disposable labor, linking him to a history of colonial relations, in which, it is arguable, the colonized have always been "available" rather than individuated and assimilated. In part, Butler's choice of Chinese protagonists defamiliarizes SF conventions, in which contact with alien others typically means the encounter of white Euro-Americans with alien "races," in a more or less explicit reenactment of imperial history in space. By making her exemplary human family Chinese, Butler precludes a reading of "Bloodchild" as a simple instance of reverse colonization, then, and insists instead on the position of the humans as a repetition with a difference of their Terran past. Butler's narrative practice of confronting nonwhite protagonists with parasitical aliens has the double effect of foregrounding the continuities between human history and the posthuman futures her work envisions while also blocking nostalgia for organic human personhood. As the subject of colonial histories, Gan contests his disposition in the economy of Terran-Tlic exchange without the possibility of reclaiming a property in the body that has accrued unevenly at best to Asian subjects in (post)colonial contexts. However obliquely, "Bloodchild" speaks to Gan's ethnicity as it links to the orientalist disposition of Asian masculinity as feminized (receptive) body and so prompts us to consider whether Gan's relation to colonial histories provides the critical edge in his refusal to equate receptive embodiment with passivity. At a minimum, the narrative ponders how the formerly/newly colonized's historically marginal relation to proprietary selfhood is a resource for them in (re)imagining the articulations of "availability" with agency.

American Studies and the State

The impetus to the reading and ruminations that have come together in this chapter was my growing suspicion that American studies has proven both more invested and more adept at thinking the continuing lure of the nation and its satisfactions than in tracing the transformation in the state's operations—particularly of what I have been calling, in Gramsci's terms, the ethical state. This is not to say that a nationalist imaginary does not continue to mediate in sometimes decisive ways our lived conditions of existence within the postnational state. As Lauren Berlant has suggested, under the disarticulation of nation and state, national political identification is not so much dissolved as relocated within the register of privatized acts and affect.[10]

Still, I wonder whether the critical investment in tracing the continuing pulsations of nationalist sentiment might contribute to producing the effect it most decries, namely, the apparent irrelevance of the state to national life, so that state power seems not simply difficult to contest but not worth contesting in the first place—as though the state's failure to satisfy were a sign of its indifference to us, of its withdrawal from the mundane lives of citizens. I have suggested that we do better to think of what the state now wants from us—what it has invested in our being (becoming) and how we may (yet) learn to be otherwise.[11] What might it mean to challenge the state's authority, not in the mode of a national subject but within the terms of the disposable pseudocitizen that, it seems to me, the state is now committed to creating? Historically, the nation-state proceeds in a kind of routinized bad faith to withhold recognition of citizenship rights that at the same time it deems inherent in the individual and thus independent of the operations of state power. If, in other words, the citizen of the nation-state has always been disposable—a propertied self derived from the power of a state that purports only to recognize and protect it—then there may be some advantage in the loss of an illusory priority, a critical possibility in the evaporation of critical distance.

Chapter 3

Eskimo Television and the Critique of Whiteness (Studies)

White people could fly circling objects in the sky that sent messages and images of nightmares and dreams, but the old woman knew how to send the destruction back on its senders...
She rubbed the weasel fur rapidly over the glass of the TV screen, faster and faster; the crackling and sparks became louder and brighter and the image of the weather map on the TV screen began to swirl with masses of storm clouds moving rapidly with each stroke of the fur. Then the old woman had closed her eyes and summoned all the energy, all the force of the spirit beings furious and vengeful.

—*Leslie Marmon Silko,* Almanac of the Dead

Lost in Space?

A project in subaltern geography, Leslie Marmon Silko's *Almanac of the Dead* emplots a five-hundred-year history of European colonialism in the Americas and a spatialized politics of fourth world resistance to the subjugation, decimation, administration, and conscription of indigenous peoples by (neo)colonial powers, whether in the name of national sovereignty or of free markets. Confronted by the territorial apparatus of nation-states established on stolen land (from the vantage of indigenous peoples, the epoch of foreign domination has never been "post-ed") and by the deterritorialized operations of transnational capital, the colonized protagonists of Silko's novel mobilize tribal affiliations and practices to define a transnational strategy of resistance to both old and new colonialisms. Critical to the character of this resistance in the novel is a refusal to position tribalism "outside" modernity (to cathect the tribal as modernity's other). Even as tribal practice in the novel counters capital's relentless tendency toward abstraction, for instance, *Almanac*'s tribal people are just as at home within the venues and idioms of commodity culture as a comprador elite and prove signally adept at circuiting tribal visions through corporate-controlled media. In *Almanac,* the assertion of tribal subalternity against a new world order involves, among other things, reinvesting the channels of mobile capital with the historical matter they traverse and annul.[1] In particular, I am interested in how the novel's mapping of tribal cultures and insurgencies within and across the centers and conduits of capitalist (post)modernity entails a critical revision of Euro-Americans' incorporations—their production of individual, administrative, and political identities. Rather than undoing the elision of white identity with the culturally normative—in what has emerged as *the* critical gesture for "whiteness studies"—*Almanac of the Dead* suggests why the assertion of white particularity is inadequate for a critical intervention in colonial formations of power and knowledge.

Tribal practices may originate in the preinvasion Americas and Africa yet are also always situated in the novel as contemporaneous with, and internal to the forms, if not the ends, of capital. In contrast to ethnonationalisms, and their sustaining rhetoric of cultural purity, tribal practices in *Almanac of the Dead* are avowedly impure, nonorganic, and noninnocent, and their subjects are media-savvy talk-show queens, computer hackers, high-tech smugglers, and smart shoppers.[2] This positioning of the novels' tribal protagonists as immersed in the circuits of information and commodity exchange supplants the primitivist imaginary and its association of the tribal with peripheral space and anterior time. In *Almanac,* the tribal is not "traditional," insofar as it is not rooted in a particular place or mode of transmission. It does not presume a stable population inhabiting a delimited region over generations—which is also to say that the tribal is not premodern and therefore not undone by the displacements and discontinuities that mark the experience of industrial and postindustrial modernity.[3] From this perspective, then, Silko's tribalism explicitly refutes a nationalist iconography in the United States, which at least since Jefferson's *Notes on the State of Virginia* has insisted that indigenous, tribal cultures are unable to withstand the transition into the progressive time and abstract space of the modern nation (even into such a pastoral version of this imagined community as Jefferson's own vision of an American yeomanry). Under the twin signs of U.S. nationalism and imperialism, the tribal is destined for assimilation, removal, or extermination (generally coded as the voluntary passage of the noble savage into oblivion). Strictly anterior to the nation-state, the tribal passes, as of its own accord, to the nation's farthest margins, or frontiers.

In *Almanac,* the distinction between the progressive temporality of the metropolitan center and the stasis of the tribal periphery ("reservation") dissolves, and the reader finds herself tracking the movements of tribal subalterns across a decentered global space, so regularly cited as a defining feature of late capitalist organization. Yet for *Almanac*'s protagonists, as for Masao Miyoshi and other theorists of flexible accumulation, this decentering is governed by social and economic practices that are anything but postcolonial.[4] Attracted to zones of nonunionized labor, below-subsistence wages, and minimal environmental regulation—conditions that it therefore seeks to perpetuate rather than redress—mobile capital has no stake in conferring the promised benefits of modernity on formerly colonized peoples whose "underdevelopment" is colonialism's legacy. At the same time, the tendency toward the spatialization of native people's historical difference that marks the nationalist/imperialist imaginary (anterior time becomes marginal space) is today amplified rather than diminished, when the most radically incommensurate cultures and experiences are reclaimed as local variations in an integrated global space.

Consequently, it has become something of a commonplace to point out that localities and place-bound identities are at least as much the product of global capital as a (potential) point of resistance to its de- and reterritorializing practices. David Harvey describes in particularly illuminating terms how the irrelevance of national borders to capitalist organization produces an equal and opposite insistence on spatial distinctions, or place. In Harvey's view, this is the "central paradox: the less important the spatial barriers, the greater the sensitivity of capital to the variations of place within space, and the greater the incentive for places to be differentiated *in ways attractive to capital*" (295–96). As one result, we witness a proliferation of historical identities slated for reproduction as local color, or style.

> The assertion of any place-bound identity has to rest at some point on the motivational power of tradition. It is difficult, however, to maintain any sense of historical continuity in the face of the flux

> and ephemerality of flexible accumulation. The irony is that tradition is now often preserved by being commodified and marketed as such. (303)

The fate of tradition, in this view, is its conscription in and by a commodity-based multiculturalism that transforms temporal relations (a lived connection to the past) into spatializations—into consumer environments (tourist destinations, theme-park installations, museum exhibits) and commodities (clothing and body fashions, crafts, music, cuisine).

Harvey prompts us to apprehend this dehistoricizing of tradition as an instance of the broader reification of lived identities under capital. No longer a function of participatory community, Harvey implies, identity transfers to the marketplace, where it is passively acquired rather than actively created and maintained; henceforth, neither the subjects of tradition, much less the consumers, can recognize themselves as historical agents. However, the novel suggests how the commodification of culture under the sign of diversity may serve a variety of political ends, as *Almanac*'s tribal protagonists exploit the market in native spirituality for their own purposes (to fund insurrection, to intrude into the commercialized public sphere a language that is never sufficiently contained by the processes of differentiation Harvey describes). I argue that this (perhaps) surprising willingness to traffic in "tradition" rests on a quite different understanding of identity, which the novel treats not as a temporal formation (the community's continuity over time) flattened, or vitiated, by capital but as a spatial construct or, rather, a territorial practice keyed to the operations of capitalist modernity. For *Almanac*'s tribal protagonists, identity is another in a series of colonial imports, a method for locating subjects within the already abstracted social space of capital rather than a historically proper technology of self-designation endangered by market forces. Consequently, the novel's tribal insurgents have little use for cultural nationalist strategies (the [re]assertion of an oppositional difference) and can traffic without compunction in "traditional ways" and "indigenous cultural identities," precisely insofar as they remain alienated from these terms, which impose on tribal peoples in the guise of benevolent recognition. This critique of identity as embedded a priori in capitalist abstraction holds significant implications for (what is now, routinely, constituted as the "field" of) whiteness studies, which has variously invested in rehabilitating and (or) repudiating white identity. More broadly, *Almanac*'s tribalism urges a reconsideration of identificatory practices on the Right *and* on the Left—not only reactionary (ethno)nationalisms but projects in racial cross-identification launched in the name of antiracist (and anticapitalist) solidarity. As it marks the limitation of identity politics for the political mobilization of tribal subalterns, the novel also marks the consequences of an identificatory politics that differentiates subaltern subjects "in ways attractive to the elite." So it is that when *Almanac*'s tribal peoples, like the old Yupik woman in the opening epigraph, "send the destruction back on its senders," they assign Euro-Americans to the blank terror of a world without others.

Tribal Epistemology

In *Almanac*, tribal practices are mobilized against the leveling and consumption of history as identity, where identity is understood on the order of the commodity, as the inert and congealed form of lived social relations. As the Yaqui arms smuggler Calabazas muses, "The tribal people were all very aware that the whites put great store in names. But once the whites had a name for a thing, they seemed unable ever again to recognize the thing itself" (224). As evidence, Calabazas cites the case of the famous Apache warrior Geronimo, who stands as the virtual incarnation of four different, living Apaches:

> "Geronimo" of course was the war cry Mexican soldiers made as they rode into battle, counting on help from St. Jerome. The U.S. soldiers had misunderstood just as they had misunderstood just about everything else they had found in this land. In time there came to be at least four Apache raiders who were called by the name Geronimo, either by the Mexican soldiers or the gringos. (224)

This conflation of four raiders into a single person, incorporated under the sign of a European saint, is not simply an act of misnaming, as Calabazas proceeds to demonstrate, except in the general sense that every European appellation, from a Yaqui perspective, is a misnomer. Rather, the invaders' identificatory magic lies precisely in the successful conjuring of the entities named; thus the U.S. military occupation can supply documentary evidence of the existence of "Geronimo," in the form of photographs.

> Each of the so-called Geronimos had learned to demand prints of themselves as payment for posing. At meetings in the mountains, they compared photographs. The puzzle had been to account for

> the Apache warrior whose broad, dark face, penetrating eyes, and powerful barrel-chested body had appeared in every photograph taken of the other Geronimos. The image of this man appeared where the face of the other Geronimos should have been. (228)

The circulation of this simulacrum under the newspaper headlines calling for Geronimo's capture and execution affords scant protection to the living Geronimos, one of whose bodies, at least, will be required to stand in for the virtual body of the photographic image. The Europeans' identifications overwrite the material world and subject the historical people they so stunningly fail to represent. Identity in *Almanac* thus functions on the order of Jean Baudrillard's "object-sign," as that which supports a thoroughly dehumanized version of human sociality:

> Human relations tend to be consumed (consommer) (in the double sense of the word: to be "fulfilled" and to be "annulled") in and through objects, which become the necessary mediation and, rapidly, the substitutive sign, the alibi, of the relation. . . . This is no longer a lived relation: it is abstracted and annulled in an object-sign where it is consumed. (*Selected Writings* 22)

From a tribal vantage, then, the accelerated commodification of traditional identity to which Harvey and Miyoshi draw attention is essentially redundant, since identity as such—the condition of being known to the colonizers—abstracts and substitutes for the heterogeneity of historical existence. Yet the point of Calabazas's ruminations, I would argue, is not to establish an opposition between the authentic tribal subject (the multiple Apache raiders) and his simulated counterpart ("Geronimo"), but rather an opposition between two epistemological regimes and their implications for the subjects of knowledge.

At the heart of Calabazas's tribal worldview, as of the novel's more generally, lies a critical analysis of colonial practice and (in) its fusion of a specular epistemology with capitalist property relations; more particularly, with the social and juridical principle of property in the self and the predication of personhood on a defining inner essence that the institutions of bourgeois culture at once require and sustain. In the world of the invaders, cognition implies incorporation: we might say that knowledge does not obtain apart from the prospect of its assimilation—into an organism (biological or social, material or virtual); a consciousness; a discipline. Knowledge in this mode arrays its subjects and its objects as necessarily commensurate; to know an object is to claim an adequate internal concept of it and so to produce the world as the objective expression of one's proper understanding. The limits of this projection also stand as the limits of colonial knowledge. Where the colonizer's proper understanding fails, he sees not an unknown but an abject—a world about which nothing can be known, other than its fallen condition. For the tribal ethnographer of Europeans, such as Calabazas, these invaders appear effectively to bypass lived relations of time and space, insofar as the world in its incommensurability falls away. Unable to distinguish between "the dark volcanic hills in the distance" and those "dark hills they marched past hours earlier," the invaders cannot encounter the invaded on their ground but must simulate the terrain to conquer it.

In its confrontation with the Europeans' abstractions and incorporations, tribal epistemology risks appearing (in a seeming affirmation of romantic racialist notions) as no epistemology at all, an unmediated relation to the world of natural objects. Thus Calabazas, holding forth to his Anglo-American gunrunner, Root, on the nuances of the Arizona desert, might be taken to argue for the givenness of the object world.[5]

> Once Root had remarked that he thought one dull gray boulder looked identical to another dull gray boulder a few hundred yards back. Calabazas took his foot off the accelerator, and Mosca had tried to save Root by adding quickly, "Maybe in the dark they look alike." But that had not prevented Calabazas from giving them one of his sarcastic lectures on blindness. . . . "I get mad when I hear the word identical," Calabazas had continued. "There is no such thing. Nowhere. At no time. All you have to do is stop and think. Stop and take a look." (201)

Yet significantly, the antidote to "blindness" is not simply vision (looking) but a particular kind of cognitive process (thinking) initiated through arrest (stopping)—through demobilizing the thinking/viewing subject. Calabazas's language presumes neither the object's transparency for a tribal observer at one with the natural world (the romance of the primitive), nor does it predicate the object on the viewing subject's self-awareness (in the tradition of Western speculative philosophy). Rather, tribal knowledge production seems to require that the producer renounce a self-referential encounter with the world that functions (not incidentally) to reproduce identities everywhere (to find the identity in objects, which Calabazas categorically rejects). The practice of "stopping" ("stopping" as cognitive practice) thus entails something like suspending for an interval the (re)circulation of language and meaning we experience as (self-) consciousness. For a tribal epistemology, the project is to think the object independently of its relation to (or value for) the thinking/viewing subject. This is, of course, not to say that tribal subjects eschew instrumental knowledge or that vision is ever untouched by desire, only that the object world does not reduce in any necessary or ultimate fashion to the tribal subject's double. There is no tribal sublime but also, and more significantly perhaps, no tribal *Aufhebung* and no tribal melancholia.

Eventually, Root learns to perceive the differences in the shape and texture of the desert rock formations. But the conditions of his reeducation further underscore that his Yaqui mentor's discernment is indebted to epistemological method rather than a natural, holistic, or local sensibility. Unlike the Euro-American New Agers who flock to a "holistic healers' convention" at the novel's end, Root neither seeks nor attains a "rooted" or integrated relation to his environment. Just the reverse, his ability to see difference—to see it outside the framework of identity and equivalence—results from a devastating motorcycle crash, which leaves his speech slurred, his foot limp and dragging, and his skull seamed with scars like "big zippers." This corporeal abjection interrupts Root's annulment and fulfillment of human relations through the object-sign of identity. And rather than strive to recapture identity through an ever more aggressive and compensatory assimilation of the world's differences, Root elects instead to inhabit his disincorporated flesh, to enter what the narrator refers to as "the world of the different" (203), by existing as a subject not always or necessarily adequate to the differences he encounters. In his unlearning of the colonizer's historical privilege, Root exemplifies the posture of Gayatri Chakravorty Spivak's postcolonial intellectual, and models for the novel's Euro-American readers what it may mean to be marked by tribal consciousness ("Can the Subaltern Speak?" 287).

Almanac of the Dead and "Whiteness Studies"

In the figure of Root, the novel offers a counternarrative to the commodity culture that so relentlessly hails white subjects with opportunities for racial self-fashioning. The novel's tribal protagonists are only too happy to exploit for their own ends the culture of racial consolation, which sends the broken inhabitants of an allegedly depthless and depleted mainstream searching for renewal on the racial margins. There is the holistic healers' convention, for example, where a benumbed metropolitan elite flocks for the spiritual affect that tribal activists gladly furnish, in exchange for substantial donations. On television talk shows, callers flood the lines as the Yaqui psychic, Lecha, solves missing-person cases; although Lecha's clairvoyance enables her only to locate the dead, the victims of stalkers, serial killers, and professional assassins, her photogenic cheekbones, the narrator affirms, lift "the chill of her grisly pronouncements" and elicit the devotion of her television public (147). As *Almanac* underscores, such mass cultural events envision and encourage the white subject's cathecting of difference, and to that extent are less removed from the various projects currently subsumed under the heading of "whiteness studies" than one might anticipate. If Root is no holistic New Ager, psychic adherent, or modern primitive, he is also not the paradigmatic subject of whiteness studies—not a "race traitor," (sub)proletarian, or consumer of nonwhite perspectives. While all these (re)constructions of whiteness posit an incorporative access to difference, Root's entry into "the world of the different" presumes instead that he relinquishes all claim to it. His nonidentitarian affiliations with tribal subalterns thus suggest some alternative directions for a critical whiteness studies.

Far from representing a monolithic endeavor, whiteness studies currently reflects a spectrum of approaches to the study of whiteness as racial formation, approaches that correlate to widely differing cultural politics. Although new (inter)disciplinary rubrics have usually been articulated by the practitioners in/of an emerging field, whiteness studies is arguably the first (inter)disciplinary project to begin its life in the commodity form, as a publisher's category. As a result, whiteness studies lacks a coherent intellectual project, representing instead a series of disparate critical endeavors, grouped together by their topical relation to whiteness. (Conversely, it is difficult for any scholarship on the topic to escape its implication in this category.) But despite this casual linkage of notably incommensurate endeavors, whiteness studies coheres to a startling degree in the inclination to array whiteness on the side of difference. This inclination entails at least three consequences. First, the discussion of whiteness becomes largely coterminous with the discussion of white *identity*.

That is, whiteness is most often considered as a form of cultural and psychic self-figuration, and an experiential content, rather than, for instance, as an effect of the technological and institutional self-mediation of Europeans and Euro-Americans (through the protocols of comparative anatomy or the legal provisions of colonial rule, for example). Second, the rescripting of whiteness comes to depend all too easily on the refiguring of white identity—on new identificatory opportunities. Third, the supposedly progressive rescripting of whiteness reiterates the white subject's acquisitive relation to difference that historically anchors white privilege.[6]

One relatively recent development within whiteness studies has been the interest in proletarian or subproletarian white identity as a supposedly privileged site for the interrogation of whiteness. While such an approach gestures at least potentially toward the mutual overdetermination of race and class, "white trash" criticism tends instead to posit a homology between (white) working-class and black identities, by virtue of their supposedly shared location on the margins of (bourgeois) whiteness. For these critics, it is the distinction of a white working class to manifest whiteness as a marked rather than a normative identity; and yet the visibility of whiteness in these analyses seems to turn on attributing to the devalued white person those racialized qualities historically assigned to African Americans and nonwhite ethnic groups, qualities such as primitiveness, hypersexuality, a tendency toward overpopulation (or excessive "breeding"), and unnatural domestic arrangements. On the proletarian subject, in other words, whiteness appears in blackface. Annalee Newitz and Matt Wray, editors of an essay collection titled *White Trash*, put it this way:

> Unlike many white people, white trash have the potential to perform the work of racial self-recognition and self-consciousness that bell hooks has found absent in dominant forms of whiteness; possibly, one might argue, it is more difficult for white trash to Other others. In part because white trash is a classed and *racialized* identity degraded by dominant whiteness, a white trash position vis-à-vis whiteness might be compared to a "racial minority" position vis-à-vis whiteness. (5)

Leaving aside the historically dubious claim that the white underclasses in the United States are less adept at "Other[ing] others," I want to stress how whiteness is apprehended in its supposed specificity within a generic discourse of "minority," posed over and against a putatively monolithic center of dominance. Newitz and Wray themselves seem to suspect the dehistoricization of social relations that attends the recuperation of white identity on the grounds of racial difference when they caution against the dangers of "victim chic" (5). In Newitz's contribution to the volume, she is at pains to acknowledge the bad faith of various cultural texts that devolve their white protagonists into the image of a despised alterity, noting how this redirection of "racism and classism at themselves" enables whites to "appear free of both while at the same time clinging to them fiercely as a basic component of their identity" ("White Savagery" 144). In more definitely political terms, we might note that the championing of minoritized whiteness within academic whiteness studies mirrors the polemic of "reverse discrimination" that has lately served the repeal of affirmative action statutes. In the discourse of "reverse discrimination," that is, all differences (all marked identities) are rendered interchangeable, so that the colonizer, having strategically relinquished his title to the norm, lines up beside the colonized to claim his reciprocal and equivalent particularity.

It is all the more startling, then, that the "new abolitionism," most frequently associated with David Roediger, Noel Ignatiev, and the journal *Race Traitor,* at once resists many of the assumptions that underwrite white trash criticism and yet drafts a remarkably similar map of social power, in which a vacuous, white center is edged by a life-restoring, racialized (and antibourgeois) periphery. In contrast to the white trash criticism, the new abolitionism specifically refuses a minoritizing construction of whiteness; as Roediger rightly insists, the presumption of black and white "sameness" covertly perpetuates the racial hierarchy by upholding the amnesiac politics of "reverse racism" (*Towards the Abolition of Whiteness* 2). Furthermore, the celebration of whiteness, albeit whiteness in trashed or trashy form, is replaced in new abolitionist work by the equally fervent indictment of whiteness, conceived as empty, parasitic, "false," and consecrated at its core to perpetuating bourgeois class hegemony. For Roediger, white labor inevitably fails to recognize its interests as a class, since whiteness on his model functions precisely to arrest the possibility of class-based solidarity across racial lines. Thus an interracial labor movement comes to depend not simply on white workers allied with workers of color but on the white subject's racial defection. In other words, the white worker's revolutionary class identification necessitates a cross-racial identification with nonwhiteness.[7]

While the new abolitionism derides the concept of marginalized whiteness central to white trash criticism, both approaches nonetheless situate the white subject in a death-defying flight toward the racial margins. This flight may be differently thematized—the white trash subject becomes visibly white within a (sub)proletarian class formation coded black, whereas the race traitor deliberately opts for blackness by renouncing bourgeois aspirations and the privileges of white skin—and yet a white/black, center/periphery binary organizes both narratives alike. The narratives prove similar in their unselfconscious reinscription of an imperialist imaginary that divides metropolis from colony as the inverse poles of a specular field (the metropolis represents progress, sublimation, enervation; the colony, lodged in a monumental temporality, offers endless possibilities for desublimation and abandon) and in so doing renders the margins accessible to the center's imaginative appetites. Significantly, Roediger himself concedes that cross-racial identification through cultural consumption is perfectly consistent with social and political antagonism toward the targeted racial group.

> There will be no simple fix for the white problem in America, and it is well to emphasize limits as well as possibilities. The "guido" subculture in Italian American New York City, well described in the writings of Donald Tricarico, stands as an ambiguous example of both those possibilities and limits. Guidos have much adopted hiphop and asserted a distinctive Italian American identity against white American "wannabes." They refer to themselves as "Guineas," turning that anti-Italian, anti-Black slur into a badge of honor. *But the break with whiteness and racism on New York's streets is less than complete.* As Tricarico nicely understates it, in many ways Guidos "resist identification with Black youth" and "bite the hand that feeds them style." (*Towards the Abolition of Whiteness* 16, my emphasis)

Roediger's phrasing proposes that the guidos' identification with blackness is simply "less than complete" and thus fails to produce the concomitant break with racism one might reasonably anticipate. Historically considered, however, white attraction to and adoption of nonwhite styles develop hand in fist with the (neo)colonial social and economic formations that support white people's theft of nonwhite populations' land, labor, and resources more generally. From this vantage, the capacity (in Baudrillard's phrase) for abstracting and annulling whiteness in the "object-sign" of blackness, which Roediger associates with treason to whiteness, reads as the sign and symptom of white privilege. After all, it is the political and juridical guarantees historically reserved for white personhood that sanction and protect a revitalizing white transgressiveness, and in their loving/thieving assumption of blackness, the guidos manifest a paradigmatically white American posture, as Eric Lott's decisive work on minstrelsy has shown.[8]

Ironically enough, Roediger's call to racial treason, grounded in a politics of socialist solidarity, champions a program of racial cross-identification not half so removed as one might have presumed from E. Ann Kaplan's liberal-multiculturalist agenda of edifying cultural consumerism. Suggesting that white people stand to achieve an enlightened racial self-consciousness by seeing themselves through the eyes of the world's nonwhite majority, Kaplan goes on to celebrate the work of nonwhite filmmakers, who offer white subjects a perspective on themselves as the repudiated other of a "reversed rejecting gaze" (*Looking for the Other* 295). Where white trash criticism seeks an alternative (antisupremacist) destiny for whiteness in its resemblance to blackness, Kaplan opens a potentially critical vantage on whiteness by vesting its futures in the black person's gaze. But this gaze is all-too-seamlessly (re)oriented in the service of a white, metropolitan bourgeoisie, for its own self-illumination. In her discussion of Tracy Moffat's *Nice Coloured Girls,* for example, a film in which three aboriginal women take vengeance on a brutish and presumptuous white man, Kaplan notes with evident satisfaction:

> Here is no "objective" camera offering the possibility of refusing the Aboriginal gaze. The spectator must see through the black women's eyes; she must see as they see. . . . In this film, the white man's body and manners are indeed disgusting, so much so that the spectator (at least this one) has no compunction in enjoying the women's stealing of his money and leaving him drunk in the bar. (296–97)

As in Roediger's analysis, the exercise of the colonizer's prerogative to be everywhere *chez soi*—equally and urbanely comfortable in the black woman's point of view and her own—is mistaken for the modest and ethical renunciation of white privilege. In this fast shuffling of the analytic cards, moreover, the directorial look is conflated with the cinematic apparatus (so that film becomes a transparent purveyor of its maker's perspective), just as the apparatus is conflated with the viewing eye (as though the spectator's perspective were one with the camera's). Such a conflation, of course, effaces from the get-go the historical difference of anything we might aspire to call the (post)colonial subject's gaze—where gaze designates a visual epistemology, operated by social technologies, in which the white tourist is precisely *not* initiated.

If the project of seeing through nonwhite eyes is not to devolve into another round of colonialist fantasy, then it is precisely the privilege of free passage that white people must unlearn, as *Almanac* suggests. A critique of whiteness would begin by unraveling the juridical, political, and social protocols that permit the possessors of whiteness to be at once nowhere (to occupy the evacuated center) and everywhere (to claim the racial margins)—and to unravel them not, or not simply, by assigning whiteness a (new) location but *by rendering white subjects accountable for the territorializing operations of specular thought.* At a minimum, such a critique would require that whiteness studies guards against the conflation of intersubjective relations (interactions with other subjects) and identificatory movement (interactions with figures and tropes of alterity)—that we distinguish between self-fashioning and a politics of racial solidarity, not because they are entirely unrelated but because they are not the same. We might remember a well-known passage from Jean-Paul Sartre, where the effect of encountering the other as subject—of seeing myself being seen—is the sudden and vertiginous loss of all that I am, not (as for Kaplan) a magical transit into the other's point of view. A critique of whiteness would thus command a critique of racial (cross-)identification, understood not (or not exclusively) as transformative social and cultural play but as a regulative grammar, which activates specific social subjects (and pacifies/instrumentalizes others).

Against Dialectics, or, Poor Marx

The resistance of tribal practice to the incorporative logic of identification—to a system of equivalence that converts the most radically exteriorized quantities into the most intimate interiorities—finds its paradigmatic articulation in the narrative of the burning children, which Lecha hears from Rose, a member of Alaska's Yupik tribe. The story of Rose's brothers and sisters suggests how tribal beliefs in the continuing presence of the dead (immediate kin and more remote ancestors) give body to the unconvertible remainder of lived social relations. As Rose recounts the events, her six younger brothers and sisters are incinerated one night, when their parents cross the river to the bootlegger's house and the eldest pours gasoline, instead of kerosene, on the fire. Asleep far away from her village, "in the girls dormitory of the school for Eskimos and Indians," Rose dreams of the fire on four consecutive nights, sees the children as they run toward the river, "in halos of yellow flame" (151). Later, after Rose has been sent south to the psychiatric hospital in Seattle, she has another dream:

> I tried to talk to the children for a long time.... I only wanted to tell them I was sorry. I would have taken care of them if I had been there. I did not want to go away.... Finally... I had a dream about them. I talked to all the children. They were standing there together, smiling at me.... Except they were all in flames, standing there on fire, but never being burned up. The old woman told me she had seen them too—on that night, and then afterwards, right before dawn, playing together along the river. They were always in flames. (151)

I would argue that the children's manifestation, as bodies always in flame but never consumed, protects them from incorporation—whether in the national context (the native as inaugural sacrifice); in the registers of commodity culture (native spirituality as redemptive self-styling); or even the context of tribal collectivity (melancholic attachment to and internalization of the martyred children)—so that in the production of tribal history, the children are *not* abstracted as the object-signs of Yupik people's suffering. Rather, the burning children write history as a trauma that can only be witnessed, not possessed. Neither introjected into Yupik consciousness (as "our" dead) nor receded in a forgotten past, the children remain proximate, present to the survivors but never reinvented in their image.

If tribal practice resists the spatialization of time and "the aestheticization of politics" that Harvey aligns with postmodernism, then it does so without simply reverting to what Harvey champions as the properly historical tendency within modernity to abolish space through time, in a universalizing movement of "Becoming" (273).[9] For Harvey, in other words, the danger lies in a postmodern loyalty to place that supersedes class affiliations and affinities as the ground of political appeal and action. For Comrade Angelita, a Mayan agitator plotting the insurrection of tribal peoples in Mexico, it is just as much the progressive temporality of "Becoming" that vexes a properly Marxist critique. In one of her frequent meditations on Marx (noting her fixation, the villagers surmise he is her lover), Angelita muses:

> Marx of the Jews, tribal people of the desert . . . Marx, tribal man and storyteller; Marx with his primitive devotion to the worker's stories. No wonder the Europeans hated him! Marx had gathered the official government reports of the suffering of the English factory workers the way a tribal shaman might have, feverishly working to bring together a powerful, even magical assembly of stories. His own children were slowly dying from cold, lack of food, and medicine; yet day after day, Marx had returned to official reports in the British Museum. Wage-earning might have saved Marx's children, but tribal man and storyteller, Marx had sacrificed the lives of his own beloved children to gather the stories of all the children starved and mangled. He had sensed the great power these stories had—power to move millions of people. *Poor Marx did not understand that the power of the stories belonged to the spirits of the dead.* (520–21, my emphasis)

Having recognized the power of the stories with a shaman's acuity, Marx assimilates them into an emancipatory narrative of the proletarian subject's entry into history and historical agency. If the dichotomy of static space (Being) and transformative time (Becoming) overlooks the extent to which places are always "constructed out of positive relations with elsewhere" and, by implication, immersed in time, never adequately "characterized by recourse to some essential, internalized moment," as Doreen Massey argues, then Angelita's musings prompt us to consider how the reverse proposition may hold, as well: how the temporal cannot escape its spatial implication and more particularly how the temporality of a dialectical becoming rests on internalizing negated quantities ("all the children starved and mangled") within a newly encompassing historical subject (169).[10] For Angelita, however, the value of the stories resides in their power to forge alliances between radically dispersed and incommensurate subjects—to effect a collective "becoming" without "the universalizing movement" endemic to dialectical process. This is not to say that the stories of the dead do not serve, for Angelita no less than for Marx, as an engine for articulating alternative futures, only to stress that for Angelita the dead are not the negative term in a dialectical progression but rather a countersanction to the synthetic logic of the specular dialectic as such.

It is worth underscoring that Angelita's critique of Marx does *not* depend, as a certain brand of romantic anthropology might surmise, on valorizing the living voice as presence, or purveyor, of lived experience. Marx's failing does not consist in substituting text for speech, in his inscription of the workers' voices and histories onto the dead letter of the page. Such a critique would seem disingenuous, at best, leveled from within the textualized form of the novel. Moreover, the novel's title refers precisely to a written history—a tribal people's almanac that includes the prophecies of the Europeans' arrival and of their eventual disappearance—which the novel at once cites (whole sections of the almanac are reproduced) and doubles (as the title implies, the novel itself is a tribal peoples' almanac). Sent on a journey north by a nearly exterminated tribe in Mexico, the almanac makes its way into the hands of the Yaqui sisters Lecha and Zeta, who, like their predecessors, both preserve and augment the document. That preserving at least some portion of the almanac is tantamount to surviving is made clear in the narrative of this dying tribe's journey: "The pages were divided four ways. This way, if only one of the children reached the safety of the North, at least one part of the book would be safe. The people knew if even part of their almanac survived, they as a people would return some day" (246).

In *Almanac,* the collective that is a tribal "people" appears no less contingent on its textualization than "the people" of the United States, whose existence, as Jacques Derrida has famously argued, is called forth by the document that declares independence in their name. For Derrida, the interesting point is that the Declaration of Independence strives exactly to conceal the predication of national identity on textual authority: the ruse of the Declaration is its representation of "the people" as, impossibly, preexisting "their" self-authorship. The text of the Declaration founds "the people," even as it effaces this figuration in the rhetorical temporality of a "fabulous retroactivity," whereby "the people" are installed as cause, rather than effect, of their naming.[11] We might also note, as Derrida does not, that in strategically misrecognizing causes and effects, the Declaration disallows reflection on *who* names—on which class of persons has been privileged to author(ize) "the people" in its own (class, gender, and race-bound) image.

In contrast, the survival of the dying tribe who move to secret their almanac in the North depends on reprioritizing the relation of people and text: the almanac explicitly writes the people, insofar as the people may be re-created (even after the tribe's extinction) from any surviving fragment of the text. The almanac of the dead thus functions as a genetic code, summoning into existence the people (imagined as the subjects of the code's histories). Yet the genetic analogy is also misleading, since the almanac's code is not a fixed or closed sequence, nor, by extension, might we use it to anticipate the form in which the people will revive. While the almanac stands as a chronicle of tribal experience—of prophecies, plagues, cataclysms pertaining to the invasion of the Europeans, their deadly reign, and its anticipated end—it is also a compendium of ephemera, "debris gathered here and there by aged keepers of the almanac after they had gone crazy," including found text ("whole sections had been stolen from other books and from the proliferation of 'farmer's almanacs' published by patent-drug companies and medicine shows that gave away the almanacs as advertisements") and the keepers' own scribbled marginalia (569, 570). The act of keeping the record, then, is inextricably linked to the act of supplementing it—an act governed by no established or continuous criteria of inclusion. In the tribal meaning of the term, the people are a function of their historical inscription, but they are *not* a constituted body (not an organic entity), since the very fact of their textuality opens every figuration of their collective existence to the dis-figuring process of an entirely contingent reinscription. It is precisely because the people embrace their open-ended textualization that they dissolve their textual constitution—that they refuse assignment to a discursive body or identity. Not defined through their administrative and imaginative interiority, the "people" are the mutable and indiscrete collective of those who further or contribute to realizing the almanac's prophecies. Thus representatives of "the people" in the novel include Clinton, an African American Vietnam veteran organizing an army of the homeless in Tucson; Awa Gee, a Korean American hacker plotting a shutdown of the power grid; even the anonymous members of Green Vengeance, a monied, "hardcore" group of "eco-warriors in the defense of the earth" (727). Rather than the claiming and defense of territory, tribal insurgency involves alliances and movements across territories, an indifference to national borders and property lines (which is not the same as the transgression and redrawing of such boundaries). Central to the novel's vision of insurrectionary prospects, for instance, is the planned migration of tribal peoples northward from Mexico and Central America to the United States under the leadership of twin brothers, Tacho and El Feo. The novel's protagonists anticipate the swamping of the sovereign borders of the "formidable neighbor" to the North as the inaugural gesture in a retaking of tribal lands that would consequently seem to entail not so much repossessing the land in the name of a competing corporate entity as releasing the land from its abstraction as property.[12] Refusing to incorporate, to maintain and multiply territorial distinctions within the already totalized terrain of global capital, the novel's insurgent peoples evade the specular difference engine—the differentiation of people and places in ways "attractive to capital"—to open up a front as broad and mobile as the flows of global capital itself.

"Tribal Internationalists"

Angelita's stance, like that of the backward "Indians" in general, exasperates Bartolomeo, the Cuban adviser to the insurgent villages, a central committee hack ambitious for an "ideological victory" in the provinces that will raise his credit in Havana and earn him a posting to Mexico City (514). Increasingly impatient with the refusal of Angelita's camp to file reports and follow committee directives, Bartolomeo threatens to cut off Cuban aid, capping his list of tribal failings with what he plainly takes to be his most devastating charge: "The Cubans had received unconfirmed reports that these mountain villages were hotbeds of tribalism and native religion. Marxism did not tolerate these primitive bugaboos" (515).

Predictably enough, tribalism for Bartolomeo marks the utter corruption and degradation of the principles of class solidarity, the backward pull of the particular against the universal or, more precisely, of course, against the centralized bureaucracy that imposes itself in the guise of international cooperation. Displaying her characteristic flair for rhetorical warfare and public spectacle, Angelita places Bartolomeo on trial, "for crimes against the revolution, specifically for crimes against Native American history; the crimes were the denial and attempted annihilation of tribal histories" (515). Angelita also emphatically denies Bartolomeo's accusations, keeping private the line of thought by which she simultaneously rescripts the meaning of both "tribalism" and "internationalism":

> "*Us? Not Us!* Their spies are *liars! We* are internationalists! We are not just tribal!" Angelita argued vehemently. She was thinking about all the "friends of the Indians" who had sent them aid from all over the world. Millions had come from a crackpot German industrialist who wanted to see the tribal people of the Americas retake their land. Millions came each year from Japanese businessmen who wanted to avenge Hiroshima and Nagasaki any way possible. They were internationalists all right! Tribal Internationalists! (515)

In Angelita's reframing of these terms, the scene of internationalism appears tribalized in the conventional sense, fragmented by old and renewed animosities that crisscross more contemporary geopolitical divides, while tribal activism (however localized in its expressions) is governed by a world-historical vision.

Tribal resisters siphon from the global flows of "aid" and arms, even as they learn to profit from the less overtly politicized operations of commodity culture. Wandering the displays of "rock crystals and wind chimes" at the natural healing convention, Calabazas observes the "slow brown hands receive cash from anxious white hands" and remarks to his associate Root that "all the time we were in the wrong business" (732). Angelita, too, turns up for a media-friendly appearance at this gathering of mostly "affluent young whites," where she imparts a message from the twins about "the great shift of human populations on the continents," a fulfillment of prophecy beyond the ability of humans to forestall (734, 735). As Angelita speaks of tribal history and insurgency in this venue of commercialized, new age spirituality, her message appears oddly uncompromised by the context of its circulation. So despite the thoroughly evacuated versions of a (supposedly) tribal holism that proliferate at the convention—Lecha, for example, wanders past "a hotel conference room full of women chanting over and over, 'I am a goddess, I am a goddess'"—*Almanac* insists that the commodification of tribal history no more "annuls" than "fulfills" the tribal insurgents' designs (719). This point finds interesting elaboration in the narrative's account of the Barefoot Hopi, the aspiring architect of an international tribal network that would coordinate insurgencies in Africa and the Americas, and prime mover behind the convergence of tribal revolutionaries at the Tucson convention. The effect of the Hopi's words is neither exhausted nor even primarily determined by the identifications that structure their reception.

> The Hopi worked only in the realm of dreams; the Hopi's letters made no mention of strikes or uprisings; instead the letters had consisted of the Hopi's stories about the Corn Mother, Old Spider Woman, and the big snake. . . . Even redneck bikers ate up the Hopi's stories, but that was because the Hopi had already infiltrated their dreams with the help of the spirit world. (620)

The Barefoot Hopi's ability to infiltrate the dreamworld tropes the limits of the colonizers' property in the self. Like the psychoanalyst, the Barefoot Hopi knows that the incorporative work of identification only palliates the truth of the subject's constitutive splitting. But what psychoanalysis poses as an ontological crisis—the subject as an effect of his self-alienation in the symbolic—the Hopi (re)defines as a historical condition: the irreducible nonequivalence of the European colonizer and the world. In Lacan's famous dictum, "the unconscious is structured like a language." But the Hopi's forays into the dreamworld of his white listeners suggest the extent to which (pace Lacan) that which speaks in the unconscious does *not* speak the father's tongue. As much as his listeners may yearn for the restorative touch of the native, the Hopi's infiltration of their dreams figures a politics of knowledge, rather than an organic embrace, which will finally set the dreamer at one with the natural world. When the colonizers dreamwalk with the Hopi, they circuit where they cannot know to find themselves: a tribal vision of the world and its futures that is profoundly indifferent to their place within it. If the Hopi's storytelling, like whiteness studies, raises a prospect of interracial solidarity, the condition of the colonizers' emergence among the ranks of "the people" lies precisely and paradoxically, perhaps, in unlearning the prerogative to remake one's self in "the people's" image (and so to make that image one's own).

Whiteout: An Epilogue

Yet ironically, the sign of the Hopi's passage through white people's unconscious may well be the moment when they start to dream of whiteout, impossible visions of white on white, a virgin landscape untouched by color. Such is the lesson, I suggest, of Eskimo television and the old Yupik woman's mediation of the "vengeful spirits" in their (re)deployment of the weather map. It is the story of the burning children that the old woman intones as she rubs the fur across the screen, and the effect of her narration is to bring down a geological survey aircraft with "a quarter million dollar sensor unit" on board (159). Trapped on a flight out of Nome with the insurance adjuster, Lecha learns the cause of the survey plane's crash: "Whiteout," [the adjuster] said. "Blue sky and sunshine at five thousand feet and then thin clouds or mist. Suddenly a cloud bank or fog. A tiny storm front—not much more than a squall. But they can't fly out of it" (160).

By halting the survey of exploitable resources, the power of the story of the burning children functions to divest those who have stolen Yupik land of the ability to appropriate, convert, and consume it. Significantly, the effect on the "white people" and their "circling objects" of the old woman's historiographical method is whiteout, a terrifying diffusion, or deterritorialization of whiteness. As the old woman feeds the story of the burning children into the satellite link, the virtual space of information flows is reinvested with tribal history, to create a feedback loop: in contrast to Root, who renounces his specular relation to the world, the fate of the surveyors is to face their own reflection, in a form unmediated by the fiction of the other.

Chapter 4

Hollywood's Hot Voodoo

To pry an object from its shell, to destroy its aura, is the mark of a perception whose "sense of the universal equality of things" has increased to such a degree that it extracts them even from a unique object by means of reproduction.
—*Walter Benjamin,* Illuminations

The soft style first crops up primarily in films made by powerful independent companies . . . or auteur directors. The main impetus for experimentation in this field came from the cinematographers themselves, and from their directors and actors, in a quest for what they viewed as quality images.
—*Kristin Thompson, "Major Technological Changes of the 1920s"*

In one of the cabaret performances folded (however loosely) into the narrative of *Blonde Venus* (1934), Helen Faraday (Marlene Dietrich) arrives on stage disguised in a full-body gorilla costume. Seemingly stalking the chorus line of nubile women in blackface, who nevertheless lead it forward in chains, the gorilla then appears to escape its bonds and make its way to stage center, where the feral body is stripped away and Dietrich rises up and out of the cast-off form. Dressed in a lavishly sequined bodice trimmed with ostrich feathers that outline and amplify her buttocks (in back) and cascade between her legs (in front), Dietrich dons a platinum blonde Afro wig (adorned with sequined arrows) and proceeds to "put over" the lyrics of "Hot Voodoo": "Did you ever happen to hear of Voodoo? / Hear it and you won't give a darn what you do. / Tomtoms put me under a cult of voodoo, / and the whole night long / I don't know the right from wrong." Certainly, this scene has not suffered from critical inattention, generating, as it has, a wide range of commentaries focused alternately or conjointly on the politics of artifice and the articulation of female sexuality with race. Bill Nichols and Robin Wood each consider how Josef von Sternberg's stress on the fabrication of the image and of the female figure at its center supports a critique of the circumscribed femininity and racist stereotypes so richly in evidence in this scene, as in the film more generally. Nichols's Sternberg "stresses the tenuous alliance between our knowledge of the illusion and our belief in its reality. He threatens to unveil a scandal before our very eyes; he invites us to play in the gap, the wedge-like opening, his style unveils," although this "decisive step toward Brecht and a political modernism is only threatened, never taken" (125–26). In Wood's account, "Hot Voodoo" cites from a primitivist tropology of sexual abandon only to collapse the effect and redeploy these figures as a measure of the sexual and racial disciplines they ostensibly repudiate. Thus Wood notes, "'Hot Voodoo' offers the *apparent* release of the forces that normality represses: beating drums; savagery (the African dancers); animalism (the gorilla); aggression (the exaggerated, jagged teeth on the native shields); eroticism (Dietrich's glittering, emphasized breasts, the words of the song).... Against all this has to be set the details that counterpoint and qualify it: the "savages" are women on display; they are chained; the gorilla also drags a chain; nothing is what it seems (the blacks are painted whites, the gorilla is Dietrich)" (61).

For other critics, "Hot Voodoo" and *Blonde Venus* chart the intersections of gender, sexuality, and race—or, more particularly, in Mary Ann Doane's formulation, "the metonymic chain... which links infantile sexuality, female sexuality, and racial otherness" (210). In a chapter whose title, "Dark Continents," cites Freud's famously racialized trope of enigmatic femininity, Doane pursues the implications of a cultural tropology that racializes female sexuality, so that the white woman "in her unknowability and sexual excessiveness" is blackened and becomes the analogue of the Hottentot rather than her opposite term (213). Even as the title of Tania Modleski's chapter, "Cinema and the Dark Continent," echoes Doane's, so too does her stress on the "vicious circularity of patriarchal thought, whereby darkness signifies femininity and femininity darkness" (*Feminism without Women* 120). "Too often," Modleski complains, "feminist film critics have alluded only parenthetically to the film's racism while devoting themselves chiefly to considering whether the film is 'progressive' in its emphasis on performance and spectacle, its subtle visual undermining of the domestic ideal that the narrative purports to uphold. Yet the racism is not an incidental, 'odd' moment to be bracketed off in order to pursue more pressing concerns, but is, in fact, central to the evocation and manipulation of desire that begins with the Hot Voodoo number" (127–28). Similarly taking up the theme that the operations of gender and race are "fundamentally allied" in *Blonde Venus,* Deborah Thomas argues, however, that the film's very insistence on this alliance joins it to a tradition of "genuinely progressive treatments" of race in Hollywood. Like Nichols and Wood, Thomas makes strong claims for the critical force of performance in the film, while she shares with Modleski and Doane a desire to interrogate, rather than to take as culturally axiomatic, the conjugation of licentious femininity with primitive blackness. In her reading, then, "the constructed images of both blacks and blondes are strongly paralleled and shown to be racist and sexist illusions, respectively, though illusions unavoidably colluded in by the 'real' blacks... and women... within the narrative, as they are given no alternative cultural space within which to create more positive self-images" (Thomas 11–12).

While the conversation on *Blonde Venus* is certainly more complex and nuanced than this brief synopsis allows, one advantage of sketching the critical terrain in such broad strokes is to make more palpable the limits of the exchange: the ways, for instance, that performance becomes synonymous with "illusion," that critique means disclosure, that race remains an exclusively thematic concern for cinema. As always, the areas of the most banal consensus register the most profound impasses—and my interest in this chapter lies with a critical conversation on race and classic Hollywood cinema that has tended to engage with race as a narrative trope that carries over to cinema from other areas of cultural representation (e.g., the visual arts, elite and popular literatures, state/administrative discourses). Thus for Modleski and for Doane, notwithstanding the considerable discontinuities in their analytic protocols and aims, race is at issue in classic cinema because women's sexuality is at issue or, in other words, because a "metonymic chain" links female sexuality to polymorphous excess and (via prostitution) to atavism and to racial degeneracy within the cultural discourse more broadly. The trouble is not with the claim itself—surely indisputable on its own terms—but with what follows: the reduction of cinema to one medium (among many) through which racial discourse circulates. So we can talk about race in cinema (as a question of representation), but there would seem to be nothing specific to the way that cinema mediates race: nothing that cinema can tell us about the (re)production and effects of racial embodiment that close study of another medium would not also reveal; nothing that cinema's mediation of race can tell us about the (re)production and effects of embodiment in film. Moving with and against the insights of feminist film scholarship, this chapter strives to rethink this curiously inert relation between cinema and race, in which each term appears historically and theoretically constituted, prior to their encounter. I argue that the blackness at once hyperbolically attributed to Dietrich in "Hot Voodoo" and emphatically (if still incompletely) purged from her shimmering white form is not simply an index to the racialization of promiscuous femininity in the cultural imaginary but the refraction of the white female body's insertion as commodity-image within the first mass medium and, more particularly, within the international circuits of distribution and consumption forged by U.S. film producers.

Images

Critical to any revisionist discussion of race and cinema is a theory of the filmic image—if only because the Metzian understanding of the image as lack has been largely hegemonic for a psychoanalytic feminist film criticism that stresses, in turn, the figuration of the female star as the embodiment of that lack. In this analytic frame, so decisively posed in Laura Mulvey's influential writing, the consideration of the white female body is oriented to investigating fetishism (the visual and narrative management of women's lack) and, by extension, to cultivating critical distance (unveiling the operations of fetishism, as the only alternative to one's conscription by the fetishizing gaze). The implications of this stance for a critical account of the *white* female body in the context of "Hot Voodoo" are briskly reviewed in Modleski's rundown of the scene's import, in the sentence that immediately follows her description of Dietrich's act: "Nowhere does Sternberg more forcefully reveal himself to be the master fetishist of the female body than in this scene, which for an adequate reading requires us to apply the insights of *both* a Homi Bhabha and a Laura

Mulvey" (127). Here a certain set of assumptions about the relation of the cinematic image to the imaginary and of femininity to the image refers the serious (nonparenthetical) discussion of race to a consideration of racial fetishism with disquieting finality.

As Steven Shaviro observes, the insistence on the image as lacking rejoins the modernist conviction in the critical force of distance, in a phobic ordering of film study that both evacuates the image and enjoins us to back away from the peculiar excess of appearance that this fundamental emptiness makes possible.[1]

> But is it really *lack* that makes images so dangerous and disturbing? What these theorists fear is not the emptiness of the image, but its weird fullness, not its impotence so much as its power. . . . Much has been written about the "lost object" as a mainstay of cinematic desire. To the contrary: the problem for the cinema spectator is not that the object is lost or missing, but that it is never distant or absent enough. Maurice Blanchot suggests that the image is not a representational substitute for the object so much as it is—like a cadaver—the material trace or residue of the object's failure to vanish completely. (17)

Drawing substantially on Walter Benjamin as well as on Blanchot, Shaviro goes on to elaborate the significance of the camera's break with systems of perception that place the human subject at their center. For Shaviro, the key point is that the camera sees blindly—sees everything. Thus "the camera does not invent, and does not even represent; it only passively records. But this passivity allows it to penetrate, or to be enveloped by, the flux of the material world. The *automatism and nonselectivity* of mechanical reproduction make it possible for cinema to break with traditional hierarchies of representation and enter directly into a realm of matter, life, and movement" (32, my emphasis). Shaviro's point, of course, is not that the image makes its object fully/newly present but quite the contrary: that it confounds the very distinction between absence and presence, Symbolic and Real. In Shaviro's account, the image is not only nonreferential but also, crucially, "nonsignifying," in the sense that the real-time cinematic images, their sensational immediacy for the spectator, and the involuntary bodily responses they provoke, remain necessarily in excess of the signifying systems to which the spectator refers her visual input in the production of meaning.

So it is that Shaviro as spectator is "confronted and assaulted by a flux of sensations that I can neither attach to physical presences nor translate into systematized abstractions. I am violently, viscerally affected by *this* image and *this* sound, without being able to have recourse to any frame of reference, any form of transcendental reflection, or any Symbolic order" (32). In this model of spectatorship, cinema suspends our constitution of the world as object, as objects dissolve into images that we can no longer hold at the proper distance, images that are at once overproximate and incalculably remote. "On the one hand," he notes, "I am no longer able to evade the touch or contact of what I see, but on the other, the image is impalpable, I cannot take hold of it in return, but *always find it shimmering just beyond my grasp*" (46, my emphasis).[2] It follows from this displacement of objects that cinema in Shaviro's reading is precisely *not* reducible to ideology—to a subject-making apparatus. Scopophilia is the inverse of "mastery," the event of the spectator's "forced, ecstatic abjection before the image," enabled by a gaze that is "passive and not possessive" (Shaviro 49, 54).

Throughout this account, Shaviro rightly stresses his debt to Benjamin, who similarly insists on the ways that "a different nature opens itself to the camera than opens to the naked eye—if only because an unconsciously penetrated space is substituted for a space consciously explored by man" (*Illuminations* 236). Benjamin's distinction between the painter and the cameraman (echoed and amplified in Shaviro's distinction between representational art and cinema) builds on an analogy to the magician and the surgeon, where the former heals through a laying on of hands that "maintains the natural distance between the patient and himself," while the latter greatly reduces the distance "by penetrating into the patient's body," but more particularly still, insofar as he abstains "at the decisive moment... from facing the patient man to man; rather, it is through the operation that he penetrates into him" (233). Benjamin goes on to differentiate between the painter and the cameraman, then, as respectively holding distant from reality and "penetrating deeply into its web." In a passage that carries special weight for Shaviro's argument, Benjamin underscores how the cinema as *mediation* thus supports an *intimacy with reality* unavailable to the more thoroughly naturalized vision of the unassisted human eye. "There is a tremendous difference between the pictures they obtain. That of the painter is a total one, that of the cameraman consists of multiple fragments which are assembled under a new law. Thus for contemporary man, the representation of reality by the film is incomparably more significant than that of the painter, since it offers, precisely because of the thorough-going permeation of reality with mechanical equipment, an aspect of reality which is free of all equipment" (233–34). But crucially, for Benjamin, the loss of distance that ensues from the mechanical reproduction of reality (and the consequent reproducibility of the film image itself) marks an intensification of abstraction, while for Shaviro, as we have seen, the film image is specifically released from the tyranny of "systematized abstraction."

In a passage never glossed in Shaviro's text but nonetheless central to the essay's exposition, Benjamin reflects:

> Every day, the urge grows stronger to get hold of an object at very close range by way of its likeness, its reproduction. Unmistakably, reproduction as offered by picture magazines and newsreels differs from the image seen by the unarmed eye. Uniqueness and permanence are as closely linked in the latter as are transitoriness and reproducibility in the former. *To pry an object from its shell, to destroy its aura, is the mark of a perception whose "sense of the universal equality of things" has increased to such a degree that it extracts them even from a unique object by means of reproduction.* (223, my emphasis)

Shaviro writes as though his terms were perfectly consonant with Benjamin's, and certainly, both are preoccupied with how cinema deranges the distance between viewing subject and aesthetic object, sacrificing the "total," humanist "picture" in the process; both are concerned with the material, tactile qualities of cinema and with how the medium overtakes the spectator, whose "thoughts... [are] replaced by moving images."[3] However, Benjamin stresses that the breakdown of the auratic object, its dis- and reassembly elsewhere/anywhere, occurs as ever-larger segments of the object world submit to capitalist abstraction, while in Shaviro's analysis, the emphasis falls instead on the ways that film, as "an art that enacts, again and again... the sacrifice of the sacred (auratic) object," invokes what is neither presence nor "systematized abstraction" but "traces and reproductions of the real" (46, 38). In other words, for Benjamin it matters that the reproductive operations of the camera are continuous with the logic of commodity production in ways that it does not seem to matter for Shaviro—which is not to say that Shaviro would necessarily care to argue the point, so much as to observe that cinema as it interests and concerns him is defined by its resistance to the reterritorializing efforts of capital, so that "every attempt to manipulate and to order the flow of images only strengthens the tendential forces that uproot this flow from any stability of meaning and reference. Cinematic vision pushes toward a condition of freeplay: the incessant metamorphoses of immanent, inconstant appearances" (39).

From this perspective, however, Mitsuhiro Yoshimoto offers an equally important updating of Benjamin, when he argues for the special properties of the "commodity-image." In an analysis of a "global image culture" that resonates complexly with Shaviro's discussion of the cinematic image, Yoshimoto notes how the advent of the digital image unmoors images from objects by unsettling distance through speed:

> The synthetic image of the computer does not represent the object's real-time presence in the past [as in the photographic image] but presents the object which does not exist anywhere except as an effect of its own image. As digitally processed images are instantaneously transmitted without a loss of fidelity, a spatial distance is replaced by speed of circulation. . . . The collapse of a hierarchical relation of the object and the image dissolves the past as a temporal category while the future is transformed into the possible present. (111)

Significantly, for Yoshimoto, the loss of distance in the production and circulation of the image is keyed to a later historical moment, inaugurated not with the advent of cinema but with the shift from analog to digital technology. Nevertheless, it is quite possible to argue that the increasing salience of "commodity-images" Yoshimoto associates both with digital processing and with flexible accumulation represents less a reordering of commodity culture than an intensification of processes endemic to capitalism itself. Yoshimoto himself is explicit on this point, when he stresses that the shift from industrial to postindustrial capital, although significant, does not alter capitalism's basic dynamic. While Yoshimoto wishes to consider how "the transformation of industrial capitalism based on Fordist mass production into a new information-based capitalism . . . cannot but affect the film industry," I suggest (and certainly nothing in Yoshimoto's exposition seems to preclude this understanding) that the commodity-images of classic Hollywood cinema already manifest several of the qualities that Yoshimoto attributes more narrowly to Hollywood in the wake of its acquisition and restructuring by multinational corporations.

Elaborating on the effects of information-based capitalism on film, Yoshimoto contends that images are not simply convertible into capital but that, like capital, they reproduce themselves through circulation:

> The image is the basic commodity in the global economy. . . . as commodities become commodity-images, new cycles of consumption and capital accumulation emerge: I-M-I (circulation of commodity-images) and M-I-M (circulation of money) [alongside and (or) in place of what Marx identifies as C-M-C (circulation of commodities) and M-C-M (circulation of money)]. One of the implications of these new formulas is the following: in the age of global image culture, *it is not only money but also image that circulates without being consumed.* While in C-M-C, the starting and end points of the cycle are qualitatively different [the process is finite, insofar as the commodity is consumed], in I-M-I as in M-C-M, that difference becomes merely quantitative. Capital now accumulates not only through the circulation of money but also through the circulation of images without end. As money begets more money, images also bring forth more images. (115–16, my emphasis)

Plainly enough, the global circulation of cinematic images in the earlier decades of the twentieth century functioned in relation to industrial commodity production and consumption more as a supplement than as an alternative: commodity-images were hardly supplanting commodities (or conversely, we might say, the commodity was not yet becoming "commodity-image"), although certainly the dissemination of commodity-images helped forge the circuits through which industrial commodities would move, as my next section details. Still, notwithstanding the altogether-rudimentary character of I-M-I after World War I, there seems little basis for claiming that the cinematic image is exhausted (consumed) in a way that the digital is not, especially if we follow Shaviro in his insistence on the nonrepresentational nature of cinema.[4] In theorizing how the mechanically reproduced cinematic image proves resistant to the spectator's consumption, Shaviro permits us (somewhat against the grain of his own intentions) to view cinema as an early instance of the "commodity-image"—an analog medium where, nonetheless, the objects that shimmer on the screen are "traces" that press too closely to be seized. To layer Shaviro's account on Yoshimoto's is to arrive at a notion of cinema as commodity-image that is all the more useful to capitalist accumulation for evading every effort to appropriate it.

Markets

In Yoshimoto's analysis, the global dissemination of the image is an index to the virtual temporality of "instantaneous transmission," which represents, in turn, the condition of possibility for globalization itself. Thus, as he notes, "to some extent, 'globalization of image culture' or 'global image culture' is a misleading phrase or oxymoron since on a fundamental level globalization and image are inseparable each from the other" (109). While Yoshimoto follows a now-standard chronology in his association of globalization with post-Fordism, Armand Mattelart suggests the extent to which mass culture as such registers and amplifies a drive toward the inter- and transnationalization of media. In a discussion of Hollywood's global reach that echoes the findings of more-conventional film historians of the period, Mattelart notes that World War I "coincided with the first great wave of the internationalization of American film, with films already amortized on the domestic market. It allowed the studios to vastly increase their production and to gain control of key positions in distribution and exhibition all around the globe" (56).[5] Unlike Great Britain and France, where state functionaries were expressly charged with overseeing the "projection" of national culture onto the international scene, "Washington did not judge it necessary to elaborate an international cultural strategy," Mattelart points out, perhaps precisely because "the film industry of the United States wasted no time pursuing its conquest of foreign markets. Hegemonic at the end of the war, as much as in the Americas as in Europe, Hollywood—aided by its hatred of protectionism—assured itself of a strong position through the purchase of cinemas, the control of distribution, and the organization of local production" (64–65).

Prior to World War I and during the early years of the war, American film had moved through the infrastructures of the British Empire to reach its (already not inconsiderable) international viewership. According to Kristin Thompson, London served as the clearinghouse for American foreign distribution between 1909 and 1916, even as Britain's own production was declining. "Given the USA's lengthy commercial domination of the world," Thompson remarks, "it seems odd to look back now and realise how naively the pre-war film export situation was managed. Apparently, in selling the British rights of their films, many firms would, for a relatively low additional fee, simply throw in the rights for, say, the Continent or the British colonies or the Far East or even the world outside North America" (*Exporting Entertainment* 31). As a result, when American producers did attempt direct sales to foreign markets, they found themselves undersold by British distributors, who offered prints of the same American films more cheaply (31, 70). "From 1916 on, however, American firms adopted new strategies, dealing directly with more markets, opening more subsidiary offices outside Europe and thereby establishing a control which other producing countries would find difficult to erode during the 1920s" (71). The crux of these "new strategies," then, was an effort to exploit the interruption of British commerce by the war and to supplant through duplication the imperial network that linked metropolitan London to the colonies. In Thompson's view, it was the diminished focus on Europe as a market and a center for distribution that enabled U.S. producers to maintain their hegemony after the war (91). The most important of the non-European markets were Australia and South America, where, according to one Latin American importer, by 1920 American films accounted for 95 percent of the screening time in South American cinemas (Thompson, *Exporting Entertainment* 139). But the U.S. product was also ascendant in parts of Asia, particularly India, which (after the opening of Universal's office in Calcutta in 1917) "would fall rapidly under an almost complete domination by American films" (76). Although U.S. film exports to Africa remained far less significant, Africa nonetheless doubled its percentage of U.S. exports several times over in the years following 1916 (92, 216–17).

As Hollywood cinema gained a controlling share of the market in Australia, South America, and certain regions of Asia through reconstituting the channels of imperial commerce, it also anticipated a broader shift from political domination to cultivating economic dependencies (from colonialism to neocolonialism) that ensued during the twentieth century with the European powers' divestment of their colonial possessions. In an essay on the marginal visibility of third world cinema to film studies, Ella Shohat and Robert Stam sketch the neocolonial dimensions of this international film market concisely:

> In the cinema, this hegemonizing process intensified shortly after World War I, when U.S. film distribution companies (and secondarily European companies) began to dominate Third World markets, and was further accelerated after World War II with the growth of transnational media corporations. The continuing economic dependency of Third World cinemas makes them vulnerable to neocolonial pressures. When dependent countries try to strengthen their own film industries by setting up trade barriers to foreign films, for example, First World countries can threaten retaliation in some other economic area such as the pricing of raw materials. Hollywood films, furthermore, often cover their costs in the domestic market and can therefore be profitably "dumped" on Third World markets at very low prices. ("From the Imperial Family" 148)

Quite simply, the point is that colonialism and its legacies are not only a theme for cinema but decisive for the medium's organization and its transglobal circulation. There is nothing astonishing about this circumstance, and it would not, presumably, merit such explicit consideration here were it not that the imperial contours of the industry have been so routinely overlooked by film studies and so, by extension, sidelined in discussions of race and film (Shohat and Stam's *Unthinking Eurocentrism* is a telling and important exception). Hollywood both participates from an early moment in the highly uneven integration we call globalization (it is suggestive, if not perhaps strictly accurate, that the post–World War I American film corporations have been described as "multinationals") and should also remind us of the extent to which globalization is imperialism by another name (Thompson, *Exporting Entertainment* 149).

Both mainstream journalism and industry publications in the post-1916 period overtly, indeed, on occasion, hyperbolically, acknowledged the relation of Hollywood cinema to the development of markets for other U.S. commodities. Observing that the Unites States would need significantly to develop its overseas trade once World War I was ended, an article in *Colliers* goes on to reflect: "Well, consider what the American moving picture is doing in other countries. It is familiarizing South America and Africa, Asia and Europe with American habits and customs. It is educating them up to the American standard of living. It is showing them American clothes and furniture, automobiles and homes. And it is subtly but surely creating a desire for these American-made articles" (cited in Thompson, *Exporting Entertainment* 121–22). This upward education is almost certainly part of what a 1915 trade publication article meant to invoke in its celebratory prediction of the postwar film industry: established in South America and in a Europe grown dependent on its products, with a "bigger than ever" domestic market, "American-made films will not only lead the world—*they will constitute it*" (cited in Thompson, *Exporting Entertainment* 54, my emphasis). Or, in Mattelart's alternate formulation that looks ahead to the culmination of this process by the decade of the next great war, "World War II would... consecrat[e] the advent of American hegemony over universality's representations, or at least representations of a certain universality" (79). The character of American hegemony as described in both contemporary trade publications and the critical work on media history is therefore distinct from what Shohat and Stam identify as the uses of cinema for the acculturation of a comprador colonial class to the specific imagined community of the colonizing power, such that "an assimilated elite [would] identify with 'its' empire and thus against other colonized peoples" (*Unthinking Eurocentrism* 102–3). At issue, instead, is U.S. cinema's articulation of modernity to consumption under the sign of a specifically deterritorialized Americanism. While Shohat and Stam ultimately tend to focus on the tropes of empire in cinema—on films where colonialism or imperialism is a more or less explicit motif; where the narrative invokes race relations or, in other words, the relation between raced subjects—at the same time, the very circumstances of media organization on which they so rightly insist would seem to invite a wider discussion of race and the apparatus of cinema, of the laws by which cinema reassembles reality, to recall Benjamin's language—so that we might learn to speak, for instance, of the very mise-en-scène in racial terms.

Bodies

The body and affect of the star have been central to mediating "a certain universality," as well as to determining a film's market value. As Tino Balio points out, while B movies were rented to exhibitors for a flat fee, the superior A product was made available for a percentage of the gross, and it was the cachet of its star(s) that largely established what the rental rate would be (144–45). Thus constituted as commodity-image—that is, as the avatar of a person "pr[ied] from [her] shell" and reckoned on a scale of abstract equivalence—the movie star was arguably the linchpin creation of the Hollywood film industry. I have argued in the introduction that, in the context of modernity, "race" (in the sense of nonuniversal, nonwhiteness) signifies the body's improper relation to capital: where the European colonizer claims an inalienable property in the body (one may commodify one's bodily or intellectual labor, but not one's flesh), the bodies of the colonized are made in varying degrees susceptible to abstraction and exchange. More particularly, my introduction addressed plantation slavery as a limit case, where the "raced" body, made legally alienable, turns inside out—because fully opened to and penetrated by the abstracting force of capital. Here my interest lies with the implications of slavery (in particular) and colonialism (more generally) for an understanding of embodiment and "image culture"—or, in other words, for an understanding of bodies as "commodity-images." What effects are engendered when the mechanically reproduced white body loses its legal and historical protections from exchange? In what sense can the mechanically reproduced body remain "white"?

In her stunning analysis of the constitution of whiteness as a "property interest" under U.S. law—an analysis to which my own thinking is broadly indebted—Cheryl Harris argues that

> because "the presumption of freedom [arose] from color [white]" and the "black color of the race [raised] the presumption of slavery," whiteness became a shield from slavery, a highly volatile and unstable form of property. In the form adopted in the United States, slavery made human beings market-alienable and in so doing, subjected human life and personhood—that which is most valuable—to the ultimate devaluation. Because whites could not be enslaved or held as slaves, the racial line between white and black was extremely critical; it became a line of protection and demarcation from the potential threat of commodification, and it determined the allocation of the benefits and burdens of this form of property. (279)[6]

Thus by custom and by law, "whiteness became the quintessential property for personhood," notwithstanding that the determination of racial identity (the state's adjudication of claims to whiteness) rested on arbitrary and ahistorical criteria (281). It would be hard to overestimate the importance of Harris's revisionist perspective on "whiteness as property," as it maps new directions for the critical study of whiteness, where stress is too often placed, and placed exclusively, on the universality of this racial identity, on the white man's status "as an overseeing subject *without properties*" (Dyer, *White* 207).[7] One significant question raised by Harris's argument is how to grasp the not merely quantitative but qualitative distinction between the atomization and reification of protected "white" persons under capital (who present as a set of market-alienable features but, also, as not reducing to them—as possessed of an inner, inalienable core) and the commodification of "life and personhood" in their entirety to which "black" people have been subject—not only during but also, arguably, in the wake of slavery. The distinction pivots ostensibly on the status of the body (the difference between selling one's bodily labor and becoming a salable body in which others may traffic), and my own procedure has been to pressure that distinction (as Harris does not), to ask after the relation between personhood and embodiment—in short, to engage the historical and critical significance of the ways that personhood in the modern West rests on a property in the body. From this vantage, I argue that what Harris identifies as a "property interest in whiteness" follows very specifically from the white person's claim on an organic embodiment, in which the body functions as a naturalized limit on capitalist abstraction or, in Benjamin's terms, as the "shell" that restricts what may be "pried" from the human subject. Read in this way (somewhat aslant of its author's own investments, though not, I think, against the grain of her intentions), a central contribution of Harris's analysis is to show how this property in the body that accrues to "white" subjects does not obtain, or does not obtain in equal measure, across racial lines.

If cinema marks the inaugural appearance of the white body in the inorganic, depthless form of the commodity-image, as I am proposing, then one might well anticipate how this body yields a set of contradictions that cannot be addressed, much less resolved, on purely narrative terms. Richard Dyer's discussion of white racial embodiment and the techniques of light takes an important step in considering how white corporeality is managed at the level of the cinematic medium. In his detailed account of the emergence and standardization of lighting patterns for white actors, Dyer demonstrates how white skin, in general, and white women, more particularly and conspicuously, are lit so as to diffuse rather than absorb the light: the white (female) star is always, to a greater or lesser degree (but it is usually greater) a radiant presence on the screen. Now for Dyer the white woman's "glow" is significant for the way it idealizes the white female subject in a gesture traceable across media, from religious iconography to Hollywood film. In a surprising turn, Dyer undercuts his welcome focus on race and the cinematic medium by claiming all the same that there is nothing specific to how cinema mediates race—that cinema simply extends the conventions developed in other representational media. But if it is true that cinema adapts its aesthetics from a wider cultural tradition, there is nothing given or self-evident in its selection of the particular codes and practices it continues (as the next section details), nor does the simple fact of continuity imply the identity of effects across media. So I draw on Dyer's account of the syntax of white embodiment in film to argue the reverse: cinema's mediation of whiteness, rather than the participation in an overarching "idealization" of whiteness that finds its genesis in something equally sprawling and transhistorical (in Eurocentrism, say), has everything to do with the organization of the cinematic medium. Primed by Dyer to remark the white body's glow (as opposed to what he describes as the black and brown body's "shine," its absorption of light), I find equally remarkable the extent to which this glowing skin remediates the white body's depthless condition as commodity-image and restores at least partially the protections of white embodiment at the very point of their erosion: visually, the radiant white body has been pried from its shell in the most literal sense (the edges of the body soften or dissolve), yet in this diffuse, unsettled, unquantifiable state it also refuses its measure on a scale of "the universal equality of things." In this way, the cinematically (re)mediated white body is overtaken by "systematized abstraction" and (seemingly) released from its condition of possibility as abstracted commodity-image. Moreover, as it suffuses and eclipses the objects that surround it, the dissipated body of the glowing star exists in a relation of spatial unrest to her mise-en-scène—an unrest that reproduces within the frame of the image the loss of proper distance that characterizes, for Shaviro, the spectator's relation *to* this image.

The Soft Style

In Hollywood trade publications of the 1920s and 1930s, as well as in the standard film histories of the period, the racial syntax that preoccupies Dyer—the lighting of white skin for glow—is addressed in specifically nonracial terms, as a preference for the "soft style" of cinematography. In their independent and collaborative writing, David Bordwell and Kristin Thompson offer an invaluable account of the changing technological environment in and sometimes against which the soft style emerged as normative for Hollywood productions. Certainly a number of factors favored the development of the soft style in its most conspicuous form during the silent era, among them the use of incandescent lighting and low-contrast developing solutions (Bordwell 342), but it is also evident that a soft, slightly (or significantly) diffused quality to the cinematic image was, more than a simple consequence of the state of the technology, a very deliberately, sometimes obsessively cultivated effect that entailed gauze filters, mesh screens, and special lenses (Thompson, "Major Technological Changes" 288). Contemporary "sources do not discuss the reasons for this usage, aside from the idea of beauty," Thompson notes. "But one purpose was probably to isolate the figures from the background, concentrating the spectator's attention on the face" (288). While "women usually got heavier gauzing" than men, "certain men were associated with glamor as well" (291). Citing an "idea of beauty" as the impetus to the soft style, these sources would seem to affirm Dyer's association of glow with idealization (less so Thompson's reference to "glamor," which carries sharper commercial overtones). Yet even the dominance of such an apparently transcendent aesthetic is more surprising, when one weighs the extent to which it slowed production, raised costs, and conflicted expressly with other emergent production norms. "Clearly, soft-style cinematography did not promote efficiency. When workers are hanging giant gauzes, calculating special exposure and developing methods, or buying extra lenses, shooting time and expenses go up" (291). Equally telling, "the soft style ... presented particular problems for the continuity system. Frequent changes in degree of contrast or fuzziness from shot to shot would call attention to editing and other stylistic devices" (292).

Citing these drawbacks, Thompson suggests that the "main impetus for experimentation in this field came from the cinematographers themselves, and from their directors and actors, in a quest for what they viewed as quality images.... [Inasmuch as t]he Hollywood cinema uses the human figure as its center of interest ... a technique that could enhance that figure might well be worth the additional expense in production" (291). With the introduction of new film stocks in the early 1930s, moreover, it became possible to achieve a more carefully modulated and moderated degree of softness. Touting the use of Eastman Super Sensitive, for instance, the American Society of Cinematographers alerted members how "with present lightings and smaller lens openings, improved definition can be obtained without sacrifice of those qualities of softness which have always been the artistic aim of cinematographers" (Bordwell and Thompson 136). The advent of sound also contributed to the standardization of a moderated soft style:

> Since sound negatives had to be developed by machine to ensure absolute uniformity of contrast in the track, cinematographers could no longer order custom hand-developing after the silent period. Instead, some studios decided to standardize a soft, slightly diffused look to their films. The result was a relatively uniform, low-contrast, slightly fuzzy gray look. Heavily gauzed close-ups would still stand out as fuzzier than the long shots, but the difference was not nearly so noticeable as it had been in the early twenties.
>
> Sound took the soft style partially out of the cinematographers' control and made it a matter of studio policy. In effect, the soft style became more pervasive, but less varied. (Thompson, "Major Technological Changes" 293)

Yet the seemingly axiomatic relation of "softness" (with or without diffusion) to "quality" and to an "art" aesthetic (referenced in both contemporary and film historical accounts) hardly settles the question of why, among the many possible indicators of "quality" that early cinematographers and directors might have selected, a (normalized) soft style would emerge as hegemonic. If cinema aspired to a level of cultural legitimacy that was threatened from the start by its development as mass medium, in other words, one can enumerate other aesthetics (besides "softness") that would equally have signaled a high cultural sensibility—and blended no less awkwardly than "softness" with other narrative and visual requirements that followed from cinema's status as commercial entertainment.

To understand the choice of this particular aesthetic (rather than simply to enumerate the aesthetic advantages of the choice), I argue that we should situate the enthusiasm for softness in the context of the deep and abiding contradiction of a medium that commodifies white bodies and in so doing threatens precisely to eradicate what constitutes the prestige and attraction of white embodiment. Whatever else its merits (its obvious signing of "artfulness," for example), the choice of a soft style allows cinema simultaneously to revoke and to extend the protections of white personhood, by opening whiteness to exchange but not to (re)appropriation. Glowing skin signals the softening of bodily limits that enables the "extraction" (through mechanical reproduction) of abstract value from the white body, even as it refuses the reduction of that body to an object among others—to a consumable artifact on the order of the cars and clothes and interior decor that surround this body on the screen. Inasmuch as the mechanically reproduced object is defined by its new and unprecedented mobility, so that, in Benjamin's phrase, it comes to "meet the beholder... in his own particular situation," we could say that cinema traffics in this encounter with (various forms of) eroticized white embodiment while also subtracting the white body from the prospect of end use, or consumption. At the same time, however, and quite apart from the workings of plot or narrative, this shimmering body visually immerses itself into the world of commodities and the (implied) pleasures of consumption. In my variation on Marx's dancing tables, the glowing white body of the star steps forth and speaks its visual hail: "You can meet me here, in this intimate darkness, but you cannot possess me (take me out of circulation and use me up). What can be yours is my ecstasy—my abandoned relation to the world of commodities."[8] My argument is that whiteness manifests in Hollywood cinema as the impossible lure of protection from the invasive forces of capital (the prying open of human shells) through ecstatic consumption.

So it may be that Benjamin's absolute distinction between aura and personality proves too unsupple, a brusque gesture of modernist distaste in an essay that otherwise displays none of, say, Theodor Adorno and Max Horkheimer's dismissive rancor about mass culture. "The film responds to the shriveling of the aura with an artificial build-up of the 'personality' outside the studio," Benjamin writes. "The cult of the movie star, fostered by the money of the film industry, preserves not the unique aura of the person but the 'spell of the personality,' the phony spell of a commodity" (*Illuminations* 231). Certainly, celebrity is mass-produced, and the obsessive sounding of the personality (the public rehearsal of the star's intimacies and inner life) renders aura as travesty. But it is also possible that the shimmering star, leading an impossibly doubled existence as abstraction and release from abstraction, represents at once the destruction of the aura and its renewal. No longer the property of certain (aesthetic) objects or persons, the aura reappears as a kind of flickering prospect that attaches to white bodies precisely in their refusal of object status—in their complete elision with the mobility of the image.

"Hot Voodoo"

In the context of these meditations on images, markets, bodies, and the soft style that normalizes the conversion of white bodies into commodity-images for a global market, I want to return to the signal moment of Dietrich's transmutation from ape to Venus. For nearly all the film's critics, this performance animates contradictions that are pivotal for *Blonde Venus* and for the broader consideration of (white) women's position within a patriarchal imaginary. In Bill Nichols's reading, "Hot Voodoo" inaugurates Helen Faraday's attempt to gain control of her performance, or more exactly to command the terms of her own fetishization. "Helen's success," he observes, "depends upon signifying that she seems to be something that she is not, and that *she* is in control of the difference" (127). Similarly, Robin Wood understands Helen's attempted emancipation as irreducibly bound by the sexual and economic disciplines that forge the very spaces through/to which Helen would escape. "The heroine's journey is through different varieties of prostitution, all male-determined; and nowhere in the film (or in Sternberg's work) does the erotic exist without contamination and constraint" (Wood 61). Acknowledging such constraint, Deborah Thomas nonetheless affirms Helen's move toward greater levels of autonomy, anchored in the increasingly "oppositional stance" of Helen's/Dietrich's musical performances (13). Critical assessments of "Hot Voodoo" thus take shape within the framework of critics' wider attention to the emancipatory possibilities and limits of (erotic) performance in the film—and, of course, it is hardly surprising that performance would emerge as a focal point of the criticism, since the narrative rides on an explicit thematics of the stage and of dichotomized public/private spaces. More startling, however, and certainly more symptomatic, is the stunning consistency with which the performance-oriented criticism situates the African Americans visible and audible at the margins of the film's semantic fields (e.g., the bandleader and bartender in the club where Helen performs "Voodoo"; the custodians outside the club owner's window; Cora, the servant in a Galveston boardinghouse) as eruptions of a social real into the domain of stage(d) illusion—as figures who expose the distance between primitivist fantasy and the "ignominy of the socialized Black American" (Wood 61), or who collapse the very distinction between stage and reality by marking the stage itself as a scene of struggle (Nichols 128), or who serve by their "mere presence... as a silent commentary on the inadequacies of the myths" (Thomas 12). In each account, in other words, black people are taken as the measure of Helen's confinement within racialized tropologies of gender and sexuality, both because authentic black bodies are positioned at the limits of the figural and because their "presence" further implies that Helen's own connection to blackness remains entirely (merely) figural.[9]

For some critics, the focus on performance leads them more particularly to consider how this (ostensible) maternal melodrama cuts against the grain of its own generic requirements by flattening Helen's affect and so rendering her inner life inscrutable. "The impassivity of faces in Sternberg is not (as is sometimes alleged) bad acting, but the means whereby ambiguity of motivation can be suggested—or at least permitted to be read," Wood remarks (61). Addressing the history of the film's censorship, Lea Jacobs astutely points out that the censors' preference for what would become the final version of *Blonde Venus* depends on the attribution to Helen of a quite particular set of desires and investments, whereas visually and narratively, the film proceeds at the very least to ambiguate every one of the censors' imputed motivations. For both Wood and Jacobs, however, this breakdown of interiority stands as a sort of narrative device (a means to put unsanctioned counternarratives in play) that appears to have no relevance to matters of race—except inversely, perhaps, since "Hot Voodoo" in Jacobs's reading identifies "the sexuality that Helen must hold back" and so stands, in essence, as an index to her "deeper" motivations that double and derail the censors' interpretation of Helen as penitent mother (28). In considering how tabloid coverage of Dietrich's romances gave viewers an alternate context for reading *Blonde Venus* as an affirmation of women's sexuality rather than maternal sentiment, Janet Staiger's essay on censorship avoids any reference at all to the film's racialization of sexuality—as though, whatever we might say of Helen Faraday, Dietrich's star persona stood clear of the ape's shadow. Thomas also tends to split Dietrich from Helen where the racial dimension of erotic performance is concerned, by reading "Hot Voodoo" in terms of the character's situation while tagging Helen's final and seemingly de-raced performance in the Paris revue as "pure Dietrich" (12).

But it is exactly the racial embodiment of the star that "Hot Voodoo" addresses, in a reflection on white femininity and the commodity form that Doane so perceptively glosses:

> Revised sexual mores connected with the emergence of the "New Woman" in the 1920s required a more flexible understanding of white female sexuality which weakened the polarization between the respectable Victorian lady and the prostitute. Marlene Dietrich is, in fact, recuperated by the nuclear family at the end of the film. Yet, the near collapse of the moral opposition between types of white femininity also threatened to collapse certain racial distinctions as well. . . . When Dietrich slowly removes the huge gorilla paws to reveal slender white hands and when she pulls off the gorilla head to exchange it for an intensely blonde wig . . . she trades one icon for another. It is as though white femininity were forcefully disengaged from blackness once and for all in the process of commodification of the image of white female sexuality. (214–15)

Only the situation is entirely the reverse: far from purging her sexuality of "blackness," Dietrich's mechanical reproduction as commodity-image imparts the condition of "blackness" that can never be adequately put aside. Doane's insight into the effects of commodification on embodiment falters at the point where she rejoins the film's other critics in thinking femininity by analogy to race, even as she refuses the other tendency so prevalent in the criticism of analogizing patriarchy to capital. Thus Doane's discussion turns on the recognition that women circulate *as* commodities within the medium, rather than simply circulating *like* commodities within the sexual economies (marriage, prostitution) represented in the narrative. Yet Doane retains the inclination to consider race as a trope of sexuality (the Hottentot as the figure of the licentious woman), with the result that the question of racial embodiment is effectively posed in advance (by the "metonymic chain"), prior to considering the white female body's mediation. In this way, the cinematic mediation of white femininity can actually appear to resolve the matter of racialized sexuality—to lift the stubborn taint of "blackness" from white women's sexual display. The critical investment in both analogies, separately and together, works therefore to block an engagement with the rearticulation of race and sexuality in cinema, specifically that would address the status of the white female star as commodity-image *and* the racial constitution of commodified embodiment.

In the end, the most telling aspect of Helen's/Dietrich's disturbing striptease in "Hot Voodoo" is the utter failure of the "disengage-[ment]" Doane presumes. Dietrich's "intensely blonde wig" is an oversized mass of kinks and curls, while the feather trim on her bodice plainly evokes the body contours of the Venus Hottentot: enormous, protruding buttocks; and distended/phallic labia. Aside from the details of dress, the placement of the camera in this scene, which sits for the most part well below and slightly to one side of Dietrich, throws her frame out of proportion: her torso and especially her head appear oddly enlarged, and her legs are largely amputated from the image. Viewed from this angle, moreover, her cheekbones create a shadow that hollows out her face and draws attention to her mouth and jaw, rather than to her eyes (as one would expect). From the spectator's point of view, Dietrich's eyes appear focused for the most part on some object above and to the left of where we sit—her look apparently trained on the wider audience, although earlier shots have established that the space of the club is quite small and most of the tables clustered in proximity to the stage. The placement of the camera thus serves to dis- and reassemble Dietrich's form, and it is, at any rate, undecidable whether the looming torso with its huge head, pronounced jaw, and eyes that refuse to meet our own presents on a more human scale than the gorilla body Dietrich cast away. If the inhuman blackness of the gorilla body has been insufficiently purged, it is also, however, partially dissolved: at the same time as the black bodice and the feathers sharply trace the outline of the Hottentot, the shiny sequins on her bodice and the almost-blinding glow of the platinum wig soften the boundaries of Dietrich's body and render the work of her mechanical reassembly incomplete. So this performance confronts us with a strangely hybrid entity: white and inhuman; brilliant and grotesque.

However joltingly, *Blonde Venus* situates Helen's/Dietrich's musical performances within a narrative of womanhood fallen and redeemed. The film begins at the moment where Helen, a cabaret performer, while swimming naked in a pond in the Black Forest, meets her future husband Ned (Herbert Marshall); the ripples of the pond water dissolve to water splashing in a tub, where Helen, now married to Ned, is bathing their son, Johnny (Dickie Moore). The child's bedtime story entails the parents' reenactment of their first meeting as pantomime, though we shift abruptly from this scene of sanctioned and reproductive domesticity to Ned's brusque efforts to "sell [his]

Helen Faraday (Marlene Dietrich) sings "Hot Voodoo" in Blonde Venus *(1932). The camera sits below and to one side of the performer.*

body for science." We learn that Ned, himself a scientist, is dying from radium poisoning and so attempting by the sale of his contaminated flesh to secure some benefit for his family. Although the doctor pronounces Ned's body quite worthless, he recommends a cure, available only in Europe and at very high cost. Helen then returns to the stage to earn the money needed for Ned's cure—and in a stunning demonstration of her body's salability, does so on the night of her first performance, by enchanting Nick (Cary Grant), a wealthy playboy/politician, who writes her a check for the full amount. Ned leaves for Europe, whereupon Helen promptly leaves the stage to move with Johnny into a lavish apartment that Nick has provided for them. Meanwhile Ned is cured, but returns home in advance of the announced date to find his own shabby quarters deserted. The affair thus brought to light, Ned reproaches Helen with her deficiency as a mother and vows to keep her away from Johnny; appalled at the prospect of this separation, she takes the child and flees south. Wanted by the police whom Ned has set in motion against her, Helen is soon forced to quit her too-visible employment on the stage and, as the film insinuates, to support Johnny and herself through prosti-

tution (in an elliptical but still-potent invocation of the fate decreed for the "tragic mulatta," when sold south, "down the river" to New Orleans). She eventually lands in a squalid boardinghouse in Galveston, where she abandons her flight and returns Johnny to his father. Although he bitterly repays her the money she had given him for his treatment, she gifts it, in turn, to a penniless old prostitute and walks away, vowing to find herself "a better bed." The film then cuts to her success montage, and we see her next as the star performer in an elite Paris nightclub, where Nick, who had fled to Europe to recover from this failed romance, seeks her out. She declines his offer to return with him to the States, but we cut from her cold refusal to Johnny and his father at the breakfast table, reading the newspaper announcement of Helen's engagement to Nick. Back in New York, Nick tries to arrange Helen's visit with Johnny for the sum of ten thousand dollars, an offer to which Ned, noting that he can "throw money around the same as" Nick can, responds by admitting her for free. Reunited with Johnny, Helen immediately begins to tend him, running his bath and bustling around the apartment, absurdly, in an evening gown. Johnny insists that his parents reenact their meeting, at which point Ned confesses his need for Helen and she consents to the reunion.

The film's overt preoccupation with domesticity and publicity, marriage and prostitution, makes it possible to read the narrative, strictly on its own terms, as concerned with an errant female protagonist, who seeks to constitute and dispose of her own value in a public, performative domain, only to be brutally, if implausibly, reprivatized in the end. To do so is to miss how the narrative attends to the circulation of the white female body as mechanically reproduced image and thus addresses the medium through which it circulates (cinema) at least as much as the arena of live performance it represents (the stage). We learn that (at the very least) two images of Helen are circulating in the press: the first, taken from the wanted poster, improbably features her in full Blonde Venus regalia; the second, which accompanies the engagement notice, is a publicity shot of the performer in a black top hat. Twice we see Johnny inspect these images of his mother, and we witness, as well, two detectives debate whether the image on the wanted poster resembles the woman they pursue. In all three instances, the focus of the commentary concerns the relation of the image to the embodied woman and the range of the responses—in contrast to the detectives, Johnny declares the image from the wanted poster "pretty good," but initially fails to recognize the top-hatted woman as his mother—suggests that the images "extracted" from the female body cannot be stabilized by reference to that body and in fact, quite the contrary, seem to render the "original" body elusive, harder rather than easier to locate in real time and space. This attention to images as mechanical reproductions of the female body that proliferate according to their own, autonomous logic (I-M-I) obtains at the visual as well as the narrative level: *Blonde Venus* is replete with images of Dietrich that cite Venus with a difference. At the moment where Helen, only just become aware of Ned's early return from Europe, is startled by his footsteps, we see her luminous face, half obscured by the outsized fur collar of her jacket; like her own skin, the irregular borders of the pelt reflect the light, so that she appears to us, once again, as bound in furs (or feathers) and yet too soft, too fluid to bind. One eye is covered, while the other again declines to meet our look and searches a distant periphery. In another, equally salient instance, where the image of Venus reproduces itself for no other reason, one can surmise, except the inevitability of its reproduction, Helen's scarves catch the breeze and we see the ostrich feathers again, at once amplifying her buttocks and raised in a phallic salute.

Helen Faraday is surprised by her husband's arrival.

Venus repeats again, dimly, in Helen's Paris performance, which stands in many respects as an apparent inversion of the motifs of "Hot Voodoo": Dietrich now appears in a rhinestone-studded white tuxedo, complete with white-silk top hat. The look is cool and cosmopolitan, instead of hot and feral; the decor spare, instead of tropical, and with the exception of the tails on the long white jacket of her suit, which again invoke, however timidly, the ostrich trim, Dietrich seems to have attained to the condition of "disengaged" whiteness that has elsewhere in the film eluded her. The glow that in "Hot Voodoo" suffused primarily her face and head here engulfs and softens her entire body; her face, in particular, manifests the softness-with-definition of a more standardized aesthetic, so that we can also read in the transit from "Voodoo" to Paris a reflection on the normalization of "glow" become possible and prevalent at the moment of the film's production.

With only a few, brief exceptions (in particular, a short sequence where it tracks her, from below, as she moves, backward, up a flight of stairs), the camera sits level with Dietrich or above her, thus returning her body to human proportions. If it is possible to read Paris as achieving the whitening of Dietrich's commodity-image, its release

Helen Faraday in the wake of a departing train.

from abstraction through (henceforth) standardized practices of softening and diffusion, still this sequence dwells obsessively—and with only marginally less anxiety than "Hot Voodoo"—on the implications of the female body's mechanical reproduction. Critics have noted Dietrich's fashioning as "mannish" woman, or lesbian, as well as the film's self-awareness on this point.[10] Yet to note that the hot femininity of "Voodoo" here gives way to the cold, lesbian styling of the Paris performance is to beg the question of how lesbianism itself codes in *Blonde Venus*. Reading the mannish attire in the context established by the lyrics, I suggest that the primary association of lesbianism is with nonreproductivity but also, by extension, with lawless reproduction. "If the hens refused to lay / Or if bulls gave milk someday / Do you think I'd care? / That's their affair, / I couldn't be annoyed"—and the lyrics proceed, in this fashion, to enumerate comic scenarios, not simply of gender inversion but of reproductive inversions, in which the copy precedes the original (in another of the verses, it is children who bring forth their parents) and bodies produce without regard for their "natural" limit(ation)s (e.g., bulls give milk). Dietrich's much-referenced "coldness" in this scene may have less to do with her apparent renunciation of affective ties and (or) with the

Helen Faraday's Paris comeback.

urbane detachment of the woman who desires "like a man" than with her studied indifference to the terms of (her) mechanical reproduction: caught up in a process of abstraction that derives from her body what was never proper to it, nevertheless, she assures us, she "couldn't be annoyed." The irony is that this cultivated distance from the image collapses the very distinction it sets out to protect; the wholly indifferent subject is finally eclipsed by the image she disowns, as subjectivity would seem minimally to require the very thing she abdicates—an investment in her being-in-the-world.

I have been arguing that the body of the star is hyperbolically white because never sufficiently white—and that Hollywood's Hot Voodoo consists in resignifying the body's invasion by capital as the condition of its emancipation. The interest of *Blonde Venus* lies in its preference for performing the ritual rather than simply effecting the voodoo—for rehearsing the production of the white female body (rather than simply producing it) and so, perversely, unlearning Hollywood cinema's grammar of white embodiment at the very moment of its most thoroughgoing institutionalization.

Chapter 5

White Women in the Age of Their Mechanical Reproduction

The image is the basic commodity in the global economy.
—*Mitsuhiro Yoshimoto, "Real Virtuality"*

The narrative cannot contain *everything.*
—*Stephen Heath,* Questions of Cinema

"Where's your wife, Vargas?"
—*Hank Quinlan (Orson Welles) to Miguel Vargas (Charlton Heston),* Touch of Evil

Not too long after Hank Quinlan's insinuating inquiry, Miguel Vargas will discover that he has no idea where his wife may be. "This can't be my wife's room," he tells the night clerk at the motel where he believed she was waiting, as he surveys in horror the devastated bed, the soiled lingerie. In apparent assent, the night clerk wails, "It stinks in here, it stinks"; rushing to open a window, he spots a half-smoked joint on the carpet and runs, still wailing, from the premises. Vargas, searching through his briefcase, discovers that his firearm is missing along with his spouse. Quinlan's question thus becomes Vargas's own ("Where's my wife?" he bellows, repeatedly, and in two languages, during the scenes that follow), although, lest we fail to grasp the implications of his loss, this question will alternate with another: "Where's my gun?"

To be sure, *Touch of Evil* would seem to offer narrative restitution to its despoiled protagonist; by the film's end, Vargas has repossessed both his abducted wife, Susie (Janet Leigh), and his stolen revolver. Nevertheless, starting from Stephen Heath's structuralist credo that the filmic narrative can never aspire to closure (cannot contain everything), I want to argue that it is the image, Yoshimoto's "basic" global commodity, which most fundamentally evades narrative capture and, furthermore, that the white female body constitutes the primary commodity-image of Hollywood cinema. To anyone versed in the most basic assumptions of feminist film criticism, such a claim may seem implausible, if not altogether unintelligible: after all, there are hardly any bodies—certainly, few white bodies—more fully surveilled, anatomized, and constrained than those of Hollywood's female stars. Yet in proposing that the white female body evades or exceeds her position within the terms of the narrative, I do not mean to imply that she eludes the disciplinary force of the camera's gaze (at least not in any consistent or predictable way). Rather, drawing on Heath's useful distinction, I wish to investigate and, hopefully, to elucidate, the discontinuities between the filmic and the cinematic production of white female embodiment. (Heath employs the term *filmic* to designate the continuous narrative, the story being told, and *cinematic* refers to the image-making apparatus: both the actual technology and the codes that govern its operation; the grammar of cinema that determines, for instance, the range of possibilities for lighting or framing a shot; the rules of editing; and so forth.) While classic Hollywood narrative compulsively posits white women's errancy—the story of a woman is, arguably, always the story of a woman gone astray—it also insists, with greater or lesser punitive glee, on the recontainment of feminine bodies and subjects. It is far from evident, however, that the cinematic apparatus shares classic narrative's investment in returning women to their consecrated positions: as wives, mothers, consumers, sexual trophies, domestic angels, symbols of the nation. And particularly in film noir, the cinematic seeps into the filmic narrative, lending to the operations of patriarchalized gender the frenzied tempo of a shell game.

Complicating Benedict Anderson's famous association of nationalist consciousness with print capitalism, Anne McClintock has recently insisted on the extent to which nationalism requires and relies on spectacle. "Anderson neglects the fact that print capital has, until recently, been accessible to a relatively small literate elite," McClintock writes. "Indeed, the singular power of nationalism since the late nineteenth century . . . has been its capacity to organize a sense of popular, collective unity through the management of mass national *commodity spectacle*" (374). Her analysis further underscores the centrality of women's participation, as symbols if not as agents, in the spectacular reproduction of nationalized social values. In redressing the central focus on print as the engine of nationalist self-making, McClintock considers how place-bound forms of popular culture such as team sports, military displays, and mass rallies engage in fabricating common origins and collective destiny. This vantage on the work of national spectacle brings into focus the status of classic Hollywood cinema as a nationally based industry of *transnational* commodity spectacle: where national spectacle evokes a uniform people on the fractured terrain of ethnic, racial, and class differences, as McClintock argues, Hollywood cinema evokes a normative consumer culture on the fractured terrain of empire. Borrowing from Gayatri Chakravorty Spivak's formulation (in which colonialism effects a "worlding of the world"), I suggest that Hollywood cinema emerges as the first in a series of image-technologies to effect a globalizing of the globe (Spivak, "Three Women's Texts").

Yet women and women's bodies are no less central to cinema's transnational commodity spectacle than they are to the national spectacles McClintock examines. Within nationalist discourse, as its feminist commentators have noted, women are assigned to figure the nation (rather than participate in it), to serve as a national resource and a national icon. Within Hollywood's global image culture, as I have argued in chapter 3, the circulation of white womanhood across national borders forges the circuits of consumer desire through which other American commodities will flow. Thus the gendered codes of property and propriety that govern national discourses and institutions, codes that assign women, and white women in particular, to a domestic function (as the keepers of home and hearth; as the cultivators of the inner person, of spiritual values and sentimental affiliations; as the legal dependents, if not the legal property, of fathers and husbands), yield to a very different logic as the white female body becomes a commercial film studio "property." Where the woman realizes value as private acquisition (through her removal from circulation), the value of the film star, on the contrary, derives from her ongoing circulation in the form of the commodity-image.

So when I suggest that women go missing in film noir—that the narrative fails to put them in their place—I do not mean simply that their sex is out of place, that they are missing *something*. Surely, this line of argument has been sufficiently explored within feminist film theory of the last two decades. And if the spectacle of the female body always signifies castration, Hollywood film culture is all too adept at disciplining women's lack, through its myriad fetishistic codes and conventions. Rather, the problem I seek to delineate is that the fetishized white female body does not circulate within the cinematic *medium* according to the proprietary relations set forth in the classic *narrative*. Where the narrative positions women as the objects of exchange between men, the medium proffers their image as an object of generalized exchange (for anyone with the price of a ticket or a tabloid). Where the narrative insists on the substitutive chain of oedipal desire (woman = castration = phallus, which ensures that desire can only attain to its signifier, never to its object), the medium proliferates visions of ecstatic consumption (shimmering white bodies become intimate with the commodities that surround them, caressing and caressed by the clothes, the interiors, the cars, and the other American products that fill the images of classic Hollywood cinema). Finally, where the classic narrative destines women for marriage, motherhood, and the reproduction of the nation's citizens ("a man would like to look after his own wife in his own country," Vargas righteously avers), the medium reproduces white women's commodity-image for distribution across national borders. In short, cinema as a global image technology—a technology of empire—confounds, even as it disseminates, the patriarchal nationalism of the filmic narrative. Hollywood cinema thus stands as another cultural institution, albeit one rarely considered in this light, where nationalism's incorporative agenda splits under the force of capital's expansionist drive. And where cinema is concerned, I would argue, the locus of this split is the body of white femininity.

White Aura, Film Noir

The ample scholarship on gender and film noir, and particularly the strain of feminist inquiry raised to prominence by E. Ann Kaplan's influential collection *Women in Film Noir* (1978), has tended to dwell on the undecidable politics of the femme fatale, who flouts patriarchal discipline only to succumb to it in the end, as well as on the dubious condition of noir masculinities, whose every fortification (most evident, perhaps, in the hard-boiled noir narrative) doubles as a measure of the white male protagonists' bodily and psychic susceptibility. As Kaplan observes in her introduction, the collection advances "no single position . . . on whether film noir as such is progressive or not" in its rendering of gender, although the contributors seek variously to chart the possibilities and limits of masculine domination and feminine resistance in specific films or sets of films. Sylvia Harvey identifies "the institution of family" and the "representation of romantic love relations" as the salient point of irreconcilable contradiction in noir. Where family in much of classic Hollywood cinema "serves as the mechanism whereby desire is fulfilled, or at least ideological equilibrium established," in film noir, by contrast, it "serves as the vehicle for the expression of frustration" (23). Janey Place also argues for noir's reversal of dominant codes, although this reversal proceeds not so much through the aggressive dismantling of dominant conventions that Harvey describes, as by the hyperbolic citation of established gender norms.

> In film noir we observe both the social action of myth which damns the sexual woman and all who become enmeshed by her, and a particularly potent stylistic presentation of the sexual strength of women which man fears. This operation of myth is so highly stylised and conventionalised that the final "lesson" of the myth often fades into the background and we retain the image of the erotic, strong, unrepressed (if destructive) woman. The style of these films thus overwhelms their conventional narrative content, or interacts with it to produce a remarkably potent image of woman. . . . In [A films of the 1930s, 1940s, and 1950s], it is the women who are portrayed as benefiting from their dependence on men; in film noir, it is clear that men need to control women's sexuality in order not to be destroyed by it. (Place 36)

A decade later, Mary Ann Doane recasts this argument in more sophisticated terms that trade Place's dichotomies of narrative and style for an account of visuality and signifying systems or, in other words, that shift attention from the dialectics of the filmic text, exclusively, to the operations of the cinematic apparatus. So in film noir, Doane contends,

> the lighting style implies a distortion of an originally clear and readable image and the consequent crisis of vision. Since the epistemological cornerstone of the classical text is the dictum "the image

> does not lie," film noir tends to flirt with the limits of this system, the guarantee of its readability oscillating between an image which often conceals a great deal and a voice-over which is not always entirely credible. Nonetheless, the message is quite clear—unrestrained female sexuality constitutes a danger. Not only to the male but to the system of signification itself. (103)

Doane and Place both posit a sustaining tension between the fundamentally unruly image of the femme fatale—an image that discloses either (at once) too much and too little—and the mandates of the classic narrative, then, where the potency or evasiveness of this image demands the brutal imposition of narrative restraints.

Unsurprisingly, critical attention to noir masculinities often centers, reciprocally, on the evacuated place of a heteronormative masculinity, when summoned purely or, at any rate, primarily to suppress the gender and sexual deviations so widely and multiply on display in film noir. As Frank Krutnik observes, "The conventionalised figuration of 'tough,' controlled, and unified masculinity is invoked not so much as a model of worthwhile or realistic achievement but more as a worrying mark of what precisely is lacking" (88). Or, in Richard Dyer's more subtle formulation, the "problematic" of film noir "can be observed in, on the one hand, the films' difficulty in constructing a positive image of masculinity and normality, which would constitute a direct assertion of their existence and definition, and, on the other hand, the films' use of images of what is *not* masculine and normal—i.e., that which is feminine and deviant—to mark off the parameters of the categories that they are unable actually to show" ("Resistance through Charisma" 91). In such analyses, the avatars of patriarchal power in noir reduce to the unstable effect of the gender/sexual insurgencies they are required to put down. Significantly, however, Dyer seems inclined to locate this instability on the side of the filmic (e.g., sexual triangulations in *Gilda*) or of the wider, ambient culture of cinema (e.g., Rita Hayworth's "star status") while aligning the cinematic with the regulation of the filmic freeplay—in referencing, for example, "generic conventions" or an "overarching" social grammar, which ensures that a man on the screen "already signif[ies] masculinity and normality," just as a woman "already signifies femininity and deviance" (98). For Place and, especially, for Doane, the situation appears largely reversed, in that it is rather the generic conventions and the epistemology of the visual image in noir that position the femme fatale in excess of what is iterable and known, while the filmic narrative "clearly" announces its disciplinary intentions with respect to deviant women.

The feminist scholarship on film noir has generally engaged the question of color—the "noirness" of noir—metaphorically or, as Manthia Diawara argues, in terms of formal properties, rather than of racial content.

> Formalist criticism links the epithet *noir* to the grotesque, to the sinister, and the image of women as treacherous. Women, bad guys, and detectives are in these films considered "black" by virtue of the fact that they occupy indeterminate and monstrous spaces such as whiteness traditionally reserves for blackness in our culture.... Through its focus on formalist devices, feminist criticism exposes *film noir's* attempt to paint white women "black" in order to limit or control their independent agency, their self fashioning. Marxist criticism also belongs to this first, formalist mode; it equates the *noirification* of film style and characters in the genre with pessimism and the decay of the capitalist system. (261–62)

This formalism never quite disposes of the racial content that it strives to remove, insofar as "blackness" remains a distinctly racial figure—a conjugation of the noir protagonists' often aggressive desublimations and devolutions with primitivist and orientalist motifs, so that (for instance) the dark underside of capital is troped through the quotidian brutalities of its functionaries (the dutiful and the disenchanted, alike), brutalities figured, in turn, as (an always already) racial atavism. Noting that film noir routinely "depict[s] Anglo protagonists who visit 'exotic' places like Latin America and Asia or who frequent Harlem jazz clubs, the Casbah, and Chinatown," James Naremore traces the racialized geographies of noir, insisting at once on the structuring dimension of "racist fantasy" that transforms these sites into the mise-en-scène for white peoples' sexual and moral abandon *and* on the articulations of such narrative motifs with international relations, finance capital, and the global market for American films (*More Than Night* 224). So, for example, he gauges the recurrence of Latin American locations in 1940s noir in terms of the primitivist tropologies that organize the filmic narrative and of Hollywood's material interests in neocolonial politics and economics.

> During the 1940s, noir characters visited Latin America more often than any other foreign locale, usually because they wanted to find

> relief from repression. This phenomenon was no doubt overdetermined by various geographic, political, and economic factors: California's proximity to Mexico; Hollywood's support for the Roosevelt government's "Good Neighbor" policy; the postwar topicality of stories about Nazi refugees in Argentina; the RKO-Rockefeller interests in Western Hemisphere oil fields; the general importance of Latin America as an export market; and so on. (229–30)[1]

From this perspective, one might speculate that the critics' predilection for treating noir as a racial figure rather than as a discourse on race and race relations (among other things)—a move that Diawara associates with the work of African American directors, or "*films noirs* by *noirs*"—has considerably to do with the way that the race relations at issue in film noir bear uncomfortably on the implication of U.S. film production in the continuation of colonialism's legacies (a continuation waged, henceforth, under the sign of development and free markets/globalization) (Diawara 263).

In the preceding chapter, I addressed the predominantly thematic treatment of race in cinema that foregrounds the recurrence of colonialist/racist tropes within specific narratives (films that reflect the ambient colonial ethos) but generally skirts consideration of cinema's participation in (neo)colonial formations or (what follows) the extent to which cinema reproduces race in ways specific to the organization of the medium. I argued that the extravagant whitening of the female star, through (increasingly) standardized lighting techniques that cultivate white feminine "glow" or radiance as a visual norm, ambivalently registers cinema's commodification of white female bodies and everything it implies: the creation of a commercial "traffic in white women" that breaches the logic of patriarchal exchange; the erosion of the historical protection from bodily commodification, which arguably constitutes a defining privilege of whiteness in the first place. I linked the whitening of the white female star to the soft style of cinematography, as it (re)enacts the breaching of bodily boundaries—the abstraction of the commodity-image from the singular human form—and remediates this abstraction, by countering the reduction of white embodiment to the inert, arrested condition of a consumable object. In this way, white skin is set in motion—a play of light in excess of the body's allocated form; it protects the white body from appropriation by others not because it constitutes any longer a limit that cannot be violated but because it signals the prior, delirious negation of limits and the (re)production of white embodiment as the figure of its own unceasing circulation. In this duplicitous fashion, I proposed, the allure of the white female body as commodity-image comes to rest on her ostensible immunity to the atomizing force of capital. Hollywood thereby contrives to sell what is most fundamentally unsalable: a body resistant to commodification; protection from the invasive logic of commodity culture through a sort of hyperbolic immersion in commodity flows.

Approaching film noir from within this set of assumptions, this chapter considers how the "noirification" of the femme fatale represents a "reengagement" (to adapt Doane's phrase) of radiant whiteness with the commodity form in which it circulates. In this regard, the chapter may complement Diawara's critique, by elaborating another alternative to a purely figural understanding of noir, a way to insert a "racial content" into the consideration of the cinematic medium. I argue that the femme fatale's unruly sexuality (her endlessly discussed evasions of patriarchal control) has at least as much to do with the mobility of her image within the medium as with her renegade persona in the narrative: the circulation of the commodity-image as a generally available sexual icon cannot fail but appear unruly from the narrative perspective of patriarchal discipline. It is the very distinction between the fatal female character and the shimmering commodity-image that tends to erode in film noir—or more exactly, perhaps, the icon overtakes the character, with the result that the figure of the femme fatale remains largely unexplained and inexplicable at the narrative level. The last thing of interest to film noir is anything that one might plausibly consider an aetiology of the fatal woman's pathology—the roots of her murderousness or perversity. The femme fatale behaves under the same depthless compulsion as the commodity-image travels; just as "money begets more money" and "images also bring forth more images," we might say that fatal feminine affect begets more fatal feminine affect or, in other words, that the sexual affect of the lawless noir female is self-augmenting, in the manner of capital itself (Yoshimoto 116). From this perspective, as well, I note that film noir's interest in "'exotic' places" ensures that the trajectories of its female protagonists often duplicate the trajectories of the commodity-image, so that the femme fatale character routinely traverses the same geographic terrain as American movies. While feminist readings of noir genders have generally pursued a distinct agenda from the (sometimes rather vaguely) Marxist readings of noir's "dark" views on capital, as Diawara's synopsis suggests, my argument here is that the question of capitalist abstraction should be central to any understanding of the gender/sexual politics of film noir. If film noir represents a kind of "marxist cinema manque," in Mike Davis's memorable phrase, the force of its (never quite realized) critique bears crucially on the matter of commodified sexualities in cinema—and on the irreconcilable imperatives of capital and patriarchal nationalism, to disseminate eroticized white femininity globally and to retain it as the exclusive property of (propertied) white men.

Inasmuch as the absence of interiority constitutes a defining quality of film noir's femmes fatales or, at any rate (what amounts to the same thing), the absence of an intelligible interiority—a sense, for example, of motivating desires and aversions and ambivalences beyond what is simply inferred from the plot (e.g., she desires her husband dead)—the recourse to psychoanalysis or psychoanalytic categories, so frequent in the feminist criticism of film noir, seems oddly misaligned with the material.[2] The point is not so much that these films resist such readings, as that they produce them in advance, in the form of fragmented citations, stylized invocations of what are already merely the clichés of popular psychoanalysis, as Krutnik has astutely observed (50–51). So femmes fatales may be figured at various moments as phallic, or as filled with castrating rage, or as smothering/engulfing their lovers in an oceanic darkness—but the assembly of such gestures into a consideration of the women's subjectivity (and/or the psychodynamics of their relations to the noir males) tends to cut against the grain of the women's performances—or, more exactly, to posit a performer where none may exist. Certainly, the standard feminist means to recuperate the femme fatale for a critical agenda has been to describe her struggle for control of her sexuality and her identity against the repressive agents of patriarchal order. Such a description seems sensible enough, and yet increasingly I wonder whether it is at the point of its most minimal assumptions about the status of character in the classic narrative that this sort of reading skirts the critical import of a genre that precisely neglects to produce a female protagonist over and above the image—a Phyllis Dietrichson or Elsa Bannister or Kathie Moffat or Cora Smith or Gilda, who would be more than this "essential luminosity" (Heath 140). It is at least arguable whether the interest of film noir for feminist critique lies exactly in the extent to which the white woman's commodity-image is cut loose from the fiction of identity—lies, in other words, in the very flatness of its characterizations. From this vantage, Walter Benjamin's claim that "personality" replaces "aura" in the "cult of the movie star" seems particularly contradicted by film noir, where it is rather the "spell of the personality" that is suspended for the duration of the noir feature.[3] If by "personality" we mean something like interiority-effect, the build-up on the surface of a (paradoxically transparent) emotional depth, then feminine personality tends to lapse in this genre that generally musters not the mildest interest in *who* its fatal women are—whether they are really fatal (only the most besotted lovers ever ponder this point) and why. The question that obsesses film noir is rather *where* the woman has gone and in whose company and who (or what) lays claim to her there, if only by virtue of a temporary proximity.[4]

My particular focus in this chapter is on films noirs that track these mobile women across national borders, or through racial/ethnic enclaves within the metropolitan United States, films that invariably linger on the spectatorship of the white female body by nonwhite people. If in classic Hollywood cinema it is at least possible to argue that white masculinity alone is identified with the power of the gaze, film noir routinely unsettles this alignment.[5] In *Gilda,* for instance, spectatorship is repeatedly divorced from the white male leads, Johnny (Glenn Ford) and Ballen (George Macready), who compete for possession of Gilda (Rita Hayworth). In several scenes where Gilda either performs (as Dyer points out, she is the only femme fatale who dances) or simply walks across the semipublic zone of Ballen's Buenos Aires casino, the camera pans across an anonymous and diverse assembly of male and female spectators, many of whom code as Latin or mestizo/a, rather than (Northern) European.[6] While these figures are sometimes emphatically marginal in relation to the white(r) audience members, whose expressions and bodily affect are more fully individuated, the peripheral Latin presence nevertheless decenters the white male viewer—quite literally so during Gilda's performance of "Amado Mío" (after her escape to Montevideo), where her newest lover's avid gaze claims the foreground, only to be ushered to one side of the frame by several distinctly "darker" male viewers. It matters, of course, that the affect of the backgrounded men and, by extension, the terms of their visual pleasure are less completely legible than those of the white man in the foreground—although this insufficient legibility should not automatically be taken as an index to the film's (relative) disinterest in what and how the (neo)colonial periphery perceives.

In any case, at the point of Gilda's final performance, which culminates in a lively, if abortive, striptease, the Latin spectators seize the foreground and the center—in particular, one leering enthusiast, who catches a discarded glove. The fact that he is short, middle aged, and considerably removed from the romantic ideal of the "Latin lover" only adds to the rage and revulsion with which Johnny (now married to Gilda) witnesses this moment, although it also bears emphasis that this shot does not simply reduce to Johnny's point of view, both because it is never explicitly assigned to him (we know in a general way that he is monitoring events on the casino floor, but there is no reverse shot to identify him with the camera at this specific juncture) and, more suggestively, because the condescension that saturates the disposition of the central figure does not sufficiently situate the meaning of the other onlookers' spectatorial affect, especially that of the tall woman with the dark mane, whose grinning face is visible just over the glove-catcher's shoulder. In other words, the camera plainly "sees" more than can be understood by reference to the angry derision of the dispossessed white male.

I cite *Gilda* as something of a representative instance not for its styling of Latin American spectators—as the next two sections suggest, film noir's rendering of spectatorship in non-Anglo settings merits attention precisely because it is *not* conventionalized—but simply to suggest something of the insistence with which film noir interests itself in this matter, even (especially) in the context of narratives where black and brown spectators remain largely mute and indecipherable figures. In *Out of the Past,* to take a rather different instance, Jeff Bailey (Robert Mitchum) follows Kathie Moffat (Jane Greer) to an Acapulco stunningly devoid of indigenous human life (with the exception of a lone tour guide named Pablo) or even of other tourists. But Kathie's entrance into the cantina where Jeff awaits her is backlit by the neon "Cine Pico" sign across the way, producing the odd impression that no one remains in the cantina to hail her silhouetted form in the doorway because they are all across the street, watching Jane Greer on the silver screen. *Out of the Past* thus invokes Mexican spectators in the purely spectral form of a visible absence, a tactic that is, perhaps, both more and less unsettling than *Gilda*'s, insofar as these spectators thereby also evade the ethnocentric gaze that discredits their "claim" to white womanhood. My own strategy in this chapter has been to privilege films—or, more exactly, a few specific scenes—where nonwhite spectators are neither (successfully)

In Gilda *(1946), audience members appreciate Gilda's (Rita Hayworth) performance.*

subordinated to the retributive discipline of Anglo patriarchy (whose authority, of course, remains largely intact in the narrative forms of classic cinema, including film noir) nor simply evacuated from the visual image, as in the eerily dehumanized cityscapes of Jacques Tourneur's Mexico.[7]

Seeing Stars in Chinatown: *The Lady from Shanghai*

Toward the end of *The Lady from Shanghai* (1948), Elsa Bannister (Rita Hayworth) pursues Michael O'Hara (Orson Welles) across the narrow, crowded streets and alleyways of San Francisco's Chinatown. It would be difficult, if not impossible, to summarize with any coherence the narrative chain of events that leads to this pursuit. For one thing, the film as a whole is a tissue of more or less surreal sequences strung along the thin narrative axis of a thriller, so that cause and effect (never mind psychological realism) seem only minimally in operation. But even a synopsis of the organizing conflicts would do little to contextualize the scene, which is in no sense required or motivated by the plot, except to the extent that it seizes on and amplifies a random detail: as the daughter of white Russian émigrés in

Shanghai, Elsa is fluent in "Chinese" (presumably Mandarin). Somehow, of course, O'Hara needs to move from the courthouse (where he is on trial for murder) to the funhouse (scene of the film's famous denouement in the hall of mirrors); and somewhere along the way, he must come to the realization that Elsa is in fact responsible for the murder. But there is nothing beyond the affinity of film noir for the "exotic place" to explain why O'Hara seeks refuge in a Chinatown theater (hardly the place for a fugitive white man to blend in with the crowd), or why his discovery of the murder weapon in Elsa's purse should take place to the accompaniment of a Chinese opera performance. Certainly, the sequence has received considerably less critical commentary than the final confrontation in the hall of mirrors, and the attention it has received tends to evince the formalism of which Diawara complains. Among the feminist scholarship on *The Lady from Shanghai,* E. Ann Kaplan's essay participates in the wider inclination to overlook the scene entirely, despite her abiding interest in the gendered operations of the gaze, that is, in classic cinema's assignment of visual and (hence) epistemological authority to men, as it regulates (or seeks to regulate) the possibilities and limits of spectators' identifications. Elsa's appearance in the theater, where she moves, blonde and conspicuous and still, apparently, *unseen,* among the cramped aisles of Asian male spectators, foregrounds considerations of visual authority and visibility in unexpected ways, yet the Asian spectators themselves remain largely invisible to the critical gaze. Starting from the claim that O'Hara's relation to Elsa is rooted in his longing for preoedipal union, which triggers his "forgetting of the world," Kaplan explores how O'Hara's idealizing gaze, and the fetishizing gaze of the other two male competitors for Elsa—her husband, Arthur Bannister (Everett Sloane), and his associate, George Grisby (Glenn Anders)—structure the imaginary field within which both male and female spectators must take up a position (*Women and Film* 63, 67–68). But the importance of the Chinese theater and of the Asian spectators who populate it lies precisely in the invocation, however ambivalent and elliptical, of radically other ways of seeing and, more particularly, ways of (not) seeing Elsa and (or) Hayworth, as she moves across the canvas of theater screens in Shanghai, Singapore, Manila, or the downtown movie houses that border San Francisco's Chinatown itself. This alternative economy of vision remains similarly unremarked in Lucy Fischer's discussion of the film, which does pause over the Chinatown sequence. For Fischer, however, Elsa's knowledge of Chinese suggests Simone de Beauvoir's claim that woman's "language is never understood," and the theater figures only as the setting for O'Hara's discovery of the "phallic" pistol in the "womblike" enclosure of Elsa's purse (44). In this reading, then, Chinatown becomes an externalized index to "woman's" enigma, a phantasmic place outside the boundaries of symbolic order or of historical time.

More plausibly, one might argue that the shadowy space of Welles's Chinatown has "lost its homogeneity, that is, the principle of its metric relations or the connection of its own parts," to borrow from Gilles Deleuze's description of the deterritorializing effects of shadow within expressionist genres more generally (109). In the confusion of the indistinguishably dim and crowded streets, for instance, it is nearly impossible to gauge Elsa's distance or proximity to O'Hara until she suddenly closes in; the sequence specifies her position in relation to his only once, by reference to a single, and primarily *aural*, marker, the neon sign of the "Shanghai Low" (easy enough to miss amid the welter of signs in the twilight) and the accompanying jazz riff that intrudes into the symphonic score. Still, Chinatown remains plainly territorialized by the flows of national and multinational capital across its boundaries. Thus the very existence of a jazz club in Chinatown signals the importance of tourism for the (prematurely) postindustrial economy of the ethnic enclave that constitutes itself as an entertainment district for a cosmopolitan bourgeoisie. Similarly, the appearance of Elsa's former "servant"-turned-gangster, Lee, whom she summons to remove O'Hara from the theater, gestures toward Chinatown's status as a switching point in the illicit transfer of people, commodities, and capital between China, Hong Kong, and the United States. Elsa's phone call to Lee is put through by Asian switchboard operators—the film cuts briefly from Elsa's face to the young female operators, while the sound of spoken "Chinese" (is it the operators themselves we are hearing, or the callers?) erupts into the soundtrack—in another detail that points up Chinatown's incorporation into national and international communications networks.

So Chinatown manifests in the film neither as the prehistory of the oedipalized Western subject nor as "the pure locus of the possible" that preoccupies Deleuze, but as a differentiated place within an unevenly integrated global space. From this perspective, it becomes harder to imagine how Elsa's circulation across this place and this space could entirely avoid reference to Hayworth's parallel movements. At any rate, *The Lady from Shanghai* produces Elsa as a trope for Hayworth, not only by eliding the protagonist with the image, as do so many film noirs, but by insisting on the domestication of Elsa/Hayworth's radiant white body at the aural/linguistic level. However unlikely Elsa's apparent fluency in Mandarin (in the colonial society of Russian and European émigrés in pre-1949 China, the upbringing of children was aggressively Eurocentric and did not, as a rule, involve facility in the language of "servants"), the American film star is always fluent in the local language, whether because the film is dubbed, or subtitled, or the local audience supplies its own dialogue, by talking over the incomprehensible English words. The terms on which Elsa presents to the Asian population on the streets of Chinatown, at once aurally Chinese and visually white/American, narratively remark the workings of a medium in which images circulate globally while sounds are more thoroughly and intractably localized. Discussions of the gaze that center entirely on the idealizing and fetishizing proclivities of the white male protagonists overlook therefore the wider apprehensions about "possession" of the too-freely-circulating white woman that register in Elsa/Hayworth's contact with the passersby and theatergoers in Chinatown.

In one sense, of course, their studied indifference to Elsa/Hayworth's presence palliates concerns over the global mediation of

Gilda (Rita Hayworth) searches out Michael O'Hara (Orson Welles) in a Chinatown theater in The Lady from Shanghai *(1948).*

femininity, by asserting that there is no such thing as Asian male (and female) spectators—or, rather, by fantasizing that these viewers are so completely sutured to the privileged position of white masculinity within U.S. cinema as to understand and perform their own exclusion from the gaze. This disavowal lines up well with the stereotype of Asian impassivity that particularly informs the disposition of the Asian men in the theater: quite unlike Hayworth's feral admirer in *Gilda,* disqualified for possession of Gilda by virtue of his all-too-explicit intentions (in this instance, the sign of "race" *is* expressivity), the Asian men in the theater are ciphers. Yet this absence of affect cuts (at least) two ways, at once affirming and suspending the ethnocentric delusion that nothing is really inscrutable to the (lens of) Euro-America's cosmopolitan elite. Rather than the specific achievement of Welles's Chinatown sequence, one could argue that this ambivalence inheres in the stereotype itself, which represents both a claim to knowledge (the Asian is illegible because irrational, so that the condition of illegibility becomes the only, the sufficient thing to know about him) and a profession of its limits (insofar as the Asian is illegible, we can know nothing of him). In any case, *The Lady from Shanghai* exacerbates this undecidability, especially in the way that

the theatergoers' blank responses to the blonde star in their midst is continuous with their blank responses to the opera performance, of which, however, it cannot (or not as easily) be said that they have no interest in the matter. In the end, and quite apart from any effects the staging and direction may have sought to cultivate, the camera renders less a disciplined vision of spectators' adherence to the right order of things, where white women remain off-limits to Asian men, than a visual fragment of another world, where Asian spectators' investments in radiant white women (as in so many things) are off-limits to Hollywood's imperialist gaze. The unsettling insight is that the apparatus of Hollywood cinema does not necessarily constitute the terms of Elsa/Hayworth's contact with the third world, where spectators are positioned in advance by an alien gaze—by other regimes of seeing and being seen—that interact unpredictably (where they interact at all) with the much-studied ways that the classic Hollywood product hails its audience.

The End of Stardom: *Touch of Evil*

A decade later, Welles's *Touch of Evil* (1958) again explores the limits of this hail and the wider consequences of the split imperative (to circulate white femininity and to prohibit its circulation) that narrative and apparatus both aspire to manage, albeit by incommensurate and often contradictory means. If film noir's ambiguous critiques of capital extend to the commodification of white femininity, so that in a general way promiscuous womanhood signifies the "promiscuity" of the commodity-image, *Touch of Evil* verges (without fully arriving) on a more-developed critique, by making the contact between the radiant white woman and the Mexican (American)s who confront this image explicitly hostile *and* central to the narrative. Along the way, *Touch of Evil* tallies, with unmerciful insistence, the psychoses of white femininity's white male keepers.

Set in the town of Los Robles, on the U.S.-Mexico border, a town whose geography is organized by the flow of commodities, legal and illegal, across the border that divides it, the film parades a set of protagonists whose involvement in the circuits of commodity exchange obsesses and depletes them. The narrative pits Miguel Vargas, a high-ranking Mexican narcotics investigator from Mexico City, against Hank Quinlan, police captain and thirty-year veteran of the force on the U.S. side of the border. Inexplicably passing through Los Robles on his honeymoon with his new American wife, Vargas suspends this romantic interlude when the car of a wealthy strip-mine owner explodes just after crossing back into the United States. Because the dynamite was planted in Mexico, Vargas intervenes to forestall an "international incident," while Quinlan also claims jurisdiction, based on the explosion's location. As Stephen Heath observes, the explosion interrupts Miguel and Susie's kiss, and it is not until the film's closing moments that the kiss will finally be consummated. The narrative itself turns on a series of subplots and subterfuges that place Susie farther and farther out of Miguel's husbandly reach. Insofar as Susie merely submits to these schemes, it is true that she stays situated on the side of the good wife rather than the fatal woman who plots her own dislocations. Yet the character remains so thin and the icon so thoroughly saturated with sexual affect, if not precisely of the lethal variety (the try-and-fuck-me allure of the classic femme fatale replaced by the flat-out fuck-me of the centerfold), as to make the matter of "Susie's" intentions largely irrelevant to the significance of her removal (the film has little interest, for example, in whether she subconsciously desires this emancipation from Miguel's proprietary embrace). In *Touch of Evil,* Susie's movements into increasingly "dark" zones have little to do with Susie herself, except insofar as the image inevitably circulates; rather, the narrative frames her abduction as the wages of her husband's irrepressibly smug and benevolent liberalism. Secure in his command of his domestic and national borders, in a hegemonic exercise of power that obviates the need for more coercive tactics, Vargas indulges in a marriage to a woman from the other side, and in a sentimental celebration of the (allegedly) "open" border (spoken, not incidentally, as he surveys the national boundary lines from the sprawling front seat of his American convertible). "One of the longest borders in the world is right here between your country and mine," he tells Susie. "Open border. Fourteen hundred miles without a single machine gun. I suppose that all sounds very corny to you."

Susie's reply—"I love being corny if only my husband would cooperate"—coyly translates Vargas's contemplative fantasy of free passage across inviolable national borders into a story of sexual possession (of intimate access to the female body). In one sense, at least, Quinlan could not agree more, since for him the border manifests precisely as the ever-present threat of getting screwed—or rather (what amounts to the same) of your wife getting screwed. Quinlan and his cohorts imply that the motive for Quinlan's fascist style of law enforcement is the rape and murder of his wife by "a half-breed Mexican," although, as the narrative at various junctures insinuates, this perpetrator is most likely fictitious and Quinlan himself the murderer. However, in the world over which Quinlan presides, to murder your wife so as to prevent some half-breed Mexican from raping her is fundamentally the same thing as having her raped and murdered by a half-breed Mexican—a logic underscored by Quinlan's apparently unerring ability to identify the guilty even, indeed especially, when any evidence of their guilt is missing. Repeatedly, we are reminded that Quinlan's crime solving consists of planting the evidence that allows him to arrest the suspects—but these same suspects, in confessing, reveal the intimate knowledge of the crime that only the perpetrator would possess, thereby validating Quinlan's famous "hunches." While Vargas domesticates difference because he presumes the border secure, well able to tolerate the flow of goods and people and sentiments while still distinguishing, absolutely, between interior and exterior domains, for Quinlan, conversely, the border, by definition, is besieged. Through the figure of Quinlan, Welles advances a rather brilliant analysis of fascism's hermeneutic, in which the distinction between real and imagined transgression collapses—in which the transgression has already occurred at the point where the law imagines it.

Vargas and Quinlan thus present as the two faces of a coin: Vargas, who cannot envision any abridgment of his property rights—his ability to look after his own wife in his own country; Quinlan, who can envision nothing else. Appropriately, then, Quinlan's plot against Vargas will require Vargas to *imagine* his wife's forced participation in what another detective later terms a "mixed party," a scene of drug use and sexual debauchery—a device through which Quinlan also hopes to frame Vargas himself as an addict. Quinlan's signature "touch" is legible in the fact that the mixed party never actually occurs but is staged through creating a trail of apparently decisive evidence. Yet in its very inauthenticity—in the perplexing narrative evocation of an event that both has and has not "really" transpired—the scene of Susie's abduction makes the most decisive narrative reference to the "abduction" of the commodity-image by black and brown spectators, unevenly receptive to the terms of its hail.

The strangeness of the scene—the tension that positions me somewhere on the cusp of laughter and revulsion—lies in its indeterminacy: are we seeing how the Mexican gangsters invade Susie's room and overpower her so as to simulate her violation, or are we witnessing the act of violation itself? Nothing and everything happens: the gang members surround the motel room, and their frozen faces, suddenly suspended in the window frames, appall Susie, who retreats to the middle of the floor. Someone manipulates the door and they file in, encircling the bed on which the wide-eyed, luminous Susie now lies. In a scant few lines of dialogue, the gang leader, Pancho, dismisses the women, who insist on staying. He instructs the others to "hold her legs," and the pack closes in, seizing Susie and lifting her off the bed. Prior to that culminating shot, when the last distance between Susie and the gang members is breached, the episode sustains its hypnotic choreography; we see them circling, approaching, circling some more. There is no incentive to speed (they are alone with Susie, the lone occupant of this desert motel), and the gang members saunter, hands in pockets—an inexorable slowness intensified by contrast to the swinging rhythms of the radio piped in from the front office (in the final moments of the encounter, the night clerk, deaf to Susie's earlier pleas for quiet, finally switches off the music, plunging the room into a now-audible silence). The gang members' aggression, then, consists primarily in deferring the point of physical contact and dwelling in the moment of visual intimacy. One of the very few fragments of dialogue in this scene concerns, appropriately, the pursuit of visual pleasure: when Pancho asks the women to leave, one of them (Mercedes McCambridge) replies simply: "No. Let me stay. I wanna watch." Finally, we stand witness less to a spectacular violation (a gang assault on Susie) than an act of violent spectatorship that assails the image of radiant femininity, by reversing the anticipated disposition of bodies and affects in the movie theater. Rather than the spectators fascinated by the shimmering white woman, here we see the shimmering white woman framed and transfixed by a circle of Latino/a bodies. And in this hallucinatory episode of spectatorship in the borderlands, mobility is on the side of the viewers, rather than the image. Here it is the spectators who traverse *and* sustain the distance to the curiously unmoving image of vulnerable white womanhood—unmoving in the double sense of stationary (each successive image of the lovely, supplicating Susie is too exactly like the one that preceded it; the flow of the medium appears halted in and around this suddenly intractable body) and lacking affective power, which is quite literally eclipsed by her captors: with the key light emanating from a point directly in front of and slightly above Susie, and a virtual absence of fill, the bodies of the circling gang members interrupt the source, throwing Susie's radiance first into partial shadow and then into unrelieved blackness (exactly as occurs in a theater, when a body is interposed between the projector and the screen).[8] In this scene, the contest between Vargas and Quinlan over the American wife (the implication is that Quinlan resents Vargas all the more for his claim on an American woman) transforms into a struggle over the effects and the reception of the commodity-image.

On one level, of course, the Mexican gang simply enacts Quinlan's plot by confronting Vargas with the evidence of his dispossession, the proof that the border cannot hold, that domestic interiority is leaky and contaminated. The gang's abduction of his wife realizes Vargas's undreamt bad dream, and the wickedness of Quinlan's lesson lies as much in his choice of agents as in the plot itself—from Quinlan's perspective, at any rate, Vargas is indistinguishable from Susie's abductors, all of them, that is, Mexicans "in possession" of a white woman. By contrast, the narrative invests in that distinction, although it also fails to sustain its investment. Thus Vargas's "Mexicanness" serves as a kind of alibi, a means to a consolationist vision

Susie Vargas (Janet Leigh) in Touch of Evil *(1958).*

of "cross-racial" sexuality that stands over and against the gang members' illicit claims on Susie—one in which Mexican men, or at any rate bourgeois Mexicans, look and act precisely as do their American counterparts; in which "Vargas" is none other than that iconic figure of patrician American masculinity, Charlton Heston, whose passionate embrace of Janet Leigh, in the film's closing moments, serves as the narrative sign of Susie's reclamation rather than as a further spectacle of miscegenated relations. At the same time, Heston's dubious incarnation as Latino does not pass unremarked, and Quinlan's trenchant reference to Vargas's appearance shortly after Vargas introduces him to Susie—"Funny. She don't look Mexican neither"—suggests the extent to which the narrative empowers Quinlan to run down its liberal palliatives. The fiction of the "good" Mexican husband stands as a disintegrating bulwark against the American viewer's implication in Quinlan's world of "half-breed" Mexican rapists assaulting American women—which is to say, our implication in a national and thoroughly institutionalized vision of the border.

For Naremore, the scene in the motel, populated by the stereotypes of Anglo-America's "racist and sado-masochistic imagination," represents a profoundly disquieting if ironized rendering of the rape fantasy that underwrites both the repressive apparatus of "respectable" marriage and the vicious tactics of Quinlan's border patrol. Noting how the "succession of hideous, glassy-eyed faces" are perceived from Susie's point of view, Naremore suggests that the audience is sutured to the position of the victim, and in this regard, he goes on to observe,

> Welles is taking one of his most considerable risks, because despite the fact that the film is made with a progressive attitude, it violates the decorum of nearly all the liberal thesis films of the late fifties. It forces us, through action with a hallucinatory power that almost parodies Griffith to imagine a white woman being raped by a Mexican thug. Indeed the fish-eye close-up of "Pancho," who gazes into the camera and flicks his tongue like a serpent, has a strong though probably unconscious resemblance to the close-ups of Battling Burroughs and Chen Huan in *Broken Blossoms:* in both cases the aggressive male looks directly into the lens, his features distorted wildly; in both cases we cut to a fearful, golden-haired girl who cringes on a bed. (*The Magic World of Orson Welles* 164–65)

One can hardly dispute that Pancho's gesture invokes a prospect of Susie's rape (another gang member suggestively licks his lips) or that this invocation depends on the broader citation of cinema's primal scenes (Griffith among others). But Naremore's account assigns a controlling coherence to a fantasy that the episode in the motel room cites in discontinuous and fragmentary form, a fantasy that markedly fails to domesticate everything that does (not) happen there. I suggest that the close-up of Pancho's stony expression is rendered less, rather than more, transparent by his flick of the tongue, a gesture that constitutes as much a refusal to disclose—throws the viewer back onto his or her own assumptions—as a compelling index to Pancho's desires and intentions. At the very least, it remains ambiguous whether this flick of the tongue signals an intention to rape or Pancho's taunting and derisive allusion to Susie's (and the viewers') expectation of rape. To paraphrase Heath, we might say that the stereotype

Gang leader Pancho (Valentin de Vargas) in Touch of Evil.

"cannot contain everything" and that something of what it can neither encompass nor expel is written across the expression of these "Mexican thugs" in the form of superfluous (from the vantage of the stereotype) and largely unintelligible affect.

Touch of Evil absorbs the viewer in the compulsive quality of Quinlan's racism—in his endlessly repetitive invocation and mastery of the chaotic forces that menace patriarchal nationalism. Yet the scene in the motel room, although staged at Quinlan's behest, registers not the already countered insurgency that Quinlan invokes but the subjects and the prospects against which his very terrors defend. The rape fantasy is the fascist's consolation, in other words, and what *this* fantasy disavows becomes most starkly apparent at the point where the woman declares her desire to watch.

The woman's self-identification as "watcher" not only underscores Susie's status as spectacle but also reminds us that the positions available to the spectators of radiant femininity are never securely anticipated in the syntax of the commodity-image. Understood within the framework of the stereotype, of course, the woman's desire to watch reads as the doubling and displacement of a sanctioned prerogative on the part of a monstrous interloper (the female voyeur). Yet this long moment of contact between Latina and Latino spectators and the commodity-image of white womanhood blocks the narrative's aspiration to closure (to recuperating sexual and national borders) precisely insofar as the gang members' look does not represent a doubling and usurpation of established positions that Hollywood

"I wanna watch": Mercedes McCambridge as an unnamed gang member in Touch of Evil.

cinema would reserve for a different race and a different class of viewers. The woman wants to watch—her eyes glitter with anticipation and her lips are wet. But we know nothing of what she sees lying prostrate on the bed, or of her pleasure in seeing it, only that the aura of whiteness has been extinguished (the light gone out). What draws and captivates her look, in other words, is a body (perhaps), a constellation of affects and effects, that constitutes the blank (blackened) part of the commodity-image.

If images necessarily beget more images, as Yoshimoto observes, so that in I-M-I (Yoshimoto's formula for the circulation of commodity-images) the difference between the beginning and end points of the cycle is purely quantitative (the image is never consumed or removed from circulation), the motel room encounter in *Touch of Evil* suggests the ways in which the difference remains also, potentially qualitative: at the juncture where cinema's mediations articulate with other regimes of vision—other assemblages of reality—what one image begets may be an image of its own violent cancellation.[9] From this vantage, the gang's assault on Susie represents not (or, not only) an invocation of racist fantasy—a sensational representation of a white woman "taken" by brown men and women—but the suspension of our own, familiar phantasms in the face of viewers whose perceptions of the cinematic image mark the limit of anything the camera can record. (If the camera sees blindly, as Steven Shaviro reminds us, it does not see everything; the mechanically reproduced image is not an archive of everything that derives from it nor of all the ways it offers to perception.) In this regard, these allegorical spectators foil Quinlan's assumptions no less than Vargas's, since the entire premise of Quinlan's law enforcement is that he knows what is coming, what has already slipped across the line *and* that he knows (he can intuit) what it wants. But Quinlan's "hunches" are correct only insofar as they operate preemptively to efface rather than to expose the insurgent subjects that mobilize along the border—which is the reason there is no distinction between Quinlan and his perpetrators, and the terror of the presumed transgression is of a piece with the terror of its containment. The scene of Susie's abduction, however, lays waste to the consoling fiction of this congruence, and the knowledge of the other it implies.

The terrain of the desolate motel where this scene transpires is presided over by the night clerk (Dennis Weaver), who accompanies Vargas on the inspection of his wife's ravaged room—and it is he who offers the film's only apparent alternative to Vargas's liberal disavowals and Quinlan's fascist ravings. At the point where the inside is turned outside, where the border patrol—like the filmic narrative—is outflanked by the expansionist imperatives of the very system it is pledged to defend, we find a curious breed of American male. At once in perpetual motion (his body quivers, jerks, seizes, dances) and perpetual arrest (he hovers on the border—the reception desk, the window sill, the threshold—seemingly loathe either to cross over or to retreat), the night clerk functions in a spatial and temporal mode of accelerated standstill. Appearing in the doorway with Susie's bed linens, he rears back, wide-eyed and terrified at the sight of her (in a posture oddly evocative of Susie's wide-eyed dismay at the invading gang). His visible recoil suggests at once a panicked recognition of her draw (he seems to anticipate his own abjection before the sensational power of this image) *and* his apprehension that mere proximity will implicate him in the (attempted) possession of something that does not belong to him. The night clerk's body and bodily affect thus register a crisis in the property relations of white masculinity: he stands dispossessed *by* white womanhood (rendered passive before the image) and *of* it, as well (he is not the white woman's keeper). At a minimum, the night clerk appears viscerally to fathom what Vargas refuses to acknowledge and Quinlan refuses to concede—that the border traverses and unsettles white men's claims; that the borderlands are everywhere (there is no possible flight to the interior). By

The night clerk (Dennis Weaver) in Touch of Evil.

turns frozen and frenzied, as though attuned to the vibrations of the ground beneath him, the night clerk alone, among the film's white male protagonists, seems to know exactly where he stands.

"More Than Most People, Even": A Coda on *Fargo*

The figure of the night clerk appears in retrospect as a salient anticipation of what becomes in contemporary neo-noir a significant modality of white masculinity. It would be flippant, but probably not wrong, to suggest that his descendants include virtually every character played by the actor Steve Buscemi or, more accurately, that the currency of Buscemi has everything to do with his aptitude for performing twitchy white men. The twitchy masculinity so richly on display in 1990s noir is a (mildly) attenuated variation on Weaver's clerk, a more-mannered loss of motor control that similarly registers the unsettling implications of the commodity-image for white men's property interest in whiteness. In tracing these implications, I mean neither to contest that enormous power and privilege remains concentrated in the hands of a white male elite nor to question that white skin continues to confer substantial legal and economic benefits on ordinary white people. Yet the circulation of whiteness in the form of the commodity-image during the past century, more or less, has eroded the *exclusive* or proper relation between white persons and whiteness. In this chapter as in "Hollywood's Hot Voodoo," I have sought to define and elucidate cinema's significance as the first medium in which whiteness (white embodiment) circulates independently of white persons—in which (to invoke Benjamin's figure once more) whiteness is "pried" from the "shell" of white bodies, extracted through mechanical reproduction. These chapters have considered the particular forms of gender trouble that ensue from the global traffic in white femininity as commodity-image, troubles compensated (perhaps) by the function of the radiant Hollywood icon in disseminating American consumer culture as the vision of modernity achieved. Contemporary neo-noir asks insistently after the consequences of this vexed triumph for nonelite white men—white men in the position of having to stake their claims to privilege (to produce their whiteness). But how to stake these claims when the gestures that served their fathers and grandfathers seem increasingly indecisive: when neither possession of white women nor other forms of consumer accumulation can establish their proper relation to white racial privilege?

Joel and Ethan Coen's 1996 neo-noir *Fargo* functions as an ethnography of middle America in which the protagonists' whiteness is constituted as ethnicity, as a henceforth particularized cultural identity—marked in their upper-midwestern (Minnesotan/Dakotan) Scandinavian-inflected speech, but also through the film's broader conversion of white-bread blandness into fascinating quirkiness. The metropolitan center is thus revisioned on the model of the colonial periphery, replete with quaint natives, going about their curious business. In *Fargo,* the whiteness of white people can be represented only as an oddity—a point on which the film is quite explicit in one memorable scene where the police investigator, Marge (Frances McDormand), interviews two astonishingly wholesome prostitutes. Asked to describe two johns now suspects in a murder, the women are completely unable to identify a single distinguishing feature, apart from remarking that one was big, one little (and the little one circumcised), until at last one of the women volunteers that the little one was "funny-looking—more than most people, even." Inasmuch as the standard, minimal description of criminal suspects (in which any viewer of American television is programmed) specifies size and race (e.g., suspect is a white male, 5′10″, 180 pounds), the woman's reference to the little man's more than usual funniness stands in for the racial identification that one might minimally expect her to produce. Because Carl Showalter (Buscemi) does not number among the natives, a difference flagged not only by his regionally unmarked speech but by his rudeness and compulsive talking, the joke is that his sur-

"More than most people, even": The girl-next-door prostitutes (Larissa Kokernot and Melissa Peterman) in Fargo *(1995).*

plus funniness derives from his more-cosmopolitan urbanity—here defined as yet another ethnic inflection of white particularity.

Yet in *Fargo*, the night clerk's nearest kin is neither the jittery and permanently dislocated Showalter (visually conjugated with parking structures, motels, and stretches of featureless, snow-covered terrain) nor the equally twitchy Jerry Lundegaard (William H. Macy), who hires Showalter and his associate to kidnap his wife (in a twisted scheme to convert a wife whose inherited wealth he cannot touch into a means of capital accumulation), but an ephemeral and quite marginal protagonist, Marge's old high-school acquaintance, Mike Yanagita (Steve Park). When the investigation of a murder takes Marge to Minneapolis, Mike's unexpected call leads to a drink in a hotel bar—"It's a Radisson," Mike comments, "so you know it's pretty good." It is not only his consummate consumerism—his faith in the quality of the brand names that signal a globalized Americanism—but his language (unlike Showalter, Mike is evidently a native) that render him aurally white, "funny" as most people in the film ("you're a super lady," he compliments Marge). The point of this meeting turns out to be Mike's excruciatingly twitchy move on Marge—closing in on her, he perches, ready to spring back; his arm edges around her, scrupulously avoiding contact—which he justifies when repelled by divulging a pathetic story of his marriage to his high-school sweetheart, Linda, and her subsequent death from cancer. He ends by

Mike Yamagita (Steve Park) in Fargo.

professing his loneliness, bursting into tears that threaten at every point to transform into some other register of convulsive affect.

Yet following this exchange, from which Marge hastily retreats, she learns that Linda, alive and well, was never involved with Yamagita, who (in the words of another old classmate) has been "having troubles." The question raised by this narrative tangent, then, is whether the Asian man's psychosis implicitly reinforces white men's proper claim on whiteness, by suggesting that an Asian's full assumption of whiteness is impossible (that he unravels under the weight of becoming what he is not) or whether, on the contrary, Mike's psychosis—his hallucinatory claim on white womanhood, for example—is precisely the sign of his successful assimilation to white masculinity. Insofar as *Fargo* upholds this second reading, it marks the extent to which film noir's enervated male protagonists—for both Krutnik and Dyer, the signs and symptoms of a strangely unrepresented and unrepresentable masculine norm—have become normative for the performance of heterosexual masculinity among the eroding middle and lower-middle classes.

Chapter 6

Fast Capitalism and Consumer Ordeals

Capitalism today quickens the pace at which significance diminishes away from text and moves toward things themselves.
—*Ben Agger,* Fast Capitalism

HOMER: You're selling what, now?
APU: Only the concept of karmic realignment.
HOMER: You can't sell that. Karma can only be portioned out by the cosmos.
APU: He's got me there.
—The Simpsons

Broadly sketched, this chapter is concerned with the status of white embodiment in a regime of flexible accumulation, where the speed at which capital overtakes corporeal identity would seem to erode quite a few of the protections that accrue to this racial classification historically and juridically. If classic Hollywood cinema is the first mass medium to overtake the white body and abstract it *as commodity,* it does so, as I have argued, through grammatical maneuvers that function to intensify rather than eliminate the aura of white skin: whiteness as global commodity-image appears as a form of embodiment immune to the abstractions of the marketplace through which it circulates. The white body in Hollywood cinema is always profoundly intimate with the world of U.S. commodities that envelops and caresses it, an intimacy made possible by its apparent ability to remain undiminished and intact even at the point of its insertion into commercial circuits through which subjects and bodies move only in pieces. But as we move from classic cinema, Fordism, mass consumption, and the rise of "Americanism" as a global force to television (and other small-screen media), mobile capital, niche marketing, and the quotidian contestations and refunctioning of "Americanism" in every quadrant of the globe, what becomes of this aura?

Although the white body is still cast within the media and genres of commodity culture as sustaining a privileged relation to the commodity, the quality of that intimacy has been altered. If the proliferation of media and media styles means that there is no longer a singular, dominant grammar of white embodiment within contemporary image culture, I would nonetheless risk a vast generalization and propose that the commodities that accompany and order the appearance of black and brown bodies on the screen are typically markers of ethnic style, while white bodies (in a prerogative established by the classic Hollywood texts) move through a field of commodities that seem to compete for their attention—to be handled, inclined to, gazed on, or in some way, however fleetingly, consumed. At the same time, the white body's immunity expires, so that the distinction between white bodies and enticing commodities breaks down—in other words, the visual grammar of white embodiment no longer guarantees this body's difference from the commodities that beckon to it. This breakdown is all the more palpable in the context of animation, a medium in which bodily aura is categorically impossible to effect. In some sense, therefore, my focus on *The Simpsons* dodges the question this chapter purports to engage, since the animated body as depthless, bounded figure necessarily forgoes the luminosity of the star. Yet in potent ways, this animated series brings to view a newer, at least partially inchoate bodily grammar, at the boundary where racial prerogatives are both maintained and eroded. As the aura of whiteness suffuses and absorbs the world of commodities in classic Hollywood cinema, in *The Simpsons,* it is the world of commodities that repeatedly seizes and prostrates white consumers, in an (ambiguously) critical reworking of consumption as trauma.

Karmic Realignment

Among the many cultural products I might propose to read, and certainly of anything I might select from the bill of contemporary television fare, the Fox Television Network's long-running animated series *The Simpsons* heralds itself with unusual vigor and consistency as a critically self-reflexive commodity. To borrow Ben Agger's useful distinction, the series *as a text* is centrally concerned with the forms, pleasures, and mind-zapping effects of the late-twentieth-century commodity culture in which the series *as a thing* is so thoroughly implicated. For Agger, admittedly, it is the failure of text and thing to remain distinct that characterizes accelerated, or "fast," capitalism, of the present moment. Under fast capitalism, "textuality, [understood as] a possible medium of critical resistance, fails to stand apart," so that texts become things, "provoking their thoughtlessly ready readings," just as things become the bearers of an already prescripted text for the world (Agger 5). If *The Simpsons* as commodity-image are paradigmatic of Agger's thing-texts, things through which circulate an increasingly circumscribed repertoire of cultural meanings, then I would argue that it is the aspiration of *The Simpsons* to make its very conscription a critical resource. In its continuous, satiric representation of corporate ethics and advertising, of the franchised suburban landscape, and of television, its representation, in short, of the "degradation of significance" in which the series itself participates (6), *The Simpsons* appears committed to assuming the intellectual's function, proffering a noniterative version (text) of its own conditions of possibility.[1]

In addressing *The Simpsons*'s self-scrutiny, I am drawn to an episode from the 1994–95 season titled "Homer and Apu," which thematizes the deterritorialized operations of multi- and transnational capital and thus resonates directly with the circumstances of *The Simpsons*'s overseas production. The episode centers on the otherwise marginal figure of the South Asian convenience store clerk, Apu, who is fired from the Kwik-E-Mart after selling tainted food products to Homer. Desperate to be reinstated, Apu undertakes a pilgrimage to Kwik-E-Mart corporate headquarters, which are located, as it turns out, on a remote mountaintop in India.[2] This representation of transnational enterprise thus furnishes a potentially retextualized frame in which the series might reflect on its own producer's practice of outsourcing animation, though only the most dedicated viewer is likely to have gleaned from the series' accelerated closing credits the notable fact of its transpacific origins. The speed at which the production credits flash by degrades the meaning of this textualized thing in the most material sense, of course, rendering nearly illegible the inscription of the commodity's relation to embodied labor. As industry sources divulge, however, Film Roman subcontracts the labor-intensive aspects of production on the series, including the drawing and coloring of cels, to one of six "animation houses" in South Korea.[3] According to studio owner Phil Roman, underpriced Asian labor has become indispensable to the animation industry in the United States: "If we had to do animation here," Roman notes, "it would cost a million dollars instead of $100,000 to $150,000 to produce a half-hour, and nobody could afford to do it except for Disney" (quoted in Edelstein 38).

Inderpal Grewal and Caren Kaplan have proposed understanding transnationalism as marking both the emergent organization of capital accumulation and a field of potential resistance to the new modalities of neocolonial domination that sustain this emerging order. The advantage of transnationalism as a model for globalization under late capitalism, they argue, lies in its capacity to query the geopolitical binaries that stand as the apparent legacy of colonialist world making: "We use the term 'transnational,'" they write, "to problematize a purely locational politics of global-local or center-periphery in favor of what [Armand] Mattelart sees as the lines cutting across them" (11). Imagined in this way, transnationalism formulates a decisive challenge to the reductive concept of "a homogenizing West" that saturates the globe with capital and commodities, remaking its historical others in its image.[4] Certainly, one contribution of postcolonial scholarship, and particularly, I would emphasize, of subaltern studies, has been to understand how the "periphery" marks the "center," as well as the "center" the "periphery."[5] Thus, as Grewal and Kaplan remind us, the West itself must be addressed, presently and historically, as no less a hybrid zone than its (former) dependencies. Building on the proposition that cultural flows are not unidirectional, Grewal and Kaplan invite a more-nuanced interrogation of global commodity culture, one in which they ask, for example: "What aspect of a commodity gets utilized in what way and where? Can we see these commodities as artifacts? How do we trace the cultural baggage of commodities from their point of origin (if this can be ascertained)?" (11).

Tellingly, as this chapter will explore, "Homer and Apu" splits itself in relation to what we might call the two faces of Grewal and Kaplan's critical project. Although the series as a whole routinely acknowledges and occasionally investigates the diasporic presence of the formerly colonized in the metropolis, in "Homer and Apu" this hybrid look of the multicultural West finds its mirror image in the westernized look of the postmodern East, so that hybridity is transformed from an index of multidirectional flows across historical divides to the paradoxical sign of global homogeneity. Homer and Apu's transglobal journey to Kwik-E-Mart headquarters reveals everywhere the same hybridity, in other words, divested of its regional/historical specificity. More particularly, in representing India, "Homer and Apu" effects its own "karmic realignment" of historical forces, conflating transnational corporatism with cosmic awareness and the hyperreality of commodity culture with the fabled Orient's monumental time. In this sanitized vision of India as the quaintly syncretic fusion of premodern holism and postmodern simulation, the question of this nation's access to the benefits of modernity is conveniently elided. Yet this degraded (if ironic) textualization of transnational capital as the newest (and the oldest) of cosmic dispensations falls under scrutiny at precisely those moments where the episode attends to the forms and practices of consumption in the West. If Marx's famous dancing table fails to divulge the social relations that animate it, commodities on this episode of *The Simpsons* seem very nearly disposed to reveal their origins and mark their destinations, to disclose their "cultural baggage" to the baffled and traumatized shopper. Furthermore, moving against the conventional association of consumerism with middle-class women, "Homer and Apu" situates white men as the paradigmatic Western consumers. Here it is specifically the white male body that is touched and refigured by its encounter with the fruits of global capital.

Who Needs the Kwik-E-Mart?

The answer to this question, sung by Apu in a toe-tapping musical sequence, is Apu himself, whose allegiance to the Kwik-E-Mart corporation turns out to be no less defining of his identity than Apu's stereotyped Indian ethnicity. After Homer's avid consumption of Kwik-E-Mart snacks lands him in the emergency room for the third time, Apu sits disconsolately on the Simpsons' roof, gazing across the suburban treetops to the neon Kwik-E-Mart sign, and croons the final line to his melody: "Who needs the Kwik-E-Mart? I dooo..." At stake for Apu is not the underpaid service position that his neighbors view as a job of last resort but the corporate membership it confers. Kwik-E-Mart personnel flown in to handle the public relations crisis generated by Homer's salmonella poisoning ritually divest Apu of his corporate insignia, including his "Try Our Fried Pickles" badge, and solemnly insist that he hand over his pricing guns, one of which Apu attempts to conceal in an ankle holster. This satiric staging of Apu's dismissal as a kind of dishonorable military discharge implicitly redefines the economic unit of the corporation as a quasi-political unit, whose employees' connections to local and national community have been supplanted by their corporate citizenship. That Apu's relation to his neighborhood clientele is subsumed by the corporate profit motive is made laughably apparent in the episode's opening sequence, in which Apu gleefully markets 29-cent stamps for $1.85 and charges $4.20 for "two dollars' worth of gas."[6] We learn that Apu is not blind but simply indifferent to the damaging effects of corporate greed on the community he supposedly serves after his dismissal, when he attempts to take his own life by ingesting a Kwik-E-Mart hot dog. His menial functions notwithstanding, Apu thus becomes representative of what Masao Miyoshi defines as an emergent transnational managerial class, culled from various nationalities and ethnicities, whose corporate loyalties displace both local and national affiliations (741).

In an initial attempt to redeem his disgrace by rededicating himself to Homer's well-being, Apu briefly labors in the Simpson household as cook, gardener, manservant, and purveyor of an enlivening and exoticized ethnicity, offered up in the form of yoga, spicy food, and the sounds of the shenai. Yet, as the melancholy Apu quickly deciphers, this overtly colonial arrangement is a poor substitute for what the episode represents by contrast as the ecstatic shopping mall multiculturalism of the transnational corporation. Apu thus resolves to petition in person for his reinstatement and purchases a pair of plane tickets for himself and Homer, who has grown attached to his domestic and insists on sharing his pilgrimage to the distant corporate offices. Briefly harassed by chanting evangelists at the airport ("Oh great, Christians!" grumbles a saffron-clad Hare Krishna with shaved head and topknot, as he pushes past them), Homer and Apu tread their way through several filmic clichés, including the train scene from *Gandhi* (the passengers ride on the outside of the car) and a desert caravan sequence, complete with romantic orchestral score, lifted straight from *Lawrence of Arabia*.

This brief transit through Hollywood's "big" pictures concluded, the duo enters the zone of generic citations: the travelogue, the mountain-climbing epic, the "lost world" romance. Standing at the base of a snow-covered mountain, Apu gestures skyward toward a modest wooden temple perched near the summit and announces with evident pride: "There she is, the world's first convenience store!" Homer demurs ("This isn't very convenient"), and the pilgrims make their way up the mountain trail, through the automatic glass doors and across a large, empty hall where Muzak plays obnoxiously. As they approach the dais at the far end, Apu alerts Homer that the aim of their quest is at hand: "Here's the benevolent and enlightened president and CEO of Kwik-E-Mart and in Ohio Stop-O-Mart. He's the one I must ask for my job back." At this point, sitting in the lotus position beneath a giant poster that cautions "The Master knows all except combination to the safe," we notice a beatific old man, in a plain white tunic, noisily slurping a Kwik-E-Mart "squishy" through a straw. Having slaked his thirst (or completed his meditation ritual), he advises the visitors that they may ask three questions. "That's great because all I need is one," Apu replies, but before he can continue, Homer intercedes:

> "Are you really the head of Kwik-E-Mart?"
> "Yes."
> "Really?"
> "Yes."
> "*You?*"

"I hope this has been enlightening for you," the sage concludes the interview, cutting off Apu's several attempted appeals with a chirpy "thank you, come again." As the doors close behind them, Homer is moved to observe: "Well that was a big bust! Is he *really* the head of Kwik-E-Mart?"

The joke, of course, is that the Indian postmodern looks exactly like a Disneyland installation of India, where holy places beckon beyond automatic doors and "thank you, come again" is repackaged as the stuff of transcendental consciousness. If the (literalized) figure of the corporate guru seems to trigger Homer's suspicions about a loss of authenticity, moreover, this ungrounding of appearances is detached from historical experience to become instead the timeless message of enlightenment that the wise man would impart to Homer. But the joke is also, in its fashion, quite pernicious. At Kwik-E-Mart headquarters, the simultaneity of electronic transfer and satellite communication, and the decentralization of production that it enables, is thematized through an orientalist construction of India's indelible antiquity.

In this way, what David Harvey terms the "time-space compression" endemic to capitalist expansion figures as a return to a phantasmic land that time forgot, rather than as a timely phenomenon linked to the formation of chronically underdeveloped zones and their differential incorporation within capital's global regime. With respect to its representation of transnational corporatism, in short, the episode draws from the colonialist archive on India in order precisely to erase the history of colonialism and its legacies. Insofar as India's colonial past reduces to decontextualized cinematic allusions, "Homer and Apu" would seem to exemplify Fredric Jameson's famous dictum that we have emerged into "a new and original historical situation in which we are condemned to seek History by way of our own pop images and simulacra of that history, which itself remains forever out of reach" (25).

It's Gonna Get You, Sucka

Multi- and transnational corporations capitalize on the cheap labor, minimal environmental regulation, and underdeveloped unionism, feminism, and civil rights consciousness that are often the colonizing nation's bequest to its former territories, in a renewal and extension of (neo)colonial practice that this episode of *The Simpsons* effaces (Miyoshi 740). At the same time, in its representation of consumerism, "Homer and Apu" registers the force (if not precisely the content) of the present and historical conditions it participates in derealizing, as though the relations of production so meticulously purged from its vision of transnational enterprise might yet somehow be grasped at the site of the commodity's consumption. In an inversion of a normative Marxist critique, which rejoins the commodity to the material scene of its production and the extraction of surplus value from the laboring body, *The Simpsons* seeks to unpack this portion of the commodity's baggage on the white consumer body and the consumer psyche. Far from sustaining a proprietary relation to commodities, white consumers in *The Simpsons* are visually *and* narratively dispossessed, overtaken and assailed by these objects to which they are by no means equal. At its worst, I suggest, this traumatization surreptitiously recoups the priority and privilege of white subjects that it appears to overturn, insofar as it rescues consumers from their depthless state, elevates them (anew) from subject-effect (a node through which capital circuits) into an authorial subject, since the experience of trauma is the victim's exclusively, and he or she alone can testify to it. In this scenario, the consumer classes (professional, administrative, and service personnel with a disposable income) are made the guarantors of subaltern histories that they participate in effacing (the laborers' prostration becomes the consumers' trauma). Yet, at its best, this figuration of trauma intrudes on consumers an awareness of their implication in the organized superexploitation of labor—in the consumption not merely of dead objects but of human lives—that is irreducible to any "testimony" of which consumers themselves would be the subject. At these moments, consumers are made the repository of potent, *unassimilated* knowledges that overload their own discursive resources and speak (in) them.

"Homer and Apu" is notably self-conscious about the consolationist ruses of commodity culture, which reckons history as loss and loss as something it can compensate. In a brief scene bearing little relation to the ostensible plot, we witness Homer watching an African American comedian on TV parody the driving habits of "black guys" and "white guys." Pointedly depicting the white male subject as anxious, defensive, and lacking in style, the comedian impersonates a white male driver by hunching over the dashboard, nervously scanning the terrain ahead, while his black male counterpart eases back into the seat, casually holding the wheel in one hand. Homer laughs delightedly at this display and affirms the comic's insight: "It's true, it's true," he chortles, "we're so lame." Homer's pleasure in the recognition of white men's inadequacy is here sustained by television's commodification of black masculinity as style, which thus becomes available to the intrepid white consumer, such as Homer. White guys may be lame, but Homer is not, exactly insofar as he can appreciate this bold racial wit, in an act of what bell hooks would call "courageous consumption." That this sketch is neither bold nor especially witty is precisely hooks's point: "The commodification of difference," hooks remarks, "promotes paradigms of consumption wherein whatever difference the Other inhabits is eradicated, via exchange, by a consumer cannibalism that... denies the significance of that other's history through a process of decontextualization.... it is by eating the other that one asserts power and privilege" (31, 36).

The inclusion of this sketch, and Homer's response, seems to register the critical impasse of the series itself, which similarly construes Apu's narrative as a palatable set of "ready readings." But "Homer and Apu" also affirms the potential failure of such consumption paradigms to divest the commodity (and the commodity-image) of the alternative significations that adhere to it, or so the episode suggests, in the form of a mute remainder. In two consecutive scenes, placed just before Apu and Homer's journey, we witness commodities inscribe the white masculine consumer with some residual yet oddly indelible matter or affect. In the first of these, Homer emerges from the shower into the waiting embrace of Apu, who (in an apparent escalation of his role as house servant) is standing at the ready with a towel. When Homer shrieks and recoils, Apu smoothly reassures him: "Relax, you don't have anything I haven't seen before." Next it is Apu's turn to be startled, however, and we see him jerk forward, gasping in confusion, "What?" The ensuing frame discloses the cause of Apu's trouble, as Homer, looking down at the lollipop embedded in his chest hair, confesses with some embarrassment, "Uh . . . I like to keep a lollipop there." Homer is thus marked and claimed by a commodity that he has either forgotten or is no longer able to ingest.

Although Apu's comic discovery of Homer's sucker invokes the myriad mobilizations of nonwhite masculinity in the colonial imaginary (as serviceable/feminized body, as homoerotic object), it also reopens the question, to put it bluntly, of who the sucker is. It is precisely not the colonial subject who sucks in this scene but the white male subject himself, reimagined as the sign and symptom of his fantastic appetites, of his propensity to incorporate others and/as objects. Apu's initial, slyly double-edged reassurance that Homer possesses nothing he has not already seen references a sexualized economy of meaning, in which one either has or is the phallus, either authorizes the meaning of things or circulates as a significant thing for others. Hinting at the banality of white bourgeois masculinity, whose eroded capacity for authorship in the already pre-scripted landscape of fast capitalism leaves him manifestly underwhelmed, Apu demotes the emblem of white male privilege to a thing like any other; and, of course, the grotesque duplication of "things" on the avid consumer body only confirms the propriety of Apu's condescension. Yet in a sense, the joke goes down at Apu's expense, not because he was wrong about Homer's condition but because he could not know how right he was. If "castration" (in Lacanian terms, the loss of the referent) marks the (male) subject's entry into language and his claim to a symbolic competence that finds its signifier (though not its referent) in the male organ (the phallus), then we might say that Homer's

"I like to keep a lollipop there": Homer in the "Homer and Apu" episode of The Simpsons *(1994).*

problem is not merely his failure to command this signifier but, worse still, his failure to undergo castration: for unlike the penis, the lollipop is oddly irreducible, not a signifier at all but a recalcitrant bit of matter of which there is nothing more to say than, simply, "there it is." Or, in Homer's vaguely anxious formulation that inserts an "I" into a sentence where none properly exists: "I like to keep a lollipop there." (More accurately, he might have said: "The lollipop keeps me there.") At a minimum, we can say that white masculinity's historical claim to embody universal corporeal norm dissolves, as Homer's consumer body assumes its comic monstrosity. But, more suggestively, this scene primes us for *The Simpsons*'s reimagination of mass consumption as trauma.

It may seem strange to speak of "trauma," considering the series' pervasively ironic tone—although certainly the claim that trauma makes irony impossible, so prevalent in the culture after September 11, has been thoroughly ironized, in turn, by the overtly cynical uses to which it was put. More to the point, perhaps, can "trauma" signify in the context of animation, where embodied subjects necessarily reduce to caricature? In some sense, of course, the trauma of the caricature becomes a caricature of trauma. This very circumstance, however, is what enables the series' treatment of the most banal experiences as traumatic—what enables, more exactly, the reenvisioning of consumerism and its endlessly iterable satisfactions as the daily contact of the eviscerated middle classes with a world of devastating objects. The narrative of consumer consolation turned consumer trauma can be told only in the mode of irony, which is not the same thing as conceding that the trauma of the animated shopper is really no trauma at all. It would be more accurate to claim that when we shop, we are all (mere) animations and that the encounter of our own inert figures with the motor force of capital marks the terrain of consumers' quotidian unmaking on which *The Simpsons* dwells.

In a discussion of trauma that represents both a synthesis of classic Freudian thought on the subject, and a somewhat polemical amplification of those aspects most responsive to the conditions of postmodernity, Cathy Caruth defines the traumatic event not by virtue of its content but by its belated temporality, its failure to signify, or signify fully, at the moment of its occurrence:

> The pathology cannot be defined either by the event itself—which may or may not be catastrophic, and may not traumatize everyone equally—nor can it be defined in terms of a distortion of the event, achieving its haunting power as a result of distorting personal significances attached to it. The pathology consists, rather, solely in the structure of experience or reception: the event is not assimilated or experienced fully at the time, but only belatedly, in its repeated possession of the one who experiences it. To be traumatized is precisely to be possessed by an image or event. (4)

From this vantage, Homer's possession by the unassimilated lollipop—this thing that he can neither experience nor elude—constitutes a visual invocation of trauma's structure, without any commensurate affect. In the end, Homer seems curiously unassailed by the presence of this accreted object, which he treats as only a minor deformation of the normative masculine body, and by no means his most potent source of corporeal shaming. But a comparison of this scene to an episode from 1997 suggests the wider import for the series of Homer's susceptibility to seizure by the world of objects.

The episode "In Marge We Trust" begins when a trip to the city dump yields a disturbing find: a box of detergent, imprinted with Japanese text and Homer's beaming face, or something that looks

In the episode "In Marge We Trust" (1997), Homer discovers a Japanese detergent that uses his face as a trademark.

remarkably like it. Rather than the jubilant assumption of the image theorized by Lacan as the mirror stage, Homer undergoes a palpable unmaking when confronted by this particular reflection, which is neither "Homer" nor "not-Homer" and so functions to dissolve rather than affirm the relations of identity and difference that (con)figure "Homer." The episode seems therefore to exemplify Hal Foster's claim that possession by an image involves the breakdown of the visual codes that screen us from the real. In Foster's paradigm, this traumatic incursion of the gaze constitutes the other face of Jean Baudrillard's ecstatic postmodernity, where the distance between spectator and scene collapses and we become immersed instead in the virtual spaces of media images and information flows. Although this hyperreality is often associated with the obliteration of the world beyond the image (our confinement in the simulacrum), Foster tellingly suggests that our impossible proximity to the image/screen also erodes its capacity to insulate us from the world's inhuman gaze:

> The breaching of the body, the gaze devouring the subject, the subject becoming space, the state of mere similarity: these are conditions evoked in much art today. But to understand this convulsive possession in its contemporary guise it must be split into its constituent

> parts: on the one hand an ecstasy in the imagined breakdown of the image-screen and/or the symbolic order; on the other hand horror at this breakdown followed by a despair about it. (121)

If *The Simpsons* is sometimes prone to revel in what the series represents as our collective dissolution in the simulated world of the image-screen, the detergent box manifests as the horrifying breach in the screen that Foster describes. Its discovery triggers for Homer an intolerable contact with the world's gaze: in the place of the object (where the object once stood) something looks back, "an impression; the shimmering of a surface that is not, in advance, situated for me in its distance" (Lacan, *Four Fundamental Concepts* 96). The gaze that emanates from the point where the object decomposes (as discrete, coherent thing) is an impossibly diffuse surveillance, antithetical to the techniques of vision, which situate social subjects in their effects. Inevitably, this episode proceeds to the only narratable outcome of the crisis, in which Homer is rescued from the abject "state of mere similarity" that characterizes his possession by the object's gaze. Homer eventually discovers that the detergent company is a joint venture of a fishery and a manufacturing firm, which have fused their respective fish and light-bulb logos into the bulb-headed, fish-eyed icon that so resembles and traumatizes him. This revelation replaces the box "in its distance" and reinstates Homer in a specular relation to the world. In a fleeting but important gesture, Homer celebrates the suspension of his trauma by overconsuming.

When Shopping Is a Baffling Ordeal

Significantly, Homer's trauma in "In Marge We Trust" seems connected to history only in the most general, epochal sense; hence its fit with Foster's analysis, which usefully insists on the relation of trauma to postmodern hyperrealities, yet dispels Caruth's emphasis on history. Indeed, for Caruth, "the surprising *literality* and nonsymbolic nature of traumatic dreams and flashbacks" renders post-traumatic stress disorder "not so much a symptom of the unconscious, but a symptom of history. The traumatized, we might say, carry an impossible history within them, or they become themselves the symptom of a history they cannot entirely possess" (5). As the stress on literality alerts us, this historicity is associated with the moments, or the places, where mediation (figuration) is suspended. It is "the overwhelming immediacy" of the traumatic event, Caruth suggests, that produces its belatedness. Turning now to the second of the two scenes in "Homer and Apu" that I invoked earlier, I want to suggest how Barney's shopping ordeal (which follows the revelation of Homer's lollipop) entails both a breakdown of the image-screen and a sudden, devastating contact with unappropriated history—and so corresponds at once to Foster's emphasis and to Caruth's.

This scene opens on Marge and Apu, who have gone on a shopping expedition to the Monstromart ("where," as the store's marquee stalwartly proclaims, "shopping is a baffling ordeal"). Boasting "great selection at rock-bottom prices," as Apu observes, the Monstromart features oversized commodities that dwarf these daring shoppers. Marge wrestles with a twelve-pound box of nutmeg almost as tall as she, and our attention is soon diverted to Barney, the town drunk, wheeling a (literally) man-sized keg of Duff beer and an equally ample container of antacid. Approaching a cluster of giant Mrs. Butterworth containers (filled, as are their more diminutive counterparts, with pancake syrup), Barney politely inquires: "Excuse me, ma'am, where are the lamb shanks?" When the figure fails to reply, he persists in drawing her attention, eventually nudging her arm and overturning the bottle, which spills its syrupy contents into the aisle. Appalled, Barney cries, "I've killed her! It's all happening again," and careens wildly into a cranberry juice display, which topples, breaks, and sweeps the shoppers away in a "cramtastic" crimson tide.

The message of love and consumer consolation that the corporate managers dispense ("Attention shoppers," the loudspeaker blares, "just a reminder that we love each and every one of you") cannot appease the passive aggression of these commodities that yearn, or so it seems, to disclose their "cultural baggage" on the (white male) consumer. Barney's encounter with a life-sized Mrs. Butterworth, whom he mistakenly addresses as a person, leads to his belated experience of homicide, though it remains ambiguous what specific murderous history has possessed him here. Does Barney's inability to distinguish between living African American women and their appearance in the dead form (the stillness) of the stereotype constitute a kind of murder? Is his victim an African American woman still marshaled under the sign of "mammy," to the extent that marginal employment in domestic service industries constitutes her primary means of survival? Or has Barney's bloated shape "killed" one of the labor force at Akom, the largest of the South Korean animation houses, where the series is produced? In any case, the "breakdown

"Excuse me, ma'am, where are the lamb shanks?" From "Homer and Apu."

of . . . symbolic order" at the Monstromart involves a decrypting of the subaltern histories sealed in the commodity-artifact. From this perspective, Barney's experience argues with Foster's account of this breakdown on much the same terms as Judith Butler contends with the orthodox Lacanian conception of the real. At issue for Butler is the opposition of history to the real, understood as an "outside" to symbolic order (what remains in a world without signifiers). While the real for Lacanian cultural analysts such as Foster is essentially timeless (historical temporality is a function of the signifier), Butler points out that the "outside" to the domain of intelligible social and symbolic formations is no more invariant than these formations themselves. In Butler's countermodel, then, the real marks the place where specific categories of historical experience and symbolic activity have been policed and subjected to their forced desymbolization.[7] Whereas the inexplicable appearance of the detergent box displaces Homer from the register of meaning (objects "in [their] distance") and thus history altogether, Mrs. Butterworth deposits her cryptic significance on Barney, who is thereby violently and involuntarily (re)inserted into a field of historically constituted social relations. If the belated structure of trauma ensures that our access to the scene of an actual killing is always barred, it is nonetheless worth stressing that the "breakdown of the image-screen" at the Monstromart triggers a resurgence of unspoken histories, rather than the further seepage of historiographical resources.

From this perspective, Barney's trauma seems less susceptible than Homer's to what Foster shrewdly identifies as the prospect of trauma's reauthentication of the subject:

> In therapy culture, talk shows, and memory mongering, trauma is treated as an event that guarantees the subject, and in this *psychologistic* register the subject, however disturbed, rushes back as survivor, witness, testifier. Here a traumatic subject does indeed exist, and it has absolute authority, for one cannot challenge the trauma of another: one can only believe it, even identify with it, or not. *In trauma discourse, then, the subject is evacuated and elevated at once.* (124)

Although the traumatic image or event seizes the subject and evacuates it, the subject revives in the act of claiming this trauma as its own—so that the subject's disappearance becomes, in Foster's critique, its own most unimpeachable experience. But insofar as Barney's traumatic contact with commodities confronts him with another person's historical trauma, it does not quite produce the vacuum into which he might then "rush back," as newly significant subject. At the very least, the burden of Foster's suspicions shifts, and we are left to ask instead how acceptable a bearer of the murdered peoples' histories the "murderer" might be? To what extent does the inscription of the laborer's trauma on the consumer render it, simply, the consumer's traumatic history, in other words? In this context, Barney's inarticulate, largely incoherent confession becomes something less final, and more hopeful, than a failing. His barely formed acknowledgment—he can say only that he is implicated in events of which he does not know—warrants this deadly history without assigning it to Barney's discursive control. His sudden, shattering proximity to this leaky commodity allows something or someone *else* (the commodity's "baggage") to manifest in Barney's breached and ruined person. If there is anything in this encounter to designate as Barney's "own" trauma, it lies with his (belated) recognition that the compulsion to consume is a compulsion to murder, in the sense of participation in a structurally mandated violence. As such, Barney's trauma is of mass proportions—a recognition of murderous complicity liable to seize any hapless shopper cruising the aisles of the world's Monstromarts.

In "Homer and Apu," as in the series more generally, the white body thus retains its intimacy with commodities, but this immersive relation disfigures the white male form, which finds itself, repeatedly, in the iron grasp of these strikingly irreducible things. In the process, I would argue, the white male body loses its organic properties, becomes a quantity of matter, rather than a discrete, self-sustaining corporeal form. Contemplating Barney alongside his consumables, for example, it is hard to discern the distinction between them—Barney's body becomes one in a series of quantifiable things (a man-sized man next to a man-sized keg), just as it is undecidable whether the lollipop is Homer's appendage, or vice versa. In some ways, this inorganicity resuscitates the white body's protections even at the point of rescinding them: in *The Simpsons,* white male bodies wear their thingness like an armor—as that, precisely, which refuses their reduction to a point of purchase, to a computer's tabulation of their consumption habits. Homer's white male body may be grotesque, but he wields his overembodiment as the most tangible proof that something unyielding remains, there where Universal Man once stood. Yet in other respects, the loss of organic embodiment deals a more decisive blow to the reproduction of white privilege, insofar as the commodities transform from thing to text, to an archive of devastating knowledges that the white consumer can neither hold off nor command.

In the end, what seems most telling about Mrs. Butterworth's agitation is its obvious kinship to the series' own. Profoundly implicated in a system of global capital that requires and perpetuates the existence of a casual, chronically impoverished labor force—for example, at Akom 1,100 of 1,200 employees are temporary workers, paid around $1.50 per cel for the tedious job of inking and painting—*The Simpsons* cannot reflect on its own transpacific origins (Edelstein 38).[8] Rather, in its representation of Barney's trauma, "Homer and Apu" seems to refer, or refract, its own critical impulse to us, as consumers. Perhaps the most interesting response to this hail for the intellectual consumer, in particular, is not to imagine our immunity to Barney's condition—not to distance ourselves from the caricature whose trauma, consequently, seems only to deride him further (like the grotesque, protruding belly, Barney's confession mocks him). To refuse the distance on which the episode's (and the series') ironic tone insists is not to deny that intellectuals hold the edge on the town drunk in commanding the social relations with which the commodity-image is freighted (although up and down the information highway, the data on transnational corporate production, on the origins and circuits of commodities, remains unevenly accessible, at best).[9] But neither is Barney the unknowing dupe of the Monstromart's consumer uplift; just the reverse, his susceptibility to the experience of consumption as trauma suggests a margin of understanding—a dim but indelible awareness of his participation in global capital's inequities. So it hardly seems to follow that a wider margin would exempt us from confronting not simply our implication in ruinous social relations but the fact that we retain no necessarily privileged vantage on our implication. This is not to advocate acquiescence in our condition or to argue that critique fails to matter. But under the conditions of fast capitalism, critique must inevitably reckon with the crimes we do not know to confess.

Notes

Introduction

1. Throughout this book, my thinking on the grammar of racial embodiment is enormously indebted to Hortense Spillers's pathbreaking reflections on the (de)constitution of captive bodies in and in transit to the New World. See "Mama's Baby, Papa's Maybe."

2. This argument builds on the critical race scholarship of Cheryl Harris, who reads whiteness from a legal standpoint as a racial "property" that confers protection from commodification on its owners. See "Whiteness as Property."

3. Klaus Theweleit makes a similar point about the racialization of the figure of the masses in *Male Fantasies.*

4. Alternately, critics have argued that the panoptic order exemplified by comparative anatomy failed to displace an earlier, specular mode of social discipline, evidenced in ongoing practices of visual display, ranging from lynching to blackface. See Robyn Wiegman, *American Anatomies* 39. See also Thomas Foster, "The Souls of Cyberfolk."

5. As Robyn Wiegman observes, "Particularity is not essentially antiessentialist, nor does it guarantee the white subject's disaffiliation from the

powers and pretensions of universality. There is, it seems to me, no theoretical, historical, or methodological escape from the impossibility of the antiracist white subject, partly because the very focus on the subject has far too much of the universal at stake" ("Whiteness Studies and the Paradox of Particularity" 147). We might reflect, as well, on the relationship between interiority and universality implicit in humanist pedagogy, where it is the inward turn of the alienated bourgeois subject that provides a sense of connection to a register of common human or national experience—so that the traditional aim of a humanist pedagogy is the cultivation of the universal in the particular; the cultivation of human truth or national tradition within the feeling individual. For a fuller discussion of subjective interiority and universality, see Simmel 217–26.

6. There is, of course, a tradition of nonidentitarian dialectics, which refuses the closure of Hegelian incorporation. It would include Adorno's concept of a negative dialectics, which foregrounds the "constitutive character" of the "nonconceptual" and thus tallies, somewhat surprisingly, with Lacan's dialectic of desire, where the subject's very being appears as the irreducibly excluded term. Judith Butler's notion of melancholic identification—an identification that marks the place of a prohibited relation—similarly emphasizes what the internalizing logic of dialectical process forecloses. These negative dialectics offer a richer analytic resource for addressing white identity as the imaginary bulwark of white privilege.

7. This despite the fact that the manifestos and other writing emerging from the cultural nationalism of the 1960s offer quite rigorous theorizations of the social, political, and economic conditions of the "internal colony." See, for instance, Carmichael and the mission statement of the Black Berets collective.

8. Yoshimoto posits that "for the purpose of shortening turnover time, image and spectacle have emerged as ideal commodities, which can be consumed and disappear instantaneously." While his argument on the shift from analog to digital, representation to simulation, and production to circulation either implicitly or explicitly aligns the filmic image with the initial term in each binary and thus with a representational economy apparently prior to the virtuality of the commodity-image, he also refuses the idea of any fundamental transformation in the organization of capital. "In terms of the basic dynamic of capital," he notes, "nothing has fundamentally changed in a transition from industrial to postindustrial or late capitalism" (115, 113). From this perspective, it becomes plausible to consider how certain aspects of Hollywood film production in the classic era announced and anticipated processes of virtualization that would become more general and more pronounced by century's end. For a fuller discussion of Yoshimoto's argument, see chapter 4.

1. Subaltern Studies in a U.S. Frame

1. As Amy Kaplan observes, "The history of American imperialism strains the definition of the postcolonial, which implies a temporal development (from 'colonial' to 'post') that relies heavily on the spatial coordinates of European empires, in their formal acquisition of territories and the subsequent history of decolonization and national independence" (17).

2. While more conventionally the advent of nationhood is seen to terminate colonialism on U.S. soil—so that, in the U.S. context, the term was understood as referring exclusively to British domination of its Anglo-American outposts—an emerging body of work in American studies has come to document and critique various forms of imperialist aggression and colonial domination, practiced by the nation-state, in the interest of capitalist development. I cite here the most salient examples of what is sometimes, and not unproblematically, termed "internal colonization," though it is in part my intention to suggest that such colonization is "internal" only if we accept the premise that U.S. sovereign territory is inhabited by a single nation. For further discussion of these examples, see Amy Kaplan and Donald Pease, eds., *Cultures of United States Imperialism;* Michael Moon and Cathy N. Davidson, eds., *Subjects and Citizens;* Hector Calderon and José David Saldívar, *Criticism in the Borderlands;* Ronald Takaki, ed., *From Different Shores;* Gloria Anzaldúa, *Borderlands/La Frontera;* Howard Zinn, *A People's History of the United States.* While my focus here rests on the dynamics of an intraterritorial colonialism in the United States, there are, of course, numerous examples of U.S. engagement in imperialist and colonial domination of a more recognizably extraterritorial form—although, significantly, this aspect of U.S. history has only recently come to be acknowledged in these terms. Although it is beyond the purview of this book, I would emphasize that any analysis of "internal" colonial practices must ultimately take into account the history of U.S. "adventurism" in the South Pacific and the Caribbean, in particular the annexations of Hawai'i and Puerto Rico.

Among the four examples of an "internal" colonialism I enumerate, the latter two are perhaps more controversial, at least in the sense that the extraterritorial dimensions of colonialism, as it is generally understood, have made it difficult to conceptualize the forced deportation of the African to American soil, as well as the controlled immigration of a Chinese labor force deemed nonassimilable under federal law, in relation to the European colonization of nonwhite peoples more generally. Ronald Takaki's work has laid important ground for a postcolonial approach to the study of Chinese and other Pacific Rim immigrations. And the importance of slavery to capitalist development in the United States has been forcefully argued by a number of cultural critics, who see in slavery neither a residual formation nor a peripheral one but a contradiction at the center of the national economic and political order. See, for example, Houston Baker, *Blues, Ideology, and Afro-American Literature,* and Carolyn Porter, *Seeing and Being.*

3. In Guha's use of the term, *the people* is synonymous with *the subaltern classes* and designates all those not included in the categories of (national, regional, or local) elite identity: "The social groups and elements included in this category [of the people] represent *the demographic difference between the total Indian population and all those whom we have described as the 'elite'*" ("Prose" 44).

4. Following Said's succinct delineation of these terms, I associate imperialism with expansionism, colonialism with occupation: "Imperialism means the practice, the theory and, the attitudes of a domination metropolitan center ruling a distant territory; 'colonialism,' which is almost always a consequence of imperialism, is the implanting of settlements on distant territory" (Said 9).

5. This essay thus arises from a sense of partial dissatisfaction with the products of a burgeoning mini-industry in the study of U.S. (post)coloniality. Although I seek to deploy subaltern studies as a kind of corrective to what strikes me as the more problematic gestures and assumptions of this "New Americanist" work, the consideration of subaltern studies in a U.S. frame clearly has implications for a revisionist approach to other established historiographical methods, including perhaps most centrally to Marxist labor historiography and its narrative of the formation of the U.S. working class. While I aim to open up the topic of subaltern studies in a U.S. frame, I neither claim nor aspire to exhaust it.

6. At issue in any claim about American studies is the delimitation of this critical field; clearly, critical work on the cultures of U.S. imperialism is being carried out within institutional spaces ambiguously related to the "American" field, such as ethnic, Afro-American, and Asian American studies, as well as in the generally comparativist context of postcolonial studies. My argument in this section refers to what I perceive as the normative construction of the field within existing institutional structures, including the delineation of an "American" curriculum within English, history, and media studies departments, as well as many American studies programs, and the operation of publishers' rubrics in the categorization of "Americanist" work.

7. For an important discussion of the resonances of this term, see Anne McClintock, "The Angel of Progress."

8. Barbara Jeanne Field's analysis of slave and free labor in antebellum and post–Civil War Maryland substantiates this point.

9. It is worth noting that Ahmad forcefully distinguishes his own position from Bhabha's and Guha's, both of whom he indicts for a privileging of Western post-structuralism in their critique of bourgeois nationalism: "Since nationalism had been designated during this phase as the determinate source of ideological energy in the Third World by those same critics who had

themselves been influenced mainly by poststructuralism, the disillusionment with the (national-bourgeois) state of the said Third World which began to set in towards the later 1980s then led those avant-garde theorists to declare that poststructuralism and deconstruction were the determinate theoretical positions for the critique of nationalism itself" (68). Ahmad goes on to situate this phenomenon in the larger configurations of a postcolonial intellectual migration: "What we have witnessed, however, is that the combination of class origin, professional ambition and lack of a prior political grounding in a stable socialist praxis predisposes a great many of the radicalized immigrants located in the metropolitan university towards both an opportunistic kind of Third-Worldism as the appropriate form of oppositional politics and a kind of self-censoring, which in turn impels them towards greater incorporation in modes of politics and discourse already authorized by the prevailing fashion in that university" (86). But in his dismissal of critics such as Bhabha and Guha, Ahmad subtly contradicts his own critique of Jameson: metropolitan academic production is here seen as wholly reproductive of late-capitalist global power relations rather than itself marked by the contradictions of imperialist practices that inform both sides of the "global divide." Post-structuralism thus incorporates the postcolonial critic but not the reverse; post-structuralism is not also incorporated in a postcolonial critical practice that might displace as well as replicate the authority of the "prevailing fashion." Similarly, although Ahmad's claim for socialism as "a resistance that saturates the globe today" would tend to imply the existence of multiple socialist practices, locally articulated in response to "the different parts of capitalist system," here "socialist praxis" is (re)constituted as a "stable" transnational standpoint.

10. As have so many others, I take exception to Eugene Genovese's argument for planter hegemony in the South. Genovese's argument hinges on a particularly elastic definition of the term, one that curiously contradicts his own perceptive formulation of the Gramscian concept in *In Red and Black*. He writes, "The success of a ruling class in establishing its hegemony depends entirely on its ability to convince the lower classes that its interests are those of society at large—that it defends the common sensibility and stands for a natural and proper social order" (408). Even supposing the planters were able to identify their own interests with "those of society at large," we might speculate that this ideological victory would have little effect on the canny perceptions of their chattel, a speculation borne out by virtually the entire corpus of antebellum writing by former or fugitive slaves. Genovese's own discussion of the plantation economy's coercive social regime obviates against the claim for planter hegemony. "The problem was that the total environment reduced the possibilities for successful insurrection virtually to zero and therefore made accommodationists out of the most high-spirited slave leaders" (138). Insofar as the slave's "accommodation" is

extracted by force—by the immediate and deadly consequences of the refusal to perform accommodation—this form of acquiescence can hardly be taken as an index to consent or complicity or to anything other than the institutionalized racial terror necessary to demobilize a captive population.

11. Judith Butler has suggested that the cultural prohibition on miscegenation intersects with the prohibition on homosexuality to found a national symbolic economy, whose privilege is thus vested in white, heteronormative masculinity and femininity: "What would it mean, on the other hand, to consider the assumption of sexual positions, the disjunctive ordering of the human as 'masculine' or 'feminine,' as taking place not only through a heterosexualizing symbolic with its taboo on homosexuality, but through a complex set of racial injunctions which operate in part through the taboo on miscegenation?" (167).

12. Critical work on *Dawn* and the other volumes of Butler's *Xenogenesis* trilogy (*Adulthood Rites* and *Imago*) has attended to its place within utopian/dystopian traditions (Miller); to the novel's critical treatment of metamorphosis as a counter to postmodern celebrations of bodily transmutation (Smith); to the biological essentialism of the trilogy's ostensible premise, in which "abandoning the human body is a necessary prerequisite for real human alteration" (Zaki 242); and, conversely, to the trilogy as self-critical "origin story" (Peppers). Butler's work is not widely cited in discussions of Afrofuturism, perhaps because it is little preoccupied with the body's *technological* (re)mediation, although her novels' concern with raced subjects and posthuman formations would seem to stake its relevance to Afrofuturist exchanges. For an excellent overview of Afrofuturism, see the special issue of *Social Text,* no. 71 (2002).

13. See Jacques Lacan, the seminar on "The Circuit" in *The Seminar of Jacques Lacan.*

14. Lilith's name, however, signals her vexed relation to origins: the first woman in the original creation account of Genesis, Lilith was made like Adam in God's image and shared political dominion with him. Refusing sexual relations in the missionary position, which she considered demeaning, Lilith fled Eden to pursue her desires freely. God subsequently produced Eve out of Adam's rib, as guarantee of her subordination to him. Expunged from the scriptures (with the exception of Isaiah 34:14–15), Lilith thus stands outside canonical Judeo-Christian history, as the delegitimating pretext of a normative origin myth.

2. After Bourgeois Nationalism

1. See Guha, "Dominance without Hegemony and Its Historiography."

2. For an excellent discussion of the interests that operate welfare reform and of its devastating social effects, see Vijay Prashad, *Keeping Up with the Dow Joneses,* especially the section "Workfare."

3. While the relations of corporate capital to the territorial nation may appear disjunctive, as Rouse observes, state administration is almost entirely given over to corporate management cadres.

4. Glossing the larger corpus of Negri's writing, Nick Dyer-Witheford in *Cyber-Marx* offers a highly readable account of Negri's views on social labor and technology, which suggests that in other forums Negri has presented a more cautious and in some respects more-nuanced version of this claim: "The 'system of social machines' increasingly constitutes an everyday ambience of potentials to be tapped and explored. The elaboration and alteration of this techno-habitat become so pervasively socialized that they can no longer be exclusively dictated by capital.... He [Negri] claims that the new communicative capacities and technological competencies manifesting in the contemporary work force, while most explicit among qualified workers, are *not* the exclusive attributes of this group, but rather exist in 'virtual' form among the contingent and unemployed labor force. They are not so much the products of a particular training or specific work environment but rather the premises and prerequisites of everyday life in a highly integrated technoscientific system permeated by machines and media" (Dyer-Witheford 84). *Cyber-Marx* also usefully situates Negri and the Italian autonomists in relation to Marx's (and Marxism's) varied and conflicting perspectives on technology. See especially chapter 3.

5. Dyer-Witheford makes a similar point that the polarization of labor within the "energy/information" and "service" sectors "raises serious questions about Negri's concept of the socialized worker" (88).

6. In Herbert Marcuse's analysis, the assertion of this inalienable core (cathected as "soul") begins as a protest against reification, only to succumb to it in the end. See "The Affirmative Character of Culture" in *Negations*.

7. Starting from Negri's analysis, Dyer-Witheford also stresses a "blurring of waged and nonwaged time," such that "the activities of people not just as workers but as students, consumers, shoppers, and television viewers are now directly integrated into the production process. During the era of the mass [industrial] worker, the consumption of commodities and the reproduction of labor had been organized as spheres of activity adjunct to, yet distinct from, production. Now these borders fray.... The world of the socialized worker is thus one where capital suffuses the entire form of life" (81).

8. Significant ethnographic work on patterns of transnational migration and the feminization of labor includes Aihwa Ong, *Spirits of Resistance and Capitalist Discipline*, Rhacel Salazar Parreñas, *Servants of Globalization*, and Lisa Lowe, "Work, Immigration, Gender."

9. In recent television series such as *Roswell, X-Files, Odyssey 5*, citizens' alienation from the state is thematized as the state's infiltration by alien forces. In these series, the state appears as operated by remote (not simply off-shore but off-world) interests, even as it is overpresent in the

protagonists' lives (their most mundane pursuits are under continuous state surveillance). Unlike "Bloodchild," however, which elucidates the critical possibilities as well as the limitations of this situation, the series generally strive to reclaim the notion of a representative state authority, by positing the existence of competing states-within-the-state. It therefore becomes the job of the heroic citizen to ferret out the legitimate avatars of government.

10. See *The Queen of America Goes to Washington City,* especially chapter 1.

11. In an essay that models such a critical practice at its best, Wahneema Lubiano considers how an African American "warrior" ethos that codes as antagonistic to racist state institutions, especially the penitentiary, is better understood as a state-sponsored identity, cultivated in and by the prison, and elevated to a sociological datum by academic knowledge producers. See "Like Being Mugged by a Metaphor."

3. Eskimo Television and the Critique of Whiteness (Studies)

1. In designating tribal (fourth world) peoples as subaltern, I draw on Ranajit Guha's alignment of subalternity with the difference, or remainder, when all forms of elite identity (national and regional) are subtracted from the totality of "the people." As I discuss in chapter 1, colonial subalternity for Guha is a condition of the nonelite, those without access to institutional power and, by extension, to those institutions that produce and archive the historical record of colonialism and its aftermath. Yet the subaltern is not simply marginal to the (post)colonial state; in fact, just the reverse: Guha predicates the normative operations of the bourgeois state and civil society—including, particularly, colonial historiography—on the work of counterinsurgency, so that subalternity is everywhere inscribed as the trace of a missing will-to-insurgency around which the disciplinary functions of the state cohere. Amply present in the record in the guise of the primitive (as hostile factors or figures rather than as insurgent subjects), yet absolutely external to the production of official history in the post-Columbian Americas, Native American peoples may be understood as subaltern on Guha's model, regardless of their visibility within contemporary commodity culture (e.g., new age aesthetics) or of the economic resources that some of Silko's tribal protagonists amass through illicit means (gunrunning and other forms of illegal traffic).

2. My emphasis throughout this chapter on the nonorganic modalities of tribal knowledge in *Almanac* places the novel (and my reading of it) in conversation with the holistic strain of Native American literary criticism, which tends to position Native American culture as the integrative other of Western epistemology's analytic protocols and its reduction of the earth's living totality to a series of inanimate component parts. Conventional, as well, within this critical tradition is the juxtaposition of European linear

time to a synchronous Native American temporality. Germinal works in this tradition include Vine Deloria's *Spirit and Reason* and Paula Gunn Allen's *Sacred Hoop,* and certainly a good deal of the criticism on *Almanac of the Dead* continues this emphasis. See, for example, Tamara Teale, "The Silk Road from Chiapas, or, Why Native Americans Cannot Be Marxist," and Deborah Horvitz, "Freud, Marx, and Chiapas in Leslie Marmon Silko's *Almanac of the Dead.*" Deloria's work, in particular, seems to me marked by the tension between a principled, critical refusal to produce "the Indian" as the other of the West and his simultaneous capitulation to this logic. Thus he insists that Native American knowledge and practice is neither premodern nor "prescientific," assertions that would imply both a teleology and a hierarchy of knowledge (i.e., Western knowledge as the more advanced). Yet to the extent that Deloria establishes a dichotomized relation between the synthetic methodologies of Native American elders and shamans, and Western analytic protocols that fragment and dissect the world's unity, he tends to reproduce under a different sign the binary opposition of cultures he sets out to contest.

In resisting the lure of such fundamentally romanticized dichotomies, *Almanac of the Dead* demonstrates the "survivance" tactics of Gerald Vizenor's "Postindian warriors." For Vizenor, the domination of Native American peoples by the political and cultural institutions of the U.S. nation-state means that tribal realities remain fundamentally unrepresentable within the discursive regimes of an institutionalized public culture dedicated to their erasure: "This is a continuous turn in tribal narratives, the oral stories are dominated by those narratives that are translated, published, and read at unnamed distances. Stories that arise in silence are the sources of a tribal presence. The simulations of dominance and absence of the other are the concern of manifest manners. The simulations of survivance are heard and read stories that mediate and undermine the literature of dominance" (12). From this "postindian" perspective, tribal realities survive in the mode of strategic countersimulations, as performative negations of their absence in (what Guha calls) "the prose of counter-insurgency." Postindian warriors "counter the surveillance and literature of dominance with their own simulations of survivance. The postindian arises from the earlier inventions of the tribes only to contravene the absence of the real with theatrical performances; the theater of tribal consciousness is the recreation of the real, not the absence of the real in the simulations of dominance" (Vizenor 5). For Vizenor as for Silko, the "Indian" is not retrievable, precisely insofar as the representational terrain of "Indian-ness" *is* the terrain of colonial domination. Thus, as Vizenor stresses, the portrait of an Indian can be captioned only like Magritte's famous pipe: "This portrait is not an Indian" (44). Crucially, however, for Vizenor as for Silko, the absence of Indians in "the simulations of dominance" (to borrow Vizenor's phrase) does not mean that anyone can become Indian. Central to *Almanac* as to Vizenor's own evaluation of "posers" is the critique of racial cross-identification as a practice of domination rather than a gesture of solidarity.

3. Certainly, much of the scholarship on Silko (as well as the cultural criticism of such Native American writers as Vizenor) now routinely distinguishes the tribal from the premodern, if only because Native American temporality is perceived as resistant to the sequential organization of time ostensibly implied by the prefixes *pre* and *post*. At the same time, the nonlinearity of Native American time is often rendered as spatial totality: Yvonne Reinecke, for instance, proposes that *Almanac* "respatializes the time of the postcolonial by incorporating (literally taking into its textual body) the term through Fourth World prophecy" (80). Similarly, Caren Irr discerns in *Almanac* "a temporality rescued from the archaicism of the eternal return to which most European traditions assign the other. Understood as an endless spatialized temporal zone, this sacred native time *encompasses Eurocentric linearity and expands beyond it*" (233, my emphasis). While eschewing the opposition of the Native American to the European American as the anterior to the modern, critics such as Reinecke and Irr nonetheless reconstitute this relation as the opposition of the temporal whole to the temporal fragment—of a Native American all time (the temporality of history) to European calendrical time, in which each moment supersedes the next (the temporality of forgetting). This surreptitious repositioning of the Native American as outside or beyond the confines of fragmented and fragmenting modernity is particularly startling in the context of Irr's ostensible investment in making the opposite point—that the simultaneity of time in Native American traditions might be allied to the critique of sequential time within the discourses of modernity itself. Even as she argues for the impact of "post-Einsteinian theories of time" on Silko's narrative method, Irr casts the "sacred time" of Native American cosmologies as anything but relativistic: "Time, in this view, is something endlessly available, something spatial; it is something through which one can travel forward and backward *like a god*" (227, my emphasis). I would argue that the tension in Irr's exposition derives from the commitment to representing the positivity of ethnic difference, so that the novel's management of its multiple temporalities reduces to the expression of an "Indian style." In this framework, as well, the articulation of Native American spirituality to oppositional social practice is presumed rather than demonstrated, since difference itself appears politically authoritative. Instead, I argue here that the novel's tribal temporality proves hostile to the figuration of time as traversible space; and, more particularly, that one casualty of an insurgent, tribal epistemology (and thus of *Almanac* itself) is the specular difference engine and its production of a representable/representative "Indian" alterity.

4. See also Inderpal Grewal and Caren Kaplan, eds., *Scattered Hegemonies,* and Aijaz Ahmad, *In Theory: Classes, Nations, Literatures.*

5. Root's Mexican great-grandfather makes him technically mestizo. But this limited Mexican lineage only provokes Root's mother to the anxious whitewashing and Europeanizing of the family tree; she forbids her children to play with Mexicans, stressing that Grandfather Gorgon was "of Spanish descent." While Root is therefore distantly related to Calabazas—most of the Southwest's "rooted" Anglo inhabitants likely bear some degree of kinship to their Latino neighbors, the novel implies—he is nevertheless raised, and raised all the more aggressively, to be white: to claim the privileges and the epistemological prerogatives of white personhood.

6. Any sketch of such a broad and varied critical terrain is necessarily reductive, and my profile of whiteness studies is intended only to remark certain more or less pronounced tendencies. There is also an invaluable critical scholarship on whiteness that makes possible my own thinking on white privilege and white embodiment. I am especially indebted on this score to the work of Cheryl Harris, George Lipsitz, Robyn Wiegman, Eric Lott, and Lee Edelman.

7. This may seem like an odd contention, given Roediger's focus in *The Wages of Whiteness* on white working-class formation. While this earlier study centers on the historical production and maintenance of white privilege rather than on a purported corrective, I would argue that Roediger anticipates his later line of argument, at least to the extent that he aligns the undoing of white privilege with the erasure of whiteness. Thus he champions the possibility that white people would cease to think of themselves as white—which is to say, that they think of themselves as something *other* than white, or as nonwhite. My point is that the unthinking of whiteness—the dismantling of its privileges—would require a critical reconstruction of whiteness. At a minimum, such a reinvention of whiteness as nonsupremacist formation would make white subjects accountable to the history (and legacies) of their privilege, rather than granting them the privilege of racial self-fashioning all over again.

8. In addition to Lott, Leslie Fiedler and Priscilla Wald have made similar arguments on how the limited or transitory assumption of nonwhite identity supports Americanization, particularly for male subjects.

9. Harvey's argument is more complex than this synopsis suggests, insofar as he sees both tendencies, toward internationalism and toward geopolitics, manifest within modernism's response to the conditions of modernity. "It would be wrong to consider these two wings of thought—the universalism and the particularism—as separate from each other. They should be regarded, rather, as two currents of sensibility that flowed along side by side, often within the same persons, even when one or other sensibility became dominant in a particular time and place" (Harvey 275). Nonetheless, Harvey does suggest that the latter tendency, toward "particularism," achieves a more general dominance within postmodernism.

10. It is worth remarking that temporality is similarly spatialized in Freud's account of psychic formation, where the earliest stimuli pass to the innermost layers of the organism. Thus temporal anteriority corresponds to spatial depth, and the record of the organism's encounters with the world (its "becoming") can be mapped onto the spatial interval between core and periphery. See *Beyond the Pleasure Principle.*

11. I draw as well on Michael Warner's elaboration of Derrida's thesis in *The Letters of the Republic,* chapter 4.

12. The formulation is José Martí's. See "Our America" 149.

4. Hollywood's Hot Voodoo

1. Shaviro's quarrel is equally with Bazin. "Bazin offers the utopian vision of an originary, phenomenological plenitude of perception, preserved and extended by the cinematic apparatus. Warhol's films ruin this idealized vision, precisely through their excessive fidelity to the Bazinian project.... Reality is not preserved and sustained so much as it is *altered* by the very fact of passive, literal reproduction—or what could better be called hypermimetic simulation" (18).

2. Despite his antipsychoanalytic, Deleuzian posture, Shaviro's formulation thus curiously echoes Lacan's in his well-known anecdote of the glittering sardine can. As he relates the story, Lacan is fishing off the coast of Brittany when his eye is caught by the glint of the light reflected from the surface of a floating sardine can. His fellow fisherman comments on how he can see the can, although the can cannot see him, a remark Lacan finds vaguely off-putting, precisely because, he insists, "it was looking at me, all the same." The anecdote anchors a meditation on the limits of subject-centered perception: "That which is light looks at me, and by means of that light in the depths of my eye, something is painted—something that is not simply a constructed relation, the object on which the philosopher lingers—but something that is an impression, *the shimmering of a surface that is not, in advance, situated for me in its distance.* This is something that introduces what was elided in the geometral relation—the depth of the field, with all its ambiguity and variability, *which is in no way mastered by me.* It is rather it that grasps me, solicits me at every moment, and makes of the landscape something other than a landscape, something other than what I have called the picture" (*Four Fundamental Concepts* 96, my emphasis). Shaviro's notion of the cinematic image is thus, in Lacanian terms, a kind of non-image—one that fails to function as a relay between the "punctiform being" (the point of perception) and the object. In Shaviro's account, the camera turns up in the place of the sardine can, as that which sees blindly, and the cinematic image, therefore, is less a screen against the real than a shutter, something that admits as much as it filters.

3. Georges Duhamel, cited in Benjamin, *Illuminations* 238.

4. A crucial point for Yoshimoto is that the quality of the analog image decays as it proliferates. "The process of analogue transcription," he notes, "moves irreversibly from the original to its copies, the quality of which progressively deteriorates as they are further removed from the original source.... Unlike an analogue transcription, a digital conversion is a reversible process, in which there is no fundamental difference between the original and its copies" (110). For Shaviro, however, the cinematic image is *not* the "mnemonic trace of the object which once existed in the past" (Yoshimoto 110), but a simulation that "disqualifies both the original and the copy" (Shaviro 19), by upsetting the hierarchical relation between them. Reading Yoshimoto from the vantage of Shaviro's claim, we would have to ask whether "the original source" is the object (supposedly) represented in the "analogue transcription" or something that we might call, at best, the original copy—the first print of the negatives (or perhaps the negatives themselves). If Yoshimoto is certainly right to point out that the analog image is not infinitely renewable (unlike the digital), it seems clear that the cinematic image is remarkably resistant to consumption—it circulates and proliferates other images through its circulation for extended periods (years or sometimes decades).

5. As Kristin Thompson specifies, "In the years after World War I, the success of the American film industry in maintaining its hold abroad was attributable primarily to its huge domestic market. Few countries in the world had enough theaters and a big enough film-going public to amortise the films they produced. Yet during an American release, a film's expenses were likely paid off and many films might begin earning profits quite apart from revenues coming in from other countries. No other industry could hope for similar returns on domestic exhibition; most, such as France, Germany, or Italy, depended on exports to help amortise films which brought in only modest amounts at home" (*Exporting Entertainment* 1).

6. Harris's understanding of "black color" as susceptibility to commodification finds interesting echoes in Eric Lott's *Love and Theft,* although this insight only hovers on the margins of his wider argument. In a discussion of Herman Melville's *Confidence-Man,* for instance, Lott observes of this protean protagonist that "commodification is, in a sense, Black Guinea's *attraction;* it is what seems *blackest* about him. It is precisely calculated to evoke the foolish pleasure of our pity, and Melville's grim irony only confirms that the attempt to reveal minstrelsy's financial purposes has itself proved to be an act of minstrelization" (62).

7. Harris's lead has been followed only fitfully within much of what currently counts as whiteness studies, whose proponents generally prefer to dwell on the vacuity of whiteness, its lack of specificity or defining properties. For a fuller discussion of "whiteness studies," see chapter 3.

8. This chapter charts a different course from much of the excellent scholarship on the production of the Hollywood star. Such work has tended to privilege the filmic and extrafilmic production of stars: the publicity machines, the production of personality in magazines and tabloids, the analysis of particular films as star vehicles, where critical attention centers either/both on narrative elements or on exceptional visual effects. See especially Dyer's *Heavenly Bodies* and "Resistance through Charisma" and Gledhill's *Stardom*. My interests here are complementary, as I attend to the cinematic production of stars: what makes a star body—*any* star body—intelligible and available as such? I can find no sustained inquiry into the production and effects of stardom at the level of visual grammar, perhaps because it is in certain respects counterintuitive to think of the institution of stardom apart from the production of particular stars. At the same time, the tendency to case studies in the crafting and dissemination of star personas marks a degree of capitulation to the star mystique—each star is different, if not unique. In any case, my aim in this chapter is to suggest the possible contours of this different sort of inquiry into the grammar of star embodiment.

9. Or, in Deborah Thomas's reading, figural *and* sororal both. Noting that Helen and her black servant, Cora, each put on an act for the detective pursuing Helen, Thomas goes on, unaccountably, to suggest that the women's shared ability to figure themselves as what they are not (as hardened prostitute, as grinning mammy) betokens (more than an ambiguously "shared" blackness), a sisterly alliance. "In marvelous paired moments, Cora and then Helen visibly alter before our eyes as they put on, like hats, the respective roles they know Wilson will expect them to play.... Cora and Helen, sisters under the skin, enact racist and sexist stereotypes (the smiling black, the femme fatale) for this representative of the law in order to use him for their own united purpose, precisely because it is both what they know he expects and what is least likely to alert his suspicions" (13–14). Just what this "united purpose" may be is nowhere explained, as Thomas avoids any further attention to the figure of Cora with the same untroubled finality as the film itself.

10. The film explicitly refers to lesbian self-fashioning in the figure of a nightclub owner who alerts Helen to her hunted status. Wearing close-cropped hair and a man's dark suit—the spectator identifies her sex through the grain of her voice, primarily, rather than any decisive visual markings—the club owner's style plainly anticipates Helen's/Dietrich's Paris avatar.

5. White Women in the Age of Their Mechanical Reproduction

1. Similarly, he notes, "in the 1960s and 1970s, when Latin America became a battleground between socialist revolutionaries and the CIA, some of the more romantic imagery of Latin countries began temporarily to disappear from U.S. screens" (Naremore, *More Than Night* 231–32).

2. To interrogate the limits of a psychoanalytic approach to noir is not to refute the wider import of psychoanalysis for feminist film criticism. My debt to feminist psychoanalysis, and especially to Laura Mulvey, is legible in my attention to the syntax of embodiment, for instance, even as I question the insistence with which psychoanalytic film criticism orders surface effects into effective subjects—conjugates affect with interiority.

3. For a more complete discussion of Benjamin's observation, see chapter 3.

4. From this perspective, film noir offers less a critique of normative masculinity than a diagnosis of the disabling conditions that defer and divert its repetition.

5. This claim finds its most potent articulation in Laura Mulvey's widely influential essay, "Visual Pleasure and Narrative Cinema."

6. Hayworth's ethnicity (she was born Margareta Carmen Cansino of Spanish parents) is bleached from the design of her star embodiment (through the reddening of her hair and the surgical alteration of her hairline, as well as the anglicization of her name). In Gilda, her dancing to Latin rhythms represents a visual and aural trace of this discarded ethnicity, in a setting where "Spanish" codes as South American creole rather than Southern European. The ethnicity obliquely recollected in her dancing (her origins and transformation were detailed in the movie magazines) carries a heightened racial taint when it conjugates with Montevideo rather than Madrid—so that Gilda's/Hayworth's "Amado Mío" may be understood as a subtler variation on Dietrich's "Hot Voodoo," in which "race" is imputed to the star *and* remediated through the overproduction of whiteness.

7. Particularly in the past ten to fifteen years, significant work has appeared both on the reception of American cinema abroad and on the practice of spectatorship by racial and ethnic minorities within the United States and other metropolitan contexts. Ella Shohat and Robert Stam have brilliantly and exhaustively mapped both the role of Hollywood as global purveyor of orientalist and primitivist stereotypes and the complex, contradictory ways in which audiences in Latin America, Asia, and Africa have submitted to, resignified, refunctioned, and (or) dismantled these racist tropologies *(Unthinking Eurocentrism)*. With a critical eye that ranges across media and performative modes, Kobena Mercer and José Muñoz have attended more particularly to the practice of disidentification—the partial and ambivalent inhabitation of toxic identities—as well as to the instability of images as they move in space and time (so that the cultural and political work of an image varies with the exhibition space, the community, or communities hailed, and the particular assembly of forces and counterforces that define a political moment). This work and other scholarship in a similar vein have enormously enhanced our understanding of the contact zone where the racial stereotype meets the raced subject. Another important direction in

film and media studies is the investigation of alternative film cultures, such as indigenous media (Shohat and Stam) or ethnic cinemas (Fregoso) by, for, and about people of color.

While my thinking about the institutional discipline of spectatorship and about the inevitable complexity and volatility of viewing practices is pervasively informed by the range of critical work I have just (all too sweepingly) described, this chapter takes a somewhat different turn: I focus neither on the way that Hollywood cinema positions nonwhite spectators nor on the reception of the Hollywood product by various historical constituencies of racial or ethnic subjects. Instead, my project takes place in the gap between these two critical endeavors, as I consider how film noir, in particular, reflects on the uncertainties of reception and on the necessary failure of Hollywood cinema to manage the encounter of Latin American, Asian, and African audiences with the white female star. At issue in film noir, in other words, are Hollywood's fantasies about nonwhite viewers and their scopic intimacy with dazzling white womanhood.

8. As Stephen Heath puts it, "Nothing happens to Susan, simply she is faded out" (140).

9. Yoshimoto's model assumes the fundamental equivalence of commodity-images, and as such—through this absolute equation of images with abstraction—steers too sharply away from Shaviro's best insights into their visceral immediacy. His model implicitly disallows the possibility that one image might overtake and dissolve another in the series, thereby introducing a qualitative distinction, as well. Chapter 3 offers a fuller discussion and juxtaposition of both Shaviro's and Yoshimoto's arguments.

6. Fast Capitalism and Consumer Ideals

1. Television scholars who read the mode of production as determining have emphasized both the limits and the possibilities of the medium for the dissemination of critical perspectives. Rather than reducing television to a univocal instrument of corporate interests, most critics have stressed its function in the ongoing work of creating and maintaining the hegemony of a heterogeneous elite. Thus, as Douglas Kellner contends, television necessarily reflects the differences among a political and corporate ruling class (9). In a similar vein, others have argued that the televisual text is positioned vis-à-vis both a television "archive" (Deming) and an "intertext" (Spiegel), or a set of ambient popular and institutional discourses, that opens it to multiple (though not unrestricted) interpretations. Within this body of scholarly work, there are, of course, important polemical variations and shadings. For some critics, consumer agency in the form of "choice" constitutes a significant variable, which drives the culture industry toward some degree of innovation (Fiske 4; Spiegel and Curtin 5). For others, the consumers are

subordinate to the medium's ideologically saturated forms and conventions (Rabinovitz) or themselves transformed into a commodity sold by the networks to the advertisers (Dallas W. Smythe, quoted in Rabinovitz).

Across the field, however, the point of resistance, such as it is, remains extrinsic to the operation of the medium itself and finds a limited reflection within it—a reflection more likely to serve than to imperil the imposition of hegemony. What interests me about *The Simpsons* is the extent to which the critical impulse seems to inhere in the series—not as a reflection of surrounding pressures, in other words, but (in Agger's terms) as a will-to-its-retextualization intrinsic to the thing itself.

2. In recent years, the Indian government has pursued a programmatic effort to attract transnational capital.

3. Headquartered in and linked to its country of origin, Film Roman is not a transnational or even a clearly multinational corporation (e.g., it does not appear to have acquired any of the South Korean animation houses, such as Akom, with whom it contracts). Nevertheless, outsourcing represents one of the defining strategies of multi- and transnational corporations.

4. See also Ella Shohat and Robert Stam, "From the Imperial Family to the Transnational Imaginary," which emphasizes local variations in the consumption of commodity-images.

5. Subaltern studies tends to frame itself as intervening in the project of nationalist historiography. Nonetheless, as Gayatri Chakravorty Spivak suggests, this method also serves to make visible the mark of the colonial subaltern on Western epistemes, which function only on condition of effacing the subaltern subject. See Spivak, "Can the Subaltern Speak?" and *In Other Worlds*, chapter 12.

6. I am grateful to Purnima Bose for alerting me that "420" refers to a section of the Indian penal code governing theft, and particularly theft by duplicity, or deceit. Inasmuch as Apu is here engaged in thievery under cover of service, one must assume the scriptwriters' rather extensive command of South Asian cultural referents. This suggests that the representation of India via Hollywood is a function of what the producers perceive as the series' generic constraints, rather than lack of knowledge of contemporary India.

7. "If we concur that every discursive formation proceeds through constituting an 'outside,'" Butler writes, "we are not therefore committed to the *invariant* production of that outside as the trauma of castration (nor to the generalization of castration as the model for all historical trauma). Moreover, it may further the effort to think psychoanalysis's relation to historical trauma and to the limits of symbolizability if we realize that (a) there may be several mechanisms of foreclosure that work to produce the unsymbolizable in any given discursive regime, and (b) the mechanisms of production are—however inevitable—still and always the historical workings of specific modalities of discourse and power" (205).

Butler's resistance to the ahistoricity of Lacanian analysis points the way to a more provisional and critical mobilization of an analytic system that presents itself—and is all too often represented—as self-contained, as an account of subjectivity (desire), language (signification), and law (prohibition) that is adequate to the measure of every fantasy, proclivity, aspiration, and movement: adequate, in other words, to the study of psychic life and political formations as such. Butler's intervention reminds us that a more selective relation to the forms of Lacanian analysis is possible—and certainly my own method has been to appropriate Lacanian categories even as I refuse to grant their transcendence (so that Lacanian analysis functions in this book as a culturally and politically situated practice itself susceptible to critical revision). If this approach seems iconoclastic, it is only on account of the unrepentant will-to-totalization that marks this particular analytic project.

8. One reader has suggested to me that by first replacing screen actors with cartoon figures and then outsourcing costly U.S. labor to South Korea, the series implicitly establishes an identity, or homology, between the Asian laborers and the two-dimensional images they draw. For this reader, the cartoon body tropes the depthless condition (the lifelessness?) of disposable labor. But in a series that is notably attentive to the numbing monotony of work and routine debasement of the labor force in the United States, the offshore laborer remains conspicuously unrepresented. And whatever may be implicit in the circumstances of its production, in the text of *The Simpsons,* as I have sought to show, the flatness of the animated image conjugates instead with the attenuated life of the consumer.

9. It is undoubtedly on account of these real methodological difficulties that the essays in Grewal and Kaplan's collection address the representation of transnationalism, rather than engage directly in the "unpacking" of transnational commodities that the editors advocate in their introduction. In a forthcoming essay, Purnima Bose meticulously models such a practice and argues for the value of constructing and circulating the commodity's archive. See Bose, "The Scent of a Conflict."

Works Cited

Agger, Ben. *Fast Capitalism: A Critical Theory of Significance*. Champaign: University of Illinois Press, 1989.

Ahmad, Aijaz. *In Theory: Classes, Nations, Literatures*. London: Verso, 1992.

Allen, Paula Gunn. *The Sacred Hoop: Recovering the Feminine in American Indian Traditions*. Boston: Beacon, 1992.

Anzaldúa, Gloria. *Borderlands/La Frontera: The New Mestiza*. San Francisco: Aunt Lute Books, 1987.

Appadurai, Arjun. *Modernity at Large: Cultural Dimensions of Globalization*. Minneapolis: University of Minnesota Press, 1996.

Baker, Houston. *Blues, Ideology, and Afro-American Literature: A Vernacular Theory*. Chicago: University of Chicago Press, 1984.

Balio, Tino. "Selling Stars." In *Grand Design: Hollywood as a Modern Business Enterprise, 1930–1939*, ed. Tino Balio. Berkeley and Los Angeles: University of California Press, 1993: 143–78.

Baudrillard, Jean. *The Ecstasy of Communication*. Trans. Bernard Schutze and Caroline Schutze. New York: Semiotext(e), 1987.

———. *Selected Writings*. Ed. Mark Poster. Stanford, CA: Stanford University Press, 1988.

Benjamin, Walter. *Illuminations: Essays and Reflections.* Ed. Hannah Arendt. Trans. Harry Zohn. New York: Schocken Books, 1969.

———. *The Origin of German Tragic Drama.* Trans. John Osborne. London: Verso, 1977.

Berlant, Lauren. "National Brands/National Body." In *Comparative American Identities: Race, Sex, and Nationality in the Modern Text,* ed. Hortense Spillers. New York: Routledge, 1991: 110–40.

———. *The Queen of America Goes to Washington City: Essays on Sex and Citizenship.* Durham, NC: Duke University Press, 1997.

Bhabha, Homi. *The Location of Culture.* London: Routledge, 1994.

Black Berets. "Black Beret Organization." In *La Causa Politica: A Chicano Politics Reader,* ed. F. Chris Garcia. South Bend, IN: University of Notre Dame Press, 1974: 405–508.

Bordwell, David. "Deep-Focus Cinematography." In *The Classical Hollywood Cinema: Film Style and Mode of Production to 1960,* ed. David Bordwell, Janet Staiger, and Kristin Thompson. New York: Columbia University Press, 1985: 341–52.

Bordwell, David, and Kristin Thompson. "Technological Change and Classical Film Style." In *Grand Design: Hollywood as a Modern Business Enterprise, 1930–1939,* ed. Tino Balio. Berkeley and Los Angeles: University of California Press, 1993: 109–42.

Bose, Purnima. "The Scent of a Conflict: Kashmir, Transnationalism, and the National Imaginary." *Passages* 1 (1999): 151–72.

Butler, Judith. *Bodies That Matter: On the Discursive Limits of Sex.* New York: Routledge, 1993.

Butler, Octavia. *Bloodchild and Other Stories.* New York: Four Walls Eight Windows, 1995.

———. *Dawn.* New York: Warner Books, 1987.

Calderon, Hector, and José David Saldívar, eds. *Criticism in the Borderlands: Studies in Chicano Literature, Culture, and Ideology.* Durham, NC: Duke University Press, 1991.

Carby, Hazel. "The Multicultural Wars." In *Black Popular Culture,* ed. Gina Dent. Seattle: Bay Press, 1992: 187–99.

Carmichael, Stokely. "Toward Black Liberation." In *Black Fire: An Anthology of Afro-American Writing,* ed. LeRoi Jones and Larry Neal. New York: William, Morrow, 1968: 119–32.

Caruth, Cathy. Introduction to *Trauma: Explorations in Memory,* ed. Cathy Caruth. Baltimore, MD: Johns Hopkins University Press, 1995: 1–12.

Castells, Manuel. *The Rise of the Network Society.* Cambridge, MA: Blackwell, 1996.

Chatterjee, Partha. *The Nation and Its Fragments: Colonial and Postcolonial Histories.* Princeton, NJ: Princeton University Press, 1993.

Davis, David Brion. *The Problem of Slavery in Western Culture.* New York: Oxford University Press, 1988.

Davis, Mike. *City of Quartz: Excavating the Future in Los Angeles.* New York: Vintage Books, 1992.

Deleuze, Gilles. *Cinema 1: The Movement-Image.* Trans. Hugh Tomlinson and Barbara Habberjam. Minneapolis: University of Minnesota Press, 1986.

Deloria, Vine, Jr. *Spirit and Reason: The Vine Deloria Jr. Reader.* Ed. Barbara Deloria, Kristen Foehner, and Sam Scinta. Golden, CO: Fulcrum, 1991.

Deming, Robert H. "*Kate and Allie:* 'New Women' and the Audience's Television Archive." *Camera Obscura* 16 (1988): 155–66.

Derrida, Jacques. "Declarations of Independence." Trans. Tom Keenan and Tom Pepper. *New Political Science* 15 (1986): 7–15.

Diawara, Manthia. "*Noir* by *Noirs:* Toward a New Realism in Black Cinema." In *Shades of Noir,* ed. Joan Copjec. London: Verso, 1993: 261–78.

Dimock, Wai-Chee. *Empire for Liberty: Melville and the Poetics of Individualism.* Princeton, NJ: Princeton University Press, 1989.

Doane, Mary Ann. *Femmes Fatales: Feminism, Film Theory, Psychoanalysis.* New York: Routledge, 1991.

Dyer, Richard. *Heavenly Bodies: Film Stars and Society.* London: Macmillan, 1986.

———. "Resistance through Charisma: Rita Hayworth and *Gilda.*" In *Women in Film Noir,* ed. E. Ann Kaplan. London: British Film Institute Publishing, 1978: 91–99.

———. *White.* New York: Routledge, 1997.

Dyer-Witheford, Nick. *Cyber-Marx: Cycles and Circuits of Struggle in High-Technology Capitalism.* Urbana: University of Illinois Press, 1999.

Edelman, Lee. *Homographesis: Essays in Gay Literature and Cultural Theory.* New York: Routledge, 1994.

Edelstein, Bill. "People Still Draw." *Variety,* June 19, 1995, 38.

Fiedler, Leslie. *The Collected Essays of Leslie Fiedler.* New York: Stein and Day, 1971.

Field, Barbara Jeanne. *Slavery and Freedom on the Middle Ground: Maryland during the Nineteenth Century.* New Haven, CT: Yale University Press, 1985.

Fischer, Lucy. *Shot/Countershot: Film Tradition and Women's Cinema.* Princeton, NJ: Princeton University Press, 1989.

Fiske, John. *Reading the Popular.* Boston: Unwin Hyman, 1989.

Foster, Hal. "Obscene, Abject, Traumatic." *October* 78 (1996): 106–24.

Foster, Thomas. "'The Souls of Cyberfolk': Performativity, Virtual Embodiment, and Racial Histories." In *Cyberspace Textualities: Computer Technology and Literary Theory,* ed. Marie-Laure Ryan. Bloomington: Indiana University Press, 1999: 137–63.

Foucault, Michel. *The Archeology of Knowledge*. Trans. A. M. Sheridan. New York: Pantheon Books, 1972.

Frankenberg, Ruth. *White Women, Race Matters*. Minneapolis: University of Minnesota Press, 1993.

Fregoso, Rosa Linda. *The Bronze Screen: Chicana and Chicano Film Culture*. Minneapolis: University of Minnesota Press, 1993.

Freud, Sigmund. *Beyond the Pleasure Principle*. Trans. James Strachey. New York: Norton, 1961.

Genovese, Eugene. *In Red and Black*. New York: Random House, 1968.

Gilroy, Paul. *Against Race: Imagining Political Culture beyond the Color Line*. Cambridge, MA: Harvard University Press, 2000.

Gledhill, Christine. *Stardom: Industry of Desire*. London: Routledge, 1991.

Gramsci, Antonio. *Selections from the Prison Notebooks*. Ed. and trans. Quintin Hoare and Geoffrey Nowell Smith. New York: International Publishers, 1971.

Grewal, Inderpal, and Caren Kaplan. "Introduction: Transnational Feminist Practices and Questions of Postmodernity." In *Scattered Hegemonies: Postmodernity and Transnational Feminist Practices*, ed. Inderpal Grewal and Caren Kaplan. Minneapolis: University of Minnesota Press, 1994: 1–33.

Guha, Ranajit. "Dominance without Hegemony and Its Historiography." *Subaltern Studies* 6 (1989): 210–309.

———. "The Prose of Counter-Insurgency." In *Selected Subaltern Studies*. New York: Oxford University Press, 1988: 44–84.

Hall, Stuart. "Gramsci's Relevance for the Study of Race and Ethnicity." *Journal of Communication Inquiry* 10 (1986): 5–27.

Hardt, Michael, and Antonio Negri. *Empire*. Cambridge, MA: Harvard University Press, 2000.

Harris, Cheryl. "Whiteness as Property." In *Critical Race Theory*, ed. Kimberle Crenshaw, Neil Gotanda, Gary Peller, and Kendall Thomas. New York: New Press, 1995: 276–91.

Hartouni, Valerie. "Reproductive Discourse in the 1980's." In *Technoculture*, ed. Constance Penley and Andrew Ross. Minneapolis: University of Minnesota Press, 1991: 27–56.

Harvey, David. *The Condition of Postmodernity: An Enquiry into the Origins of Cultural Change*. Cambridge, MA: Blackwell, 1990.

Harvey, Sylvia. "Woman's Place: The Absent Family of Film Noir." In *Women in Film Noir*, ed. E. Ann Kaplan. London: British Film Institute Publishing, 1978: 22–34.

Heath, Stephen. *Questions of Cinema*. Bloomington: Indiana University Press, 1981.

Honig, Bonnie. "Immigrant America? How Foreignness 'Solves' Democracy's Problems." *Social Text*, no. 56 (1998): 1–27.

hooks, bell. *Black Looks: Race and Representation.* Boston: South End, 1992.

Horvitz, Deborah. "Freud, Marx, and Chiapas in Leslie Marmon Silko's *Almanac of the Dead.*" *Studies in American Indian Literatures,* 1st ser., 10, no. 3 (1998): 47–63.

Irr, Caren. "The Timeliness of *Almanac of the Dead,* or, a Postmodern Rewriting of Radical Fiction." In *Leslie Marmon Silko: A Collection of Critical Essays,* ed. Louise K. Barnett and James L. Thorson. Albuquerque: University of New Mexico Press, 1999: 223–44.

Jacobs, Lea. "The Censorship of *Blonde Venus:* Textual Analysis and Historical Method." *Cinema Journal* 27, no. 3 (1988): 21–31.

Jameson, Fredric. *Postmodernism; or, The Cultural Logic of Late Capitalism.* Durham, NC: Duke University Press, 1991.

Kaplan, Amy. "Left Alone with America." In *Cultures of United States Imperialism,* ed. Amy Kaplan and Donald Pease. Durham, NC: Duke University Press, 1993: 3–21.

Kaplan, E. Ann. Introduction to *Women in Film Noir,* ed. E. Ann Kaplan. London: British Film Institute Publishing, 1978: 1–5.

———. *Looking for the Other: Feminism, Film, and the Imperial Gaze.* New York: Routledge, 1997.

———. *Women and Film: Both Sides of the Camera.* London: Routledge, 1983.

Kellner, Douglas. *Television and the Crisis of Democracy.* Boulder, CO: Westview, 1990.

Krutnik, Frank. *In a Lonely Street: Film Noir, Genre, Masculinity.* London: Routledge, 1991.

Lacan, Jacques. *The Seminar of Jacques Lacan: Book 11,* ed. Jacques-Alain Miller. New York: Norton, 1988.

———. *The Four Fundamental Concepts of Psychoanalysis.* Trans. Alan Sheridan. New York: Norton, 1981.

Layoun, Mary. "The Female Body and 'Transnational' Reproduction; or, Rape by Any Other Name?" In *Scattered Hegemonies: Postmodernity and Transnational Feminist Practices,* ed. Inderpal Grewal and Caren Kaplan. Minneapolis: University of Minnesota Press, 1994: 63–75.

Lipsitz, George. *The Possessive Investment in Whiteness: How White People Profit from Identity Politics.* Philadelphia: Temple University Press, 1998.

Lott, Eric. *Love and Theft: Blackface Minstrelsy and the Making of the American Working Class.* New York: Oxford University Press, 1993.

Lowe, Lisa. "Work, Immigration, Gender: New Subjects of Cultural Politics." *The Politics of Culture in the Shadow of Capital,* ed. Lisa Lowe and David Lloyd. Durham, NC: Duke University Press, 1997: 354–74.

Lubiano, Wahneema. "Like Being Mugged by a Metaphor: Multiculturalism and State Narratives." In *Mapping Multiculturalism,* ed. Avery Gordon and Christopher Newfield. Minneapolis: University of Minnesota Press, 1996: 64–75.

Macpherson, C. B. *The Theory of Possessive Individualism: From Hobbes to Locke.* London: Oxford University Press, 1962.

Marcuse, Herbert. *Negations: Essays in Critical Theory.* Boston: Beacon, 1988.

Martí, José. "Our America." In *The America of Jose Marti,* trans. Juan de Onis. New York: Noonday, 1953: 138–51.

Marx, Karl. *Capital.* Vol. 1, trans. Samuel Moore and Edward Aveling. New York: International Publishers, 1977.

Massey, Doreen. *Space, Place, and Gender.* Minneapolis: University of Minnesota Press, 1994.

Mattelart, Armand. *Mapping World Communication: War, Progress, Culture.* Trans. Susan Emmanuel and James A. Cohen. Minneapolis: University of Minnesota Press, 1994.

McClintock, Anne. "The Angel of Progress: Pitfalls of the Term 'Post-Colonialism.'" *Social Text,* nos. 31–32 (1992): 84–98.

———. *Imperial Leather: Race, Gender, and Sexuality in the Colonial Context.* New York: Routledge, 1995.

Mercer, Kobena. *Welcome to the Jungle: New Positions in Black Cultural Studies.* New York: Routledge, 1994.

Miller, Jim. "Post-Apocalyptic Hoping: Octavia Butler's Dystopian/Utopian Vision." *Science Fiction Studies* 25 (1998): 336–60.

Miyoshi, Masao. "A Borderless World? From Colonialism to Transnationalism and the Decline of the Nation-State." *Critical Inquiry* 19 (1993): 721–51.

Modleski, Tania. *Feminism without Women: Culture and Criticism in a "Postfeminist" Age.* New York: Routledge, 1991.

Moon, Michael, and Cathy N. Davidson, eds. *Subjects and Citizens: Nation, Race, and Gender from Oroonoko to Anita Hill.* Durham, NC: Duke University Press, 1995.

Mulvey, Laura. *Visual and Other Pleasures.* Bloomington: Indiana University Press, 1989.

Muñoz, José Esteban. "'The White to Be Angry': Vaginal Davis's Terrorist Drag." *Social Text,* nos. 52–53 (1997): 81–103.

Naremore, James. *The Magic World of Orson Welles.* Dallas: Southern Methodist University Press, 1989.

———. *More Than Night: Film Noir in Its Contexts.* Berkeley and Los Angeles: University of California Press, 1998.

Nelson, Alondra, ed. "Afrofuturism," special issue. *Social Text,* no. 71 (2002).

Newitz, Annalee. "White Savagery and Humiliation, or A New Racial Consciousness in the Media." In *White Trash: Race and Class in America,* ed. Annalee Newitz and Matt Wray. New York: Routledge, 1997.

Newitz, Annalee, and Matt Wray. Introduction to *White Trash: Race and Class in America*. New York: Routledge, 1997.

Nichols, Bill. *Ideology and the Image: Social Representation in the Cinema and Other Media*. Bloomington: Indiana University Press, 1981.

Ong, Aihwa. *Spirits of Resistance and Capitalist Discipline: Factory Women in Malaysia*. Albany: State University of New York Press, 1987.

Parreñas, Rhacel Salazar. *Servants of Globalization: Women, Migration, and Domestic Work*. Stanford, CA: Stanford University Press, 2001.

Pease, Donald E. "National Identities and Postnational Narratives." In *National Identities and Post-Americanist Narratives*, ed. Donald E. Pease. Durham, NC: Duke University Press, 1994: 1–13.

Peppers, Cathy. "Dialogic Origins and Alien Identities in Butler's *Xenogenesis*." *Science Fiction Studies* 22 (1995): 47–62.

Place, Janey. "Women in Film Noir." In *Women in Film Noir*, ed. E. Ann Kaplan. London: British Film Institute Publishing, 1978: 35–67.

Porter, Carolyn. *Seeing and Being: The Plight of the Participant Observer in Emerson, James, Adams, and Faulkner*. Middletown, CT: Wesleyan University Press, 1981.

Prashad, Vijay. *Keeping Up with the Dow Joneses: Debt, Prison, Workfare*. Cambridge, MA: South End, 2003.

Rabinovitz, Lauren. "Sitcoms and Single Moms: Representations of Feminism on American TV." *Cinema Journal* 29 (1989): 3–19.

Reinecke, Yvonne. "Overturning the (New World) Order: Of Space, Time, and Prophecy in Leslie Marmon Silko's *Almanac of the Dead*. *Studies in American Indian Literatures*, 1st ser., 10, no. 3 (1998): 65–83.

Roediger, David. *Towards the Abolition of Whiteness*. London: Verso, 1994.

———. *The Wages of Whiteness: Race and the Making of the American Working Class*. London: Verso, 1991.

Rouse, Roger. "Thinking through Transnationalism: Note on the Cultural Politics of Class Relations in the Contemporary United States." *Public Culture* 7, no. 2 (1995): 353–402.

Rowe, John Carlos. "Melville's *Typee:* U.S. Imperialism at Home and Abroad." In *National Identities and Post-Americanist Narratives*, ed. Donald E. Pease. Durham, NC: Duke University Press, 1994: 255–78.

Said, Edward W. *Culture and Imperialism*. New York: Vintage Books, 1994.

Shaviro, Steven. *The Cinematic Body*. Minneapolis: University of Minnesota Press, 1993.

Shohat, Ella, and Robert Stam. "From the Imperial Family to the Transnational Imaginary: Media Spectatorship in the Age of Globalization." In *Global/Local*, ed. Rob Wilson and Wimal Dissanayake. Durham, NC: Duke University Press, 1996: 145–70.

———. *Unthinking Eurocentrism: Multiculturalism and the Media*. London: Routledge, 1994.

Silko, Leslie Marmon. *Almanac of the Dead.* New York: Penguin, 1991.

Simmel, Georg. *On Individuality and Social Forms.* Ed. Donald N. Levine. Chicago: University of Chicago Press, 1971.

Smith, Stephanie. "Morphing, Materialism, and the Marketing of *Xenogenesis.*" *Genders,* no. 18 (1993): 67–86.

Spiegel, Lynn. "White Flight." In *The Revolution Wasn't Televised: Sixties Television and Social Conflict,* ed. Lynn Spiegel and Michael Curtin. New York: Routledge, 1987: 46–72.

Spiegel, Lynn, and Michael Curtin. Introduction to *The Revolution Wasn't Televised: Sixties Television and Social Conflict,* ed. Lynn Spiegel and Michael Curtin. New York: Routledge, 1987: 1–18.

Spillers, Hortense. "Mama's Baby, Papa's Maybe: An American Grammar Book." *diacritics* 17, no. 2 (1987): 65–81.

Spivak, Gayatri Chakravorty. "Can the Subaltern Speak?" In *Marxism and the Interpretation of Culture,* ed. Cary Nelson and Lawrence Grossberg. Urbana: Illinois University Press, 1988: 271–313.

———. *In Other Worlds.* London: Routledge, 1988.

———. "Three Women's Texts and a Critique of Imperialism." *Critical Inquiry* 12 (1985): 243–61.

———. "Who Claims Alterity?" In *Remaking History,* ed. Barbara Kruger and Phil Mariani. Seattle: Bay, 1989: 269–92.

Staiger, Janet. "The Romances of the Blonde Venus: Movie Censors versus Movie Fans." *Revue Canadienne D'Etudes Cinematographiques* 6, no. 2 (1997): 5–17.

Takaki, Ronald, ed. *From Different Shores: Perspectives on Race and Ethnicity in America.* New York: Oxford University Press, 1987.

Teale, Tamara. "The Silk Road from Chiapas, or, Why Native Americans Cannot Be Marxist." *MELUS* 23, no. 4 (1998): 155–65.

Theweleit, Klaus. *Male Fantasies.* Minneapolis: University of Minnesota Press, 1987.

Thomas, Deborah. "Blonde Venus." *Movie* 34–35 (1990): 7–15.

Thompson, Kristin. *Exporting Entertainment: America in the World Film Market, 1907–1934.* London: British Film Institute Publishing, 1985.

———. "Major Technological Changes of the 1920s." In *The Classical Hollywood Cinema: Film Style and Mode of Production to 1960,* ed. David Bordwell, Janet Staiger, and Kristin Thompson. New York: Columbia University Press, 1985: 281–93.

Vizenor, Gerald. *Manifest Manners: Postindian Warriors of Survivance.* Hanover, NH: University Press of New England, 1994.

Wald, Priscilla. "Terms of Assimilation: Legislating Subjectivity in the Emerging Nation." In *Cultures of U.S. Imperialism,* ed. Amy Kaplan and Donald Pease. Durham, NC: Duke University Press, 1993: 59–84.

Warner, Michael. *The Letters of the Republic: Publication and the Public Sphere in Eighteenth-Century America*. Cambridge, MA: Harvard University Press, 1990.

Wiegman, Robyn. *American Anatomies: Theorizing Race and Gender*. Durham, NC: Duke University Press, 1995.

———. "Whiteness and the Paradox of Particularity." *Boundary 2* 26, no. 3 (1999): 115–50.

Wood, Robin. "Venus de Marlene." *Film Comment* 14, no. 2 (1978): 58–63.

Yoshimoto, Mitsuhiro. "Real Virtuality." In *Global/Local: Cultural Production and the Transnational Imaginary*, ed. Rob Wilson and Wimal Dissanayake. Durham, NC: Duke University Press, 1996: 107–18.

Zaki, Hoda M. "Utopia, Dystopia, and Ideology in the Science Fiction of Octavia Butler." *Science Fiction Studies* 17 (1990): 239–51.

Zinn, Howard. *A People's History of the United States*. New York: Harper and Row, 1980.

Films

Blonde Venus. Dir. Josef von Sternberg. Paramount, 1932.

Fargo. Dir. Joel and Ethan Coen. Polygram Film, 1996.

Gilda. Dir. Charles Vidor. Columbia, 1946.

The Lady from Shanghai. Dir. Orson Welles. Columbia, 1948.

Out of the Past. Dir. Jacques Tourneur. RKO, 1947.

The Simpsons. "Homer and Apu." Original broadcast, October 8, 1994.

The Simpsons. "In Marge We Trust." Original broadcast, April 27, 1997.

Touch of Evil. Dir. Orson Welles. Universal, 1958.

Index

Eva Cherniavsky is the Hilen Professor of American Literature and Culture at the University of Washington at Seattle. She is the author of *That Pale Mother Rising: Sentimental Discourses and the Imitation of Motherhood in Nineteenth-Century America,* and has published essays on affect, nationalism, embodied identities, and visual culture in *boundary 2, Cultural Critique, GLQ, Feminist Studies,* and *Angelaki.*